Proclaiming the Gospel

Proclaiming the Gospel

Preaching for the Life of the Church

EDITED BY BRIAN K. PETERSON

Fortress Press

Minneapolis

Library of Congress Cataloging-in-Publication Data
Proclaiming the Gospel : preaching for the life of the church / edited by Brian K. Peterson.
    p. cm.
  Includes bibliographical references and index.
  ISBN 978-0-8006-6331-5 (alk. paper)
  1. Preaching. I. Peterson, Brian K.
  BV4222.P743 2009
  251—dc22
                             2009013735

Contents

Foreword

MARCUS MILLER

For since, in the wisdom of God, the world did not know God
through wisdom, God decided, through the foolishness of our
preaching, to save those who believe.—*1 Corinthians 1:21*

Any preacher who ponders Paul's words will shudder. It is a
sobering and amazing claim that the apostle makes: God's decision is to
save those who believe through the foolishness of preaching. While it
may be sobering and amazing, we believe it to be true.

This enterprise of proclaiming God's precious and saving word to
hungry souls week in and week out is the central task of the church. It
follows that, if we organize our common life around God's saving act
toward people, preaching is the vocation of the church.

One of the great surprises of my life came only a few years ago, well
into my sixth decade of life. This surprise came when I was no longer
a parish pastor, on one of those rare Sundays when I as a bishop had a
chance to attend the liturgy at my home congregation. For years I had
been preaching week after week. Sometimes I wondered if the words I
spoke made any difference at all; other times I confessed before going
into the pulpit my sloth in preparing the proclamation for that week.
There were times when that proclamation just did not fit together at all

until I preached it, and other times when I thought I had just the right way of saying it until the words actually exited my mouth.

Faith Lutheran Church in Fairlawn, Ohio, was our congregation and my schedule allowed me to be there only occasionally. As I walked through those heavy wooden doors, and after I had greeted a few folks I had not seen for some time, I headed toward my seat. I felt a gnawing hunger in my soul to hear the word preached to me. I needed to hear firsthand that God had my salvation, and the salvation of those who worshiped around me, and the salvation of the whole world in mind when God sent Jesus into the world to take up the cross. I yearned for those words, and I had always heard Pastor Hansen say those good words as if they were directed specifically to me.

I have wondered if the hearing of that good news is why people return week after week to worship. I have discussed this with other hearers and have watched the faces of people during the preacher's sermons, particularly at those moments when the gospel is spoken with clarity, and have concluded that for many it is the hearing of the good news that brings them back every week. The burdens, confusions, and troubles of everyday life are lifted with the joyful hearing and reception of that good news. I also recognize the various pressures that there are on the parish pastor who is called to preach this word week in and week out. It is a great temptation to skip the text study with colleagues. It is a great temptation not to do the exegetical work that the sermon requires. It is a great temptation to believe that the foolishness of stories we tell (sometimes too often about ourselves) will substitute for the real foolishness we are called to proclaim.

The faculty of Lutheran Theological Southern Seminary acknowledged the challenge and centrality of the task a while back and began work on this collection of essays as our gift to the preachers of the church. This is our encouragement to you in your important task of proclaiming this foolishness. From our various disciplines and backgrounds, teachers at Southern Seminary offer their perception and understanding of preaching. It is not intended to burden the preacher further with one more perspective to which you must attend, but, rather, to assist the preacher in seeing and hearing again from teachers of the church the importance of your task.

These essays are also written for the seminary student and for homiletics classes. As you learn the art of writing the sermon, we trust that this will offer you some guidance and encouragement as well. As you learn to love this weekly work, we trust these words will be an encouragement to you to be a preacher all week long, weaving the texts and sermon from Sunday into your pastoral visits, into your confirmation instruction, into your parish meetings, and into your life as student.

When we say that preaching is the central task, we assert that not only is it the most important task, but that all we do as pastors has a focus in preaching and in the Lord's Day Eucharist. Evangelism, stewardship, conflict resolution, pastoral counsel, catechesis, social ministry, parish gatherings, and all that we do as a congregation have a stake in our preaching. It is the most important task because it is in this Sunday liturgy that everything we do is put into perspective.

It is all about words, after all. It is about how we put them together, how they reflect the world in which we live and give witness, the promises of God to us, and the hope of salvation for those who believe. It is about how those words carry the weight of God's eternal love for God's creation.

God is at work in our preaching. An acquaintance of mine told me that when he retires for the night on Saturday he looks forward to hearing his pastor preach the next day. "He is such a good preacher," he told me. "Did you ever tell your pastor this?" I asked. "Oh, no," came the reply. "Why not?" I asked. "I guess I just never thought about it," was the reply.

My guess is that more people than we care to acknowledge anticipate our words the next day or later that morning or whenever we preach. So, from these words on these pages we hope you will find encouragement. From the theologians and historians, from the exegetes and the administrators, from those who teach preaching and those who listen to preachers, we offer these words to you.

We hope that these essays can be used in clergy groups and in parish adult studies. We hope that you will read these as you have time and talk back to us. We want to hear from you and listen to what you have to say and what your experience is with preaching, so please e-mail any of us (first initial followed by last name@ltss.edu; for example, MMiller@ltss.edu). We would welcome the conversation.

I am grateful to every one of these treasured colleagues who have taken the time from busy schedules to write these essays. We gathered in the faculty dining room and critiqued each other's work. We listened attentively as colleagues told us what they thought. These and faculties at other seminaries have been called to be teachers of the church. They are the ones who taught us as we journeyed through those years of study and they are the ones who continue to teach us.

May God's Spirit continue to bless and use the words of your preaching.

Introduction

BRIAN K. PETERSON

For as the rain and the snow come down from heaven, and do not return there until they have watered the earth, making it bring forth and sprout, giving seed to the sower and bread to the eater, so shall my word be that goes out from my mouth; it shall not return to me empty, but it shall accomplish that which I purpose, and succeed in the thing for which I sent it.—*Isaiah 55:10-11*

With the conviction, hope, and prayer that their words actually do convey the word of God, preachers hold on to this promise from Isaiah, though many preachers' experience is that they often affirm this promise despite all evidence to the contrary. What good is preaching, anyway? The time when the faithful few are gathered together is short and precious, and there are no small number of suggestions being promoted (and sold) for what might captivate, motivate, entertain, and thus keep them coming back for more. In the spiritual marketplace of twenty-first-century Western culture, what does a bit of preaching accomplish? What is it even supposed to accomplish? And how does the preacher faithfully become a part of God's Word accomplishing that which God purposes?

This book began with the suggestion from one of our faculty members that, as a group, we share a vision of what theological education should be about, and that at its core is the call to proclaim the gospel clearly and persuasively. We share a conviction that preaching is at the

I

heart of the church's life and ministry. And in our teaching we affirm that preaching is not simply a skill to be learned like repairing small engines, but an art that is informed and shaped by all the various disciplines of a theological education. The church deserves and needs preaching that is nothing less than this, and preachers should settle for nothing less from themselves. This book formed around the hope that if the faculty focused attention on this task of preaching from the whole spectrum of theological education, something useful might be offered to the church and particularly to those called to preach to and for the church.

As our essays developed and our discussions with one another continued, one point kept surfacing as central and decisive: preaching is for the sake of the whole life of the church. That is, preaching has as its primary audience the community of faith as a community, and not simply as an aggregate of individuals who happen to be listening to a speech in the same building to address their personal or even private needs. The biblical texts and the theological tradition of the church do not only address individual fears, hopes, and identity, but aim to shape us into a particular kind of community with one another. That community's worship practice shapes and guides its preaching and hearing. Preaching grows out of and reinforces the relationships of pastor, congregation, and context. The long history of the church binds us into a single community across differing cultures and distant centuries as we hear and witness to the one gospel of Jesus Christ. Thus, preaching not only declares God's justification of the individual sinner, but is concerned with and integrally connected to the ongoing life, maturity, and sanctification of the community. In preaching we are being shaped into the community that God calls us to be.

Academic life and schedules being what they are, this project stretched across a time of significant transition within the faculty. One-third of the faculty retired during the writing and discussion of these essays. The voices of those who had long and faithfully served on this faculty are represented here, but so are some of the new faculty members who came to fill those positions. The resulting mix of voices adds depth and diversity to this effort. Change is a constant part of the mix in which proclamation takes place. Yet what has remained constant amidst the leavings and comings is the shared conviction that preaching is central to the church's life, is informed and shaped by the whole breadth of theological education, and above all is the life-giving activity of God at work in, and for, and through the church. It is our hope that this volume is an encouragement and an aid toward that end. *Soli Deo Gloria.*

PART ONE

Gospel Proclamation and Its Purpose

Called and Sent to Preach the Gospel of God

1

TOM RIDENHOUR

To begin this essay I want to remind us all of some important items from the biblical and confessional tradition.

The apostle Paul in Romans 1:16-17 wrote, "For I am not ashamed of the gospel; it is the power of God for salvation to everyone who has faith, to the Jew first and also to the Greek. For in it [the gospel] the righteousness of God is revealed through faith for faith; as it is written, 'The one who is righteous will live by faith.'"

In 2 Corinthians 3:5-6 Paul wrote, "Not that we are competent of ourselves to claim anything as coming from us; our competence is from God, who has made us competent to be ministers of a new covenant, not of letter but of spirit; for the letter kills, but the Spirit gives life." The letter that kills is the letter of the law. In Galatians 3:10-14 Paul makes a similar claim.

Article 4 of the Augsburg Confession presents the Lutheran proposal of dogma to the church catholic. That is the article on justification. Article 5 then reads, in part:

> To obtain such faith God instituted the office of preaching, giving the gospel and the sacraments. Through these, as through means, he gives the Holy Spirit who produces faith, where and when he

wills, in those who hear the gospel. It teaches that we have a gracious God, not through our merit but through Christ's merit, when we so believe.[1]

Article 6 of the Augsburg Confession says, "It is also taught that such faith should yield good fruit and good works and that a person must do such good works as God has commanded for God's sake but not place trust in them as if thereby to earn grace before God."[2]

Article 7 of the Augsburg Confession says:

It is also taught that at all times there must be and remain one holy, Christian church. It is the assembly of all believers among whom the gospel is purely preached and the holy sacraments are administered according to the gospel. For this is enough for the true unity of the Christian church that there the gospel is preached harmoniously according to a pure understanding and the sacraments are administered in conformity with the divine Word.[3]

The explanation of the Third Article of the Apostles' Creed in the Small Catechism says:

I believe that by my own understanding or strength I cannot believe in Jesus Christ my LORD or come to him, but instead the Holy Spirit has called me through the gospel, enlightened me with his gifts, made me holy and kept me in the true faith, just as he calls, gathers, enlightens, and makes holy the whole Christian church on earth and keeps it with Jesus Christ in the one common, true faith. Daily in this Christian church the Holy Spirit abundantly forgives all sins—mine and those of all believers. On the Last Day the Holy Spirit will raise me and all the dead and will give to me and all believers in Christ eternal life. This is most certainly true.[4]

As I hear these words from Paul and the Lutheran confessions, I hear a clear, direct, and unambiguous word that God is the subject of the action directed to the individual person, to the church, and to the world. Or as my older son, Tom Junior, says, "Daddy, I don't understand why every Lutheran preacher can't have at least three or four sentences in every sermon in which God is the subject of an active verb." Yea, verily! Then why is it that in my life within the Lutheran church I hear so much preaching of oughts, musts, shoulds, and conditionality as though my behavior determines what God will or will not do?

The issue for me is not focused on Lutheran preaching of the law/ gospel distinction in the church, but, rather, the lack of direct, clear, and unambiguous proclamation of the good news of what God has done, is doing, and promises yet to do.[5] The grammar of the gospel is indicative, not imperative. The gospel is the announcement of God's action to reconcile, redeem, justify, and save the cosmos, the church, and individual people. The basic biblical pattern is a "Because . . . , therefore . . . ," as in Exodus 20:2: [Because] I am the LORD your God who brought you out of the land of Egypt, out of the house of slavery, [THEREFORE (I wish this were in four-foot-high red letters)] you shall have no other gods before me. You shall not take my name in vain. You shall remember the Sabbath day. You shall honor your father and mother. You shall not kill, not commit adultery, not steal, not bear false witness, and not covet.

The Pauline corpus reflects the same indicative-imperative, "because . . . , therefore . . ." pattern. In Romans 1–11 Paul proclaims what God in Christ Jesus has done, is doing, and promises yet to do. This proclamation is the "because." Then in Romans 12:1-2 Paul moves to the "therefore," which calls those justified by God to have obedient and faithful lives in response to God's gracious gift of new life as the Spirit empowers us. The section of exhortations continues through chapter 16 of Romans.

The same "because . . . , therefore . . ." pattern is seen in Mark's Gospel. As Mark begins his Gospel narrative of Jesus, the first actor is God:

> See, I am sending my messenger ahead of you, who will prepare your way; the voice of one crying out in the wilderness: "Prepare the way of the Lord, make his paths straight." (Mark 1:2-3)

The "I" here is God. God is the actor who sent John the Baptizer to prepare the way for Jesus. Then after John was arrested Jesus begins his ministry by preaching.

> Jesus came to Galilee, proclaiming the good news of God, and saying, "The time is fulfilled, and the kingdom of God has come near; repent, and believe in the good news." (Mark 1:14-15)

In this text in Mark the preaching of Jesus has the indicative of God's action preceding the imperative of our responses. The "because . . . , therefore . . ." pattern is clearly implied here.

The issue for me is again not the law/gospel distinction but the absence of (or at least the very muted word of) the gospel. Often I ask myself, "Do Lutheran pastors actually believe the gospel of God they are called and ordained to proclaim?" If we believe the gospel, then why is there so little clear and direct announcement of God's activity and more focus and emphasis on what we human actors are to do?

One Christmas Eve not long ago, I heard a sermon that began by quoting an editorial writer of the *New York Times* who had asked, "What if Mary had said no to God?" The sermon then claimed if Mary had said no to God, then God would have been prevented from giving Jesus. But, the sermon said, Mary said yes to God and Jesus was born. Jesus also said yes to God. We should also say yes to God. Our saying yes to God was then described in terms of ministries to be done within the congregation itself. I did hear two brief sentences in which it was said that God enables our saying yes to God. But there was no clue in the sermon about how and where God enables us to say yes. At that worship service there was the Sacrament of the Altar, God's action to forgive our sin of saying no to God and to empower us to say yes to God. To have made that homiletical move and pointed to the connection between our saying yes and God's grace at the table would have announced the indicative of God's action that empowers our faithful response to God.

The focus of the text in this sermon was on the human actor Mary. The sermon then moved to focus on our behavior and to exhort us to do what Mary did and say yes to God, to be obedient to God. Because Jesus had said yes to God, by implication we were called to imitate Jesus. I left that Christmas Eve worship service very much weighted down. I left weighted down because the clear, unambiguous announcement of God's gracious action of coming to be with God's people in the birth of Jesus was not made. If there was a word of good news it was so muted as not to be heard.

In my view the first question always to put to a text of Scripture for preaching is: "What does the text say God is saying or doing?" There is then the possibility of proclaiming the gospel. To ask this question focuses on discerning what the text says concerning God as the subject of active verbs. And if the text is a piece of exhortation, then exegetically I am called to look at the broader context in which the text appears in order to discover the "because" in which that "therefore" is rooted.

To focus on the human actor in the text leads, I think, invariably to preaching an imperative or exhortation for us either to behave like the human actor or not to behave like the human actor in the text. And that is not, in my judgment, good news.

So, what of vocation? If the Scriptures and Confessions are appropriate in their witness, then God is the primary (only?) actor to make us new creations and thereby enable us and empower us to respond in faithful obedience to God's calling, sending and inviting us to join with God where God already is at work in the world and in the church. We are made new creations in baptism, given the gift of faith, brought into the church of Christ, Christ's body, to be nurtured, nourished, assisted, and empowered to discern what the call of God is to us, for us, with us—and for the whole community of new creations in that community. And when we do not respond in faithful obedience, when our sinnerhood controls our living, then God's grace still comes to us to forgive us our sins and to strengthen our faith through the foretaste of the eschatological free lunch, the Lord's Supper.

In the Lutheran theological tradition the law has a political use and a theological use. In the political use of the law God's will is for there to be order and peace with justice and righteousness in the human community for all its inhabitants. And as a new creation I am called by God to participate in that community, seeking justice and righteousness for all people.

The theological use of the law is to serve as a sledgehammer or cattle prod to confront us with our sinnerhood, our unfaithful discipleship, our rebellion against God, and to point us to Christ Jesus who has forgiven us, who is forgiving us, and who will forgive us our sins and renew us to be faithful disciples of our Lord. Another image of the law in this function is to describe it as a mirror that shows us our brokenness, our unfaithfulness, our hopelessness, or whatever our fallen condition is as unfaithful or faithful sinners. The gospel promise is then proclaimed to point to and declare how and where God has acted, is acting, and will act to overcome our broken reality.

There is in our Lutheran tradition dispute about whether or not there is a third use of the law—that is, a continuing function of the law to guide the faithful behavior of the church. My personal view is that I would rather speak of a gospel imperative, a "therefore" that follows the "because" of what God has done, is doing, and promises yet to do. There will be imperatives here, but the imperative is rooted in and empowered by the indicative statements of God's gracious action for us, to us, with us.

Some might call to my attention the words of the preexilic prophets of Israel who announced God's call for justice, righteousness, and steadfast love to be done by God's people or God would bring judgment upon God's people. And if that is how we understand what the prophets did or if that is what we today would call prophetic preaching, I have some difficulty with such an understanding. That understanding is to preach imperative and not indicative-imperative. The prophets did proclaim to God's people that God desired them to act with justice, righteousness, and steadfast love. Prophets did proclaim God's impending judgment upon an unfaithful covenant partner. But implicit or explicit in the message of the preexilic prophets, there is that "because . . . " of God's having freed Israel from Pharaoh's brickyard, of cutting covenant with Israel, and continuing to care for Israel. I find the "because . . . , therefore . . ." pattern in the prophets. Two examples are from Amos and Hosea.

> Hear the word that the LORD has spoken against you, O people of Israel, against the whole family that I brought up out of the land of Egypt:
>> You only have I known of all the families of the earth;
>> therefore I will punish you for all your iniquities. (Amos 3:1-2)

The Lord God speaks to Israel in Hosea:

> When Israel was a child, I loved him
>> and out of Egypt I called my son.
> The more I called them,
>> the more they went from me;
> they kept sacrificing to the Baals,
>> and offering incense to idols.
> Yet it was I who taught Ephraim to walk,
>> I took them up in my arms;
>> but they did not know that I healed them.
> I led them with cords of human kindness,
>> with bands of love.
> I was to them like those
>> who lift infants to their cheeks.
> I bent down to them and fed them.

> They shall return to the land of Egypt,
> and Assyria shall be their king,
> because they have refused to return to me. (Hosea 11:1-5)

The indicative of God's gracious, caring, saving action for God's people Israel was the call for Israel to be faithful and obedient. Yet when Israel was not faithful and obedient God invoked the curses of the covenant upon them to chastise and punish them. But the word of judgment from God is to a people who have been loved and graced by God.

It is also the case that not all the prophets of Israel busted Israel's chops for being unfaithful. Prophetic preaching (certainly by exilic and postexilic prophets) proclaims God's gracious action to renew Israel, to forgive Israel, and to bring Israel home to the land promised to the ancestors. The prophets do proclaim that Israel's God is the God who is active in and concerned for the totality of life lived in the cosmic structure of reality and cannot be confined only to some sort of religious cult. The New Testament makes the same proclamation. God's activity is for the sake of the whole cosmos that God has made and loves and cares for. As God's new creations the church is called and sent to serve and minister in justice, righteousness, and steadfast love in the world as an empowered response to God's love and grace.

There is one other deeply held conviction I have concerning preaching. Preaching and teaching that focuses on the "therefore," or the imperatives, on oughts and musts and shoulds, does not empower the church to be faithful disciples of the Lord Jesus. I am convinced that persons who are faithful church folk and who attend worship on a regular basis know what God wills and desires of them in the living of their lives of faithful discipleship. The problem is not lack of knowledge! The lack is a lack of power, of energy that enables the church to do what God calls and sends the church to do. A more robust, lively, and faithful proclamation of the gospel of God could and will empower and energize the church to grow in grace—to be faithful, obedient disciples, servants of the Lord Jesus Christ in the totality of our life in the world. I claim this because I firmly believe that Paul is absolutely on target when he says in Romans 1:16 that "the gospel . . . is the power of God for salvation to everyone who has faith." The clear and unambiguous proclamation of the good news of God is the energy and the power that can and will propel the church in ministry and discipleship.

Lutheran Preaching and the Third Use of the Law   2

SHAUNA K. HANNAN

Lutheran preachers claim that preaching should contain both law and gospel since that is the nature of God's word. A traditional homiletical form (oversimplified here) begins by describing brokenness in the world (judgment) before proceeding to proclaim to that broken world God's free gift of healing in Jesus Christ (grace). For some preachers, however, this is not the end of the sermon. Once the gospel has been proclaimed, the preacher charges the congregation members with practical suggestions for living as Christians in the world. "Freed by the gospel, now go and [*insert imperative*]," is commonly used to frame the final minutes of the sermon. Such a format (law gospel law?) may not be as innocent as it seems. In fact, a long-standing debate stands behind these final exhortations: namely, the debate regarding the third use (that is, function) of the law.

In this article I hope to (1) show that, despite the longevity of this debate, it is still alive and pertinent to twenty-first-century preaching; (2) provide a brief summary of the history of the Lutheran debate over third use of the law in relation to preaching; and (3) encourage preachers to engage questions about the third use of the law and preaching, articulate their viewpoints, and examine their sermons in relation to these articulated viewpoints.

It is no secret that our theological convictions affect our preaching. Unfortunately, it is not always as transparent to preachers when such theological convictions are not mirrored in their preaching. For example, a preacher may be committed to preaching in line with the central Lutheran tenet that affirms that we are justified by grace through faith. Yet, her equally laudable commitment to encourage hearers to service of the neighbor results in sermons that consistently end in a list of summary exhortations. This seemingly innocent template may, over time, lead her congregation members simply to listen for what actions they are to be doing as committed Christians at the expense of hearing that Christ's death and resurrection justifies their being. It may even be that repeatedly closing sermons in this way undermines the centrality of the preacher's conviction that good works do not earn salvation.

What are your theological convictions regarding the third use of the law and how do they manifest themselves in your preaching? My hope is that you will take seriously the invitation to reflect on this question. As you begin to articulate your response, consider the following subquestions: (1) How does the law function in your preaching? (2) To what extent do you subscribe to the Lutheran confessions? (3) To what extent do you follow the thinking of Martin Luther?

While one may think the starting point for this engagement is whether one will be an opponent or proponent of the third use of the law, an even more basic question is whether or not one thinks the law functions in a third way at all. One would think this would be easily resolved given the following paragraph from Article VI of the Formula of Concord in which the uses of the law are clarified:

> The law has been given to people for three reasons: first, that through it external discipline may be maintained against the unruly and the disobedient; second, that people may be led through it to a recognition of their sins; third, after they have been reborn—since nevertheless the flesh still clings to them—that precisely because of the flesh they may have a sure guide, according to which they can orient and conduct their entire life.[1]

There it is, seemingly clear as ever, the civil, theological, and pedagogical uses of the law. And yet you may find yourself in the camp that claims that there is no positive use of the law. After all, *lex semper accusat*, the law always accuses. How might this conviction coincide with the affirmative response all ordained Lutheran pastors must give in response to the ordination question, "Will you therefore preach and teach in accordance with Holy Scriptures and these creeds and confessions?" This potential contradiction calls for deeper reflection on confessional subscription.

Confessional Subscription

While this is not the place to parse thoroughly the issue of confessional subscription, provided here are a few angles that will help preachers examine their own convictions. First, C. F. W. Walther has distinguished between a *quia* fashion of subscription and subscribing to the confessions *quatenus*. Whereas *quia* (Latin for "because") suggests that "Lutherans pledge themselves to the content of the Lutheran Confessions *because* [my italics] they are true and correct expositions of the Word of God," *quatenus* (Latin for "insofar as") suggests subscribing to the confessions *insofar as* they reflect the Bible's own teaching (which some may argue is no subscription at all).[2] The latter group leaves room to choose the Bible's teaching over that of the confessions when they are believed not to be synonymous. The argument of this group is that simple repristination is problematic because it naïvely assumes there is only one unequivocal meaning to the words in the confessions. Even more, this group argues that such "nostalgic romanticizing of the past seldom serves the past well and never serves the present or future."[3]

A second typology complexifies the preacher's possible intensity of confessional subscription. Erik Samuelson has divided the "Lutheran Confessional Spectrum" into five types.[4] The two extreme positions include *Type One* (Unconditional Doctrinal Authority) and *Type Five* (Historical Source among Many). *Type One* claims that the Lutheran confessions are authoritative in much the same way they were in the sixteenth century. Those who fall in *Type Five* say that because the confessions were written for a particular time and place, they have historical but not doctrinal significance.[5]

Samuelson offers two not-so-extreme positions in types two and four. Those who fall in *Type Two* (Historically Conditional Authority) claim primarily that the Lutheran confessions are normative for present theology and doctrine. There are, however, certain elements that are products of their own context and must be reinterpreted for our time.

Type Four (Primary Theological Source) differs from its more extreme ally, *Type Five*, in that the Lutheran confessions are relevant when they are helpful; that is, when they speak to current situations.

Samuelson proposes for his readers' consideration a "golden mean" in *Type Three* (Roadmaps to Grace). As roadmaps to grace, the Lutheran confessions are "both products of their context and normative for doctrine and theology." They "provide a theological framework and are an interpretive lens for reading scripture." Even more, confessional theology "informs, challenges, and is a resource for preaching, teaching, and pastoral care."[6] This type is evidence of neither a "wavering doctrinal confidence" nor "capitulation to the contemporary context."[7] In other words, the confessions have to meet a standard in much the same way that present church practices must meet the standard of the Lutheran confessions. That standard, according to Samuelson, is "the ability to proclaim the Triune God, made manifest in the Word made flesh, in this time and place."[8] Ultimately, Samuelson counsels, even those who understand the confessions as roadmaps to grace need as conversation partners those who place themselves in the other categories.

Which of the five types resonates with your theological convictions? While you explore a response to this question, be forewarned that not only will you have to recognize the way in which you subscribe to the confessions, but also to *which interpretation* of the confessions.

Martin Luther

Have you ever responded to a question such as, "What is your theology of proclamation?" with something like, "Well, Martin Luther would say . . . "? Lutherans often default to the views of Martin Luther even though this is not as straightforward as one might think (not least because the interpretations of Luther are widely divergent). We could do as Samuelson did and map out a spectrum of ways in which to subscribe to Luther. Some Lutherans have chosen Luther as the trump card even over the confessions. Of course, suggesting that the confessions and the opinions of Luther are not one and the same complicates the issue and, thus, requires ongoing examination and interpretation of Luther. This is the case, in particular, with regard to the third use of the law. Let it be said that both proponents and opponents of the third use of the law in preaching cite Luther as their guide.

The following section will provide a brief history of the relationship between Luther and the eventual development of the statement regarding the uses of the law in the Formula of Concord. Note that some of the same viewpoints that challenged those in the sixteenth century creep into our debates over the third use of the law still today. Perhaps you will recognize yourself, your colleagues, and/or your parishioners in some of these viewpoints. Note that there will be places along the way for you to stop and consider how you would enter the debate.

Sixteenth-Century Germany

Luther's views on the structure of law and gospel had become well known via his sermons, lectures, and pamphlets. Given Luther's status as a frontrunner in the Reformation, it is not surprising that his views are assumed to be reflected in the documents that were presented at the 1530 imperial diet in Augsburg, Germany. Emperor Charles V had summoned the diet in order to present to the Turks a unified front of religious practices in the empire. Since Luther had been banned from this gathering, his younger colleague and an emerging evangelical theologian in his own right, Philipp Melanchthon, became the main author of the Augsburg Confession and its subsequent "contemporary commentary" known as the Apology (defense) of the Augsburg Confession.[9]

In the Augsburg Confession, Melanchthon addresses law and gospel in relation to repentance. More specifically, he highlights the law's role in indicating the need for repentance and forgiveness. Melanchthon's conviction that repentance comes from preaching law did not go unchallenged. Three positions in particular opposed the conviction that forgiveness is available to sinning Christians who repent. These arguments fed the subsequent antinomian controversies and their remnants continue to sneak into our contemporary debates. (As you read these positions, consider whether they reflect statements you have heard people make or you have made yourself.)

The first position was taken by some Anabaptists who denied any use for the law to accuse baptized Christians of sin or to make them aware of sin. This was based on their belief that Christians, *qua* (insofar as) they are Christians, have no sin.

A second group of people who similarly opposed Melanchthon's convictions, but for different reasons, were the sixteenth-century followers of Novatian (a third-century Roman presbyter), who denied that baptized Christians needed either law or gospel to lead them to repentance. Their claim was that if Christians committed sin, repentance was unnecessary because forgiveness would not be granted anyway. Because the Novatians denied absolution to Christians who committed serious sins, they were eventually deemed heretical. To clarify, while both positions insist that preaching the law is unnecessary, their reasons are different. Anabaptists claimed preaching the law is unnecessary because once baptized, individuals have no sin. Novatians deemed such preaching unnecessary because, if a Christian sins, there is no chance for forgiveness.

Finally, the medieval sacrament's "requirement of satisfaction" continued to play a role. It undermined the comfort of absolution by imposing additional demands on the penitent.

> By keeping the commandments, with the aid of grace, people accumulated merit that qualified them to receive eternal life. No one asserted that keeping the Ten Commandments alone was enough, but their use as a *basis for punishment* and as a *supplement to grace* placed the law at the forefront of the Christian life.[10]

I rarely hear Lutheran sermons that suggest the positions of the Anabaptists or the Novatians. However, I do hear the occasional keeping of the law as a supplement to grace. This is a specific issue for preachers to examine in their sermons, which will be addressed in the final section of this essay.

Antinomian Controversies

Despite the Reformers' hopes that the distinction of law and gospel would make clear the role of each, the role of the law sparked more controversy. It became necessary to define further the nature of the law and its various functions. Note that there is rarely any division regarding the first two uses of the law, namely, the civil use and the theological use. This is not the case, however, with the pedagogical use (also referred to as reformative, didactic, or instructional). Three major controversies stemmed from the concern over the third use of the law. It is critical to note that all three antinomian controversies pertained to the relationship between the third use of the law and preaching.

The first antinomian controversy actually occurred prior to the Diet of Augsburg.[11] Already in 1527, Melanchthon had been challenged by Johann Agricola (Luther's colleague at the University of Wittenberg), who said that "preaching the law would not lead people to repentance but either to pride or to despair."[12] True repentance, Agricola insisted, comes from the gospel itself. Only after the people hear God's promise and love for them in Jesus Christ are they truly sorry for their sin and ready to receive forgiveness. Note that Agricola is not declaring that Christians have no sin (Anabaptist) or that Christians have no hope to be saved from sin (Novatians). Rather, he is essentially assigning a motivating function to the gospel. The gospel, not the law, is the agent for transformation.

This is a good place for preachers to stop and reflect upon whether or not they consider the possibility of preaching the law for the sake of leading people to repentance and, if so, on what basis. Do you agree with Agricola that preaching law would lead either to pride or despair and that it is the gospel that leads people to repentance? Is it the law or the gospel that is the agent for transformation?

Melanchthon strongly disagreed with Agricola's low view of the law's function. Luther played the role of mediator for their debate until, finally, as has been shown in the consequent documents (Augsburg Confession and Apology), Melanchthon's views won the day.

Ten years later, in 1537 (seven years after the Augsburg Diet), the intra-Lutheran debate over the law erupted again. (Note that ours is not the only era in which debates in the church are constantly revisited.) Agricola still questioned the preaching of the law to Christians. Melanchthon stood his ground regarding the need to "point people to the law." This debate lasted for three years until Luther's public criticism of Agricola provoked him to leave his preaching post. One might fittingly draw the conclusion that Luther and Melanchthon were united in their disagreement with Agricola, and denied that the gospel has a motivating function.

It was not until after Luther's death (1546) that attacks fell once again on Philip Melanchthon. The Gnesio-Lutherans, with their leader Matthias Flacius at the helm, endorsed what they considered to be a "pure" version of Luther's viewpoints and, therefore, argued against Melanchthon's high regard for the law. This is interesting, since in 1537 Luther and Melanchthon seemed to be on the same side in order to team up against Agricola. Only ten years later some were pitting Luther and Melanchthon against one another. One begins to think that since it was difficult to ascertain a unequivocal interpretation of Luther's views only a decade after his death, it is no surprise that there are divergent interpretations fifty-five decades later.

The Gnesio-Lutherans trusted the gospel's ability to cause spontaneous works by those who truly believe.[13] This perspective does seem to be synonymous with the following statement by Luther:

> Faith is a living, daring confidence in God's grace, so sure and certain that the believer would stake his life on it a thousand times. This knowledge of and confidence in God's grace makes men [*sic*] glad and bold and happy in dealing with God and with all creatures. And this is the work which the Holy Spirit performs in faith. Because of it, without compulsion, a person is ready and glad to do good to everyone, to serve everyone, to suffer everything, out of love and praise to God who has shown him this grace. Thus it is impossible to separate works from faith, quite as impossible as to separate heat and light from fire.[14]

Formula of Concord

A generation after Luther's death, many of the same issues resurfaced. Lutherans were threatened by factions; namely, the Gnesio-Lutherans (those led by Matthias Flacius who claimed, as already mentioned, to adhere "purely" to the writings of Luther) and the "Philippists" (followers of Philipp Melanchthon). A group of second-generation Lutherans desired for all Lutherans to come to agreement on major issues including the function of the law in preaching. (Recall that this is what Emperor Charles V desired when he summoned the diet in Augsburg over four decades earlier.) Thus, the conversations began and culminated in the writing of the Formula of Concord. The subtitle of the Formula of Concord reads (note the confidence with which the writers claim this to be the definitive account):

> A Thorough, Clear, Correct, and *Final* [my italics] Repetition and Explanation of Certain Articles of the Augsburg Confession

on Which Controversy Has Arisen for a Time Among Certain Theologians Adhering to This Confession, Resolved and Settled according to the Direction of God's Word and the Summary Formulation of Our Christian Teaching.[15]

The impetus for this agreement occurred in 1573 when Württemberg theologian Jakob Andreae wrote "Six Sermons on the Disputes Dividing the Theologians of the Augsburg Confession." After formalizing the sermons into a statement and upon numerous revisions (bearing various names such as the Swabian Concord, Saxon-Swabian Concord, Maulbronn Formula, Torgau Book, and Bergen Book), attempts at working toward Lutheran concord had begun to succeed. Eventually, the book that bore many names in its various amended states came to be called the Solid Declaration. That, along with an epitome (essentially a "Reader's Digest Condensed Version" of the Solid Declaration), formed the Formula of Concord. After three years of revisions, the Formula of Concord was signed by 8,188 theologians, ministers, and teachers. Exactly fifty years to the day after the Augsburg Confession was read before Charles V (June 25, 1530), the Lutheran Confessions, entitled *The Book of Concord*, now including the Formula of Concord, was completed. It is to this library of documents that Lutherans regularly and with fervor refer when debates arise regarding Lutheran identity.[16]

Twenty-First-Century Debates

Debates over Lutheran identity continue even today. It is crucial that preachers are able to articulate a stance (even if it is admittedly a work in progress) on issues such as the third use of the law in preaching in order to participate in the conversation. One's perspective will most certainly take its cue in part from a particular interpretation of and level of subscription to the confessions and the writings of Martin Luther. Other angles of exploration include how one (1) understands the law in relation to the gospel, (2) defines the law, and (3) views the two Lutheran aphorisms: *lex semper accusat* and *simul iustus et peccator*. In addition to doctrinal convictions, individual scriptural pericopes shape one's preaching. (Given the latter, it is worth considering whether or not it is ever fitting or faithful to have unyielding theological convictions when interpreting individual texts.)

These rich and complex matters require much more attention than can be given in this space. Suffice it to say, it is my conviction that "nostalgic romanticizing of the past" (that is, simple repristination) is not helpful. It is important for preachers to know why they say and do what they say and do. It has been my hope that this article gives preachers some angles of exploration in order to articulate these convictions. Whether or not preachers are able to do so, theological convictions will emerge from their sermons. For this reason, in addition to knowing the *why*, it is important for preachers actually to explore *what* they say and do in their sermons. Yes, this may seem ridiculously obvious. Even so, you may be surprised. If you are able to articulate your views on the third use of the law in preaching, do not be afraid to double-check that such views are mirrored in your sermons. If you are unsure at this point how to articulate your views, you will certainly discover what others see to be your views by analyzing your sermons.

My suggestion to you, the preacher, is that you tend to your own sermons in order to interpret your theological convictions regarding the third use of the law just as you would the sermons of Martin Luther, for example, in order to interpret his theological convictions. Choose a handful of sermons you have written (better yet, gather the audio versions) and go through them with the following tasks and questions in mind:

1. Consider the Scripture text.
2. Consider the context. What was going on in your congregation, in the world, and with you at the time? You may recall, for example, being frustrated at a lack of participation on the part of your members. Did this lead you to exhort more than usual? (Note that despite Luther's search for a gracious God, some of his sermons seem to be tirades against the hearers. This is especially true in Luther's sermons after the 1529 Church Visitations. In other words, context shaped Luther's preaching tremendously.[17])
3. Read through your sermons with an eye toward a discernable pattern. Do your sermons follow the pattern given earlier—namely, judgment followed by grace and concluding with something akin to, "Freed by the gospel, now go and [*insert imperative*]"? Or perhaps your sermons begin with a proclamation of the gospel. As you detect patterns in your sermon form,

imagine how such a pattern affects your hearers. Ask how your sermons function for your hearers. That is, what do you think a particular sermon *did* (note: not *said*) to them in its hearing? Might they have been comforted? Motivated? Judged? Convinced? Saved?

4. The two extremes in the debate over the third use of the law are *antinomianism* and *legalism* (or, as Jane Strohl calls them, "the barely concealed nihilism of the self-indulgent and the tunnel vision of the arbiters of Christian virtue"[18]). What dangers persist at these extremes? Do your sermons avoid both antinomianism and legalism? If so, how? If not, how might you be attentive to this in subsequent sermons?

The following questions were introduced earlier in this essay:

5. Is there anything in your sermons that suggests that keeping God's commandments is either a supplement to grace or that not keeping God's commandments is a basis for punishment (recall the medieval requirement for satisfaction)? My suspicion is that you might skip over this question assuming that you would not dare suggest such a thing. Do not skip this step. If you must, lock your office door so that no one will know you are doing this, but do it. If you notice even a hint of our works supplementing God's grace, ask yourself what the theology is behind such words and whether or not you agree with such theology.

6. Do you preach law in your sermons? If so, what does it sound like? And what was your reason for doing so? Is the reason, as Melanchthon suggested, to lead people to repentance? What effect might this have on your hearers? Did preaching law, as Agricola suggested, lead your hearers to pride? To despair?

7. Related to the previous question, do your sermons suggest that it is the gospel or the law that motivates the hearer? By "motivates," I mean, Does it move or compel the hearer to repentance or good works or belief? Another way to ask this is, How in your sermons have you encouraged hearers to service of the neighbor without undermining the conviction that they are justified by grace through faith and not by works?

8. It is worth considering whether or not your congregation members ever think (or, at least, if you think they think) that *if* they act a certain way (for example, serve at the local homeless shelter, teach Sunday school, attend worship) they "accumulate merit" in order to "qualify them to receive eternal life." On what do you base your answer?

While this is not an exhaustive list, it will get you started. You will be well on your way to an understanding of how your theology regarding the third use of the law shapes the word choice, structure, movement, stages, and rhythm of your preaching. Like any good practical theologian, you will discover how your actual preaching informs your theology (with regard to the third use of the law, this is particularly noticeable in the closing of sermons). Your participation in this conversation will inform generations of Lutheran preachers just as conversations of the second generation of Lutherans that led to the Formula of Concord have informed us. Even more, your participation in this conversation will grace and inform those who hear your preaching.

Finally, the kind of thorough examination and clear articulation proposed here is only *prolegomena* to a vital task. In order to find out how preaching is heard by congregation members, preachers must ask them. It is a ripe time for you *and* your parishioners to enter the conversation about the third use of the law. Articulate your theology of proclamation to your hearers and invite them to give you feedback. They will, in turn, begin to develop their own theology of proclamation. Let the conversation begin.

Preaching Justification   3

MICHAEL ROOT

What is it to "preach justification"? That question would seem so obvious and important for the Reformation that Lutherans should have settled it almost immediately. In fact, preaching justification has been a problem for Lutherans almost from the beginning.[1] When is justification rightly preached? How does it relate to the preaching of the law? How does the preaching of justification relate to the preaching of sanctification? Such questions have been central to intra-Lutheran debates since the Wittenberg disturbances of 1521–1522.

In this brief essay, I will outline an understanding of what it means to preach justification. Inevitably, in an essay of this length, only an outline can be provided, not a full development. What is provided is intended as an alternative to perhaps the most widely influential understanding of "preaching justification" in contemporary American Lutheranism, that of the late Gerhard Forde. The eloquence and rhetorical force of Forde's presentation of the nexus of preaching and justification is not to be denied. As will be noted, there are crucial points at which his understanding is to be affirmed. Nevertheless, I believe that the understandings of justification and preaching that he presents are exemplary forms of trends in modern Lutheranism that are deeply destructive of both the catholic and the evangelical core of the Reformation. Again, the critique of Forde here cannot be fully developed, but will be laid out in an excursus toward the end of the essay.

Justification and Its Proclamation

All too often, discussions of questions related to the doctrine of justification never stop to define what is meant by the phrase "doctrine of justification." Lutherans especially have a tendency to use the phrase as an accordion concept, expanding and shrinking its meaning as argument requires. Sometimes the doctrine is quite narrow (for example, in distinction from sanctification); at other times it seems to be equivalent to the gospel as a whole.

In this essay, I will use the term *justification* to refer to a specific aspect of soteriology: justification concerns how the sinner is accepted by the righteous God. Is the sinner transformed into a righteous person? Is the sinner forgiven in the sense that God simply overlooks, forgets, or disregards the sinner's sinfulness? What are the roles of God, of the sinner prior to acceptance, and of the person (no longer a sinner?) after acceptance in this coming-to-be-accepted? This nexus of questions constitutes the concern of the doctrine of justification.

This topic is significantly limited. It does not even cover the whole of soteriology, which can utilize concepts other than those related to justification to describe salvation (for example, liberation or deification) and address problems other than how the sinner comes to be accepted by the righteous God (for example, how one escapes captivity to the devil or the forces of this world, or how justice is established within humanity). Every soteriology assumes some particular portrayal of the human predicament, to which its central soteriological concepts form a solution.[2] The centrality of justification assumes the centrality of the problem of the sinner before God's righteousness.

A Reformation understanding of justification involves not only a particular understanding of how the sinner is accepted by the righteous God (by grace through faith because of Jesus Christ), but also a particular understanding of the importance of justification. The totality of salvation cannot be reduced to justification, but no account of salvation can avoid the problematic of sin and righteousness. In addition, any account of salvation must deal with this problematic in a way that centers on Christ as sheer gift. Any theological scheme that does not do so is unevangelical and thus unacceptable. Thus, while justification is one specific soteriological theme, it has a far wider—in fact, an unlimited—criteriological extension within theology: "It is an indispensable criterion that constantly serves to orient all the teaching and practice of our churches to Christ."[3]

Against the background of this understanding of what is meant by justification, what would it be to "preach justification"? On the one hand, "preaching justification" might refer to preaching that takes justification as its topic, preaching that focuses on the theme of justification. Such sermons can easily be found, going back to the earliest days of the Reformation (for example, Luther's 1518 sermon on "Two Kinds of Righteousness"[4]).

On the other hand, "preaching justification" might be taken to refer to preaching that *effects* justification, preaching that brings about (or sustains or at least contributes to) the sinner's being accepted by the righteous God. In the *Apology to the Augsburg Confession* [12:29], Melanchthon states: "[T]he sum of the preaching of the gospel is to condemn sin and to offer the forgiveness of sins, righteousness on account of Christ, the Holy Spirit, and eternal life, so that having been reborn we might do good."[5] The "sum of the preaching of the gospel" involves two actions: to condemn and to offer. Preaching is not reducible simply to stating a particular content, but to addressing that content to the sermon's hearers in a particular way (to use standard Lutheran terms, as law and gospel). In making this address, the content is realized: the sinner stands condemned and the sinner receives an offer. When the sinner hears that preaching with faith, then the address reaches its intended end: the condemnation is accepted as just and the offer of forgiveness, righteousness because of Christ, the Holy Spirit, and eternal life is received. When that offer is received, the hearer is justified; as forgiven and possessing righteousness because of Christ, he or she stands accepted before the righteous God. Preaching justification is preaching that does this.[6]

Such preaching might explicitly use the term *justification*, but it need not. Famously, Luther's Small Catechism makes no use of terms directly related to justification; the term *justification* and forms of the verb *justify* do not appear. Instead, it speaks of dependence on Christ and the Spirit, human inadequacy, and the forgiveness of sins. In doing so, it states the promise and elicits the faith that constitutes justification.

Understood along these lines, the referent of the term *justification* might be understood in three slightly, but significantly, different ways. First, it might be understood to refer to *an event*, the event of the sinner coming to stand accepted before the righteous God. As such an event, justification might be datable: person x was justified on date y. As such a datable event, justification might come to be seen as an event that occurred in a person's past.

Second, *justification* might be understood to refer to *a relation*, the relation of standing accepted before the righteous God. One might still refer to the event of coming-to-stand in that relation (or coming to stand in that relation for the first time), but the relation is not itself a datable event, but an ongoing reality. Justification could become a reality of the past only if one were to fall out of that relation.

Third, *justification* might be understood to refer to *a state within the justified*, the reality or quality within the justified that forms the human pole of the relation of standing accepted before the righteous God. Justification then refers to an aspect of the "having been reborn" in the quotation given above from Melanchthon.

These three possible referents are not mutually exclusive. They are best understood as three aspects of the reality of justification, aspects that must each be explored and described in any fully developed doctrine of justification. Much is at stake, however, in how these three possible referents are interrelated. Lutherans historically have been suspicious of an emphasis on justification as a quality within the justified, worrying that such an emphasis might lead to the view that the sinner is accepted by the righteous God *because of* some quality within the justified.[7] But does the relation or event of justification produce no quality or state within the justified? If it does not, then is justification at best strictly external and at worst a legal fiction?

Similarly, an emphasis on justification as a datable event can lead to a practical deemphasis on justification within the Christian life. I was justified; that is in the past; I now must concentrate on something else—on sanctification or good works or holiness. Justification becomes analogous to birth. It was of decisive importance to me that I was born, but that is not something that greatly concerns me in the present. John Wesley has a tendency at times to speak this way about justification.[8]

How we understand preaching as effecting justification will be shaped by how we understand justification as event, relation, and/or

quality. Does preaching seek to bring about an event? Or sustain a relation? Or nurture a quality? Or all three in some sense?

A final aspect of the preaching of justification needs to be noted.
Almost all preaching in the narrow sense of the term—a sermon delivered
in the context of a Christian worship service of some sort—is preaching
to a congregation composed mostly of persons who are already believers in Christ. Very little preaching is "conversion preaching," aimed at
the unbeliever and seeking to persuade the unbeliever to come to faith.[9]
Rather, as Michael Reu states at the beginning of his influential early-
twentieth-century Lutheran textbook on preaching, the sermon, beginning with the church of the New Testament and consistently thereafter,
was typically "an address to Christian *brethren*; not to *catechumens*, who
needed previously to be instructed and prepared for full participation in
the service and fellowship of the congregation, nor to *those without*, in
whose hearts the decision to join themselves to the congregation must
first be awakened, but to *mature Christians*, who were already members
of the congregation, and whose Christian consciousness did not need to
be aroused, but was to be deepened and strengthened."[10]

Most preaching is to the justified. Our analysis of what it means to
preach justification must take this reality into account.

Preaching Justification as Preaching Christ

So far, the analysis of preaching justification has been abstract. The
subject matter of justification has been stated—the acceptance of the
sinner by the righteous God—but little has been said about the nature
of that acceptance or how it comes about. What it means to preach
justification can only be given concreteness when justification itself is
more precisely discussed. This discussion must be brief and without
extensive documentation. What is presented is, I believe, in accord
both with recent ecumenical developments (especially the Lutheran-
Catholic *Joint Declaration on the Doctrine of Justification*) and with recent
trends in the interpretation of Luther.[11]

Already in his early commentary on Romans, Luther said: "The
Gospel is nothing else but the preaching of Christ."[12] This statement
may seem theologically innocuous, but it contains the seed of the central Reformation insistence: the righteousness of the Christian, the
only righteousness that will avail before the judgment seat of God, is

the righteousness of Christ. *Coram Deo*, no righteousness that is simply a predicate of the Christian, not even a righteousness brought about by God's grace, is adequate in itself. Only the righteousness that is primarily a predicate of Christ can stand before God's judgment.[13]

If the righteousness of the Christian is always (even eschatologically) the righteousness of Christ, the righteousness of another, then justification must primarily refer to a relation. Some relation exists between the Christian and Christ such that the righteousness of Christ applies to or covers the Christian. That relation is faith. Faith brings the sinner into a new relation to Christ, such that the righteousness of Christ now is also the righteousness of the Christian. Faith justifies because of the relation it establishes (or which is established through it) between the one who has faith and the object of faith (that is, Christ), not because of any quality inherent in faith as a human action, disposition, or attitude. An early Lutheran scholastic such as Leonhard Hutter could list faith, along with the grace of God and the merit of Christ, as a cause of justification because "faith alone is that *means* and *instrument* by which we can appropriate and receive the grace of God, the merit of Christ, and that righteousness found in him which alone can endure God's judgment."[14]

To say that justification is a relation and that faith justifies because of its object and not as a disposition of the self is not to deny that faith in fact *is* a disposition of the self, that faith has a reality in the self. Lutherans have classically described this reality as that of knowledge, assent, and trust (*notitia, assensus, fiducia*).[15] The relation that constitutes justification has a human pole, a reality within the justified self, which distinguishes the justified from the nonjustified. The Lutheran suspicion of an emphasis on this human pole is rooted in a fear that the character of faith as a form of trust in and dependence on another may be obscured. If faith becomes self-regarding, if it comes to trust or depend on itself, then it ceases to be trust in Christ and thus ceases to be the means and instrument of justification. Faith as the pole of a relation cannot exist on its own, apart from the relation that constitutes it. Faith is linguistically displayed, especially in the first person, by not talking about itself, but by talking about Christ.

A further step must be taken in the description of faith, one of great consequence for our understanding of preaching. The relation that constitutes justification involves a true union between Christ and the justified. The ascription of Christ's righteousness to the Christian is not a legal fiction, a piece of divine bookkeeping that takes place in heaven. Christ's righteousness becomes that of the justified because Christ and the justified have become, in a specific sense, one. Christ and the Christian remain distinct; the Christian does not dissolve into Christ in such a way that the distinct human identity of the Christian is lost. Nevertheless, Christ and the Christian are one in such a way that the righteous God rightly, justly, accepts the Christian as standing in Christ. In "The Freedom of the Christian," Luther describes this union in marital terms: faith "unites the soul with Christ as a bride is united with her bridegroom. By this mystery, as the Apostle teaches, Christ and the soul become one flesh."[16] Later Lutheranism spoke of a mystical union of the self with Christ that is simultaneous with justification, inseparable from it, and a ground of its reality.[17] Christ is present through the Holy Spirit in faith and faith cannot be separated from the indwelling of Christ in the justified.[18]

Closely tied to justification and the indwelling of Christ is the death of the old self and the resurrection of a new self in Christ.[19] Union with Christ is union with his death and resurrection, as Paul makes clear in Romans 6. Describing the theology of Martin Luther, Paul Hinlicky states: "[F]orgiveness and the new birth are double-sided aspects of the one saving event of encounter and union with Christ in divine faith through the gospel, such that the sinner dies and the believer is born."[20] The new self is the agent of the human act of faith, moved by the indwelling Spirit, who is a second agent of the same act. "Becoming the temporal object of the Father's eternal love for the Son, she [the Christian] therewith becomes a new subject in the Spirit's trusting apprehension."[21] However we theologically understand the language of "new person," it points to the reality of faith as the act of a human agent.

Justification is thus a particular way of interpreting the Christian's life in Christ. It emphasizes the sheer gift character of that life and the utter dependence on Christ within that life. Only as the Christian has "put on Christ" can he or she stand before God.

Preaching as Communicating Christ and Conforming the Hearer to Christ

If preaching not only speaks about but effects justification, and if justification is our participation in Christ and his righteousness, then what more can be said about preaching justification?

Preaching justification must speak *about* Christ, so that it might *speak* Christ, and thus *communicate* Christ. Preaching justification must be *about Christ*, for trust in Christ is at the center of justifying faith. Preaching cannot elicit trust in Christ without speaking about Christ. As noted in the quotation given above from Melanchthon in the *Apology*, however, preaching involves not simply speaking about something, preaching itself does something: it condemns sin and offers salvation. The condemnation and offer it proclaims are not of a sort that can be proclaimed on mere human authority. Rather, when the gospel of justification is proclaimed, Christ is himself speaking through the preaching, rejecting sin and opening the gates of heaven. The sermon then not only speaks about Christ, it *speaks Christ*. The sermon is then truly word of God.[22]

When that word of address from Christ, in the Spirit, is heard by faith, then the sermon itself *communicates* Christ. Christ dwells in the justified in their faith. Faith trusts in Christ by trusting Christ's word of promise that is proclaimed in the sermon. The sermon is thus not simply information about Christ, who is communicated to the self through some other channel, through mystical experience or through the sacraments. Rather, the sermon is itself a means of the communication of Christ. Working in and through the sermon that proclaims Christ, the Spirit communicates Christ to the faithful self. A Reformation understanding of the Eucharist, the service of Word and Sacrament, must always insist that Christ comes to the believer no less in the sermon than in the bread and wine, even if he comes in different ways in each. The sermon has itself a quasi-sacramental nature.[23]

In communicating Christ, the sermon is thus an instrument of that union with Christ, that is foundational for justification. As noted above, however, the majority of those who hear a sermon preached in the context of a worship service are persons who already believe, who presumably already dwell in Christ by faith. What is the specific function of preaching justification to the justified?

Preaching justification to the justified renews and nurtures justification. Justification is, by its nature as a relation of trust and dependence, never a secure possession. If justification were a secure possession, then I would be able to depend on my being justified, rather than depend on Christ. Faith must depend on Christ for its continued existence, otherwise it would lose its nature as trust. This trust is not anxious. It is intrinsic to faith to trust, and trust confidently, in Christ's continued work in me to preserve me in faith. A security, however, that would go beyond confidence and assurance and become certainty about a given fact is beyond our reach. Paul's message to "watch out that you do not fall" (1 Cor. 10:12) always remains relevant. Herein lies the sense of Luther's admonition that faith must always begin anew.[24] Faith cannot rest on its past existence; it must be renewed by a present, active trust.

Preaching is to renew that trust. To again quote Reu: "The mighty works of God need to be presented again and again even to the believing congregation, in order that by means of such preaching of the Gospel its faith may be renewed from day to day; for faith lives only so long as it is daily produced anew by God through the Gospel."[25]

But how is that renewal to be understood and preached? In the *Apology* [4:78], Melanchthon can equate justification with regeneration.[26] Luther speaks similarly: "Justification is in reality a kind of rebirth in newness."[27] Justification is inseparable from the reality of this new person. Nurturing that person is nurturing justification. The new person in Christ is thus the addressee of preaching that nurtures and renews justification. As Reu states: "The old Adam in the Christian is overcome only by means of the heightened efficacy of the motives controlling the new man, and it is this new man who must be the object of all preaching of repentance, comfort and sanctification to the children of God."[28] Reu can thus present edification as the central purpose of the sermon.[29] Edification nurtures what is present. New life "is not to be implanted by edification but existing as it does in whatever degree, it is to be strengthened, deepened, increased, advanced."[30]

Equating such edification with preaching sanctification is a significant theological mistake. It isolates justification from the ongoing Christian life. If justification is a relation that must be constantly renewed and preaching justification is preaching that maintains and nurtures that relation, then such edification is certainly a form of preaching justification when it preaches Christ as the one in whom the new self lives. The life of the new self is a life of being conformed to Christ. We are "to be conformed to the image of his Son" (Rom. 8:29). As Christ is formed in us, that relation of trust and dependence that is faith and that constitutes our justification is strengthened.

The entire range of what can be called "preaching Christ," the entire range of imaginatively presenting Christ to the congregation as the object of Christian trust, should be seen as participating in that conforming the person to Christ. On this subject, Reu quotes the nineteenth-century Reformed theologian R. L. Dabney: "The preacher's task may be correctly explained as that of (instrumentally) forming the image of Christ upon the souls of men. The plastic substance is the human heart. The die which is provided for the workman is the revealed Word; and the impression to be formed is the divine image of knowledge and true holiness."[31] This "imprinting" should not be seen simply as an exercise of moral influence, but as shaping the self of the hearer into Christ. The Catholic theologian Susan Wood notes: "Just as the early monks memorized the scriptures in order to interiorize them for the purpose of praying unceasingly, the Christian repeatedly participates in the liturgy so as to imprint that economy in his or her very being."[32] The reference to "economy" is here important. One way that conformity to Christ is developed is by the location of the self within the divine economy, narrated with its center in Christ. The weekly preaching of the word places the self within that narrative as it imaginatively develops that encompassing narrative world as the world within which the hearer lives.

Preaching justification is, then, preaching that speaks about Christ in such a way that it speaks and communicates Christ as the reality in whom the old self dies and the new self lives. The life of that new self, which is the realization of justification, is a life of being conformed to Christ. It involves not only an ever-anew dying and rising but also the present realization—however limited by the realities of sin and of this world—of the new, risen self who lives in anticipation of the last day, when the death of the old self and the perfection of the new is complete.

Excursus: Contrast with Gerhard Forde

This understanding of edification of the new person as an aspect of preaching justification is sharply contrasted with the understanding of preaching justification put forward by Gerhard Forde and some of his followers.[33] For Forde, as for many others in recent Lutheran theology, the "begin anew" passage in Luther's Romans lectures becomes the springboard for a view of the existence of faith (and the new self that comes to be in faith) as a series of utterly discontinuous moments.[34] "Being a Christian means ever and anew to be blasted by that divine lightning (for we always forget) and to begin anew."[35] For Forde, the sermon is always implicitly addressed to the old person, who must be slain. The new self is always rising, but never risen, and thus cannot be the addressee of the sermon.

This aspect of Forde's theology is not marginal to its logic. As David Yeago demonstrates, for Forde this world is not one in which God's eschatological action can take on an extended reality. For Forde, "while the eschatological event, the eschatological word of justification together with the eschatological faith which it elicits, occurs concretely in history, it does not itself *become historical*."[36] Thus, for Forde, "that being-blasted which is the end of the Old Being is at the same time the whole content of the New Being."[37] This exclusion of the new self from this world is clear in Forde's first book: "Man's acting and thinking in this life remain an acting and a thinking in this age, under the eschato-logical limit. The fact that it is also total grace means that man can be content to allow his acting and thinking *to remain as it is*, totally in this age; he can trust in Christ entirely for the gift of the new age."[38] Faith does not transform—all is "to remain as it is"—for when the new takes shape within this world, it can only be presumption and thus invites the divine lightning. Herein lies what Yeago analyzes as the profoundly Gnostic character of Forde's theology.[39] Unfortunately, Forde's theol-ogy, while unusually pointed in its conclusions (its single-minded focus is a part of its attraction), is representative of central trends in Lutheran theology of the last 150 years.[40]

Conclusion

What is it to preach justification? It is to preach Christ as the one in whom we live and move and have our being and thus the one in whom is our righteousness. When Christ is preached as the one on whom we can depend in every need, and in particular as the only one on whom we can depend in the decisive crisis of God's judgment, then justifica-tion is preached.

PART TWO

Gospel Proclamation and Scripture

Preparing to Preach the Gospels

4

Interpreting the Unity and Diversity of the Fourfold Gospel Canon

IRA BRENT DRIGGERS

Even a casual reader of the New Testament Gospels will notice that they each tell the same basic story, but with many differences, both small and large. To borrow the scholarly jargon, the Gospels exhibit a "unity in diversity." If our casual reader is religiously uncommitted, reading the Gospels out of mere curiosity or academic obligation, then she will probably find this just an interesting observation, on par with the similarities and differences in Dostoevsky's great novels. For the Christian who grants the Gospels scriptural authority, however, the matter merits further attention. How can the Gospels exhibit differences, even tensions, while being equally true? Are the differences themselves important for understanding the truth of a particular Gospel, and if so, why? This essay attempts to answer these questions with an eye toward a common pastoral scenario: the preacher-exegete preparing a sermon.

I begin by briefly describing the challenge of honoring differences between the Gospels. For the contemporary preacher, it is the challenge of interpreting each Gospel on its own terms. I next place this challenge within the larger history of interpretation, pointing out that the church has always acknowledged tensions in Scripture. The primary vocation of the ancient church, however, was to discern beyond those tensions a unified story of salvation, thus setting the wide boundaries of orthodoxy within which the contemporary preacher interprets Scripture. Next I analyze the tension between Matthew 16:13-28 and Mark 8:27—9:1 (Peter's so-called messianic confession) to show how each Gospel exhibits its own distinctive narrative logic. Interpreting each Gospel on its own terms is a matter of tending precisely to this distinctive narrative logic, thus ensuring the preacher's consideration of the full range of homiletic possibilities for her congregation. In conclusion I offer some final clarifications on the relationship between exegesis and sermon writing. By the end, readers should better understand how the underlying unity of the Gospels does not preclude our acknowledgment of their very real differences, and how careful attention to those differences can produce sermons consistent with the orthodoxy that unites them.

The Challenge of Preaching a Fourfold Gospel

At some point every seminarian faces the question of how the church benefits from a plurality of Gospel narratives and how the differences between them do not undermine the church's claim to a single, non-contradictory, gospel story. The analogy I initially use is one of four people viewing the same sculpture from different angles. Each will view the sculpture differently and, if asked to draw what she sees, will arrive at a rather different picture. So it is with the evangelists. Even in the many cases where they share the same basic oral tradition (for example, a specific miracle story or teaching), they will often narrate that tradition differently in accordance with the specific concerns they have for their respective hearers. The stories are shaped in different ways so as to edify the church in different ways. Yet all the stories render the same Christ truthfully.

Most of the seminarians whom I teach are following a call to ministry in a traditional parish setting, so they will be asked to interpret Scripture with the aim of preaching to their congregations on Sundays. In teaching them the basic exegetical skills that go into sermon preparation, I am fond of saying things like, "If the text is from Matthew, make sure you're interpreting Matthew, and not Luke or John." This is because the tendency for many students is to assume that all four evangelists mean the same thing, or close to the same thing, in virtually every instance. On the one hand, they rightly understand that the Gospels, and in fact the entirety of Scripture, exhibit an underlying theological coherence. On the other hand, however, they are prone to let this understanding blind them to an evangelist's distinctive mode of discourse. They are not accustomed to interpreting each Gospel *on its own terms*. One sees this especially when the text in question is difficult to interpret or simply unsuited to the student's heretofore unchallenged assumptions. In these cases it is easy to resort to what another evangelist says in a parallel scene, either for clarification or escape. Only with reinforcement in lectures and practice in exegesis do students begin to understand that the basic theological coherence of the four Gospels does not mean agreement in every instance. Parallel episodes can in fact "mean" different things in different Gospels.

The Church's Discernment of a Unified Scriptural Story

The idea of tension does not always sit well with seminarians, particularly those less familiar with academic biblical criticism. That is why it helps them to know that the church has always acknowledged tension among the Gospels, and indeed throughout Scripture. The famous defense of the four Gospels by Irenaeus, second-century bishop of Lyons, was given at a time when the church was still finding its way on this issue and when many believed that a plurality of Gospels was problematic.[1] Irenaeus notes that Docetist Christians read only Mark, that Ebionite Christians read only Matthew, that Valentinian Christians gravitated toward John, and that Marcion rejected all three in favor of an altered version of Luke.[2] Meanwhile, Tatian opted to harmonize all four Gospels into a single narrative (the *Diatessaron*), thereby eliminating the distinctive sequencing of each, and with the likely intention of supplanting them as autonomous narratives.[3] Finally, Gnostic Christians read and transmitted distinctively Gnostic Gospels such as *The Gospel of Thomas* and *The Gospel of Truth*. Thus, Francis Watson writes that the gradual and collective decision to adopt the four now-canonical Gospels was "an attempt to impose order in response to the threat of chaos."[4] The need for order, however, was not one of obsessive compulsion but of right theology. The church discerned over time, in other words, that together these particular Gospels captured the truth about what the God of Israel did, does, and will do in Jesus Christ.

The crucial point here is that the church, in adopting a fourfold Gospel canon, claimed that a *diversity* of witnesses was essential for understanding the life, death, and resurrection of Jesus Christ. There was one gospel "according to" (κατά) four different inspired writers. Even more to the point, there was one gospel according to the whole chorus of scriptural writers—that is, the entire biblical canon pointed to Jesus Christ. Moreover, tensions between the biblical documents were less an *obstacle* to understanding than an *impetus* for discerning a larger overarching narrative. The ancient church believed, in other words, that all the biblical documents, despite their divergent authors, audiences, and circumstances, pointed to a unifying story of God, a story that no single document fully captured but that was sufficiently reflected in the collection as a whole. This overarching story came to be known as the "Rule of Faith," and it was through this Rule (exemplified today, though with significant theological development, in the Nicene Creed) that the church in turn interpreted Scripture, not as a way of harmonizing divergent documents into a single scriptural text but as a way of *honoring the diversity itself.* The larger story of God's salvation in Christ was the most important thing; and insofar as it was a story about God it could not be contradictory. The purpose of Scripture was seen as bearing witness, through various and divergent voices, to the larger divine story.[5]

It is well known that the ancient and medieval church frequently used allegorical interpretation as a way of addressing tension in Scripture. It was through allegory that seemingly problematic passages (problematic when read in the "literal sense") were brought into conformity with the Rule of Faith. What is often missed, however, is the extent to which such recourse to allegory honored the diversity of the scriptural witness. It was not a form of harmonization on the level of Tatian's *Diatessaron*, which created a single narrative out of four. It was rather a way of upholding the sufficiency of the biblical canon—tensions and all—in bearing witness to a God in whom there is no contradiction. While modern historical criticism helped the church distinguish between the allegorical meaning of a passage and the likely "intended" meaning of its human author, it was not equipped to render a verdict on the truthfulness of any given allegory in relation to the Rule, much less render a verdict on the truthfulness of the Rule itself. It simply approached the issue of diversity—which the church had always embraced—in terms of strictly human history. It stressed the importance of historical context as a way of preventing the mere imposition of meaning upon the text. But the possibility of a theologically truthful interpretation not "intended" by an historical author, or not likely considered by an "original" audience, lay outside its method of investigation.[6]

This requires a crucial clarification. It would be wrong to assume that the church's traditional focus on the overarching story of God signifies disinterest in history, as if the Rule simply pointed "above" Scripture to some heavenly, otherworldly reality. Rather, the Rule tells a thoroughly historical story by forwarding an interpretation of a particular flesh-and-blood person who lived in a particular time and place within human history. In fact, an underlying motivation for the crafting of the first written Gospel (Mark) may very well have been the reinforcement of Jesus' real flesh-and-blood existence, discouraging Christians from conceiving him in strictly spiritual terms or altogether anti-materialist terms. The difference from the modern historical-critical approach, then, is actually not one of greater or lesser concern for historical reality. The difference is primarily over whether we go on to make sense—that is, theological sense—of historical reality: What is the ultimate *meaning* of Christ's flesh-and-blood existence? One could argue that this approach actually reflects a *greater* concern for history to the extent that it seeks to understand its full significance.

To be clear though, I am not suggesting that allegorical interpretation simply replace standard academic exegesis, especially when it comes to the task of sermon preparation (the next section exemplifies a rather historical mode of exegesis to accentuate tension between the Gospels). My point is simply that seminarians confronted with tension between the Gospels are not being exposed to some uniquely modern discovery or concern. They are, rather, entering into a conversation as old as the church itself.[7] Still, while the tradition of allegorical interpretation will continue to edify the church, it cannot serve as the preacher's primary approach to scriptural tension. Allegory played an indispensable role in the ancient church's discernment and defense of the Rule, and this in a pagan culture that often pointed to scriptural tensions as a way of refuting Christianity (yet was fortunately open to allegory). It was thus a means of both doctrinal development and institutional survival. But there have always been important voices within the church warning against the overuse of allegorical interpretation at the expense of Scripture's "literal" sense.[8] In many respects modern historical criticism represents a continuation of this concern; it is part of, and largely consistent with, much of the church's history of interpretation. And while the truthfulness of the Rule lay outside its philosophical purview, historical criticism has forced a healthy reconsideration of the relationship between the Rule and the task of exegesis.

What I mean is that the preacher's exegesis must honor the tensions between the Gospels in a different way, not with the intention of bringing the text into strict conformity with the Rule (since no single document can carry its full weight), but with the understanding that the Rule establishes certain limits to what she can eventually proclaim out of her exegesis. The Rule does not represent a hermeneutic tightrope. Rather, it establishes the wide boundaries for orthodox proclamation of the one gospel.[9] Within these boundaries, exegesis employs its linguistic, historical, and literary tools to explore the text's significance for "the one holy catholic and apostolic church" that spans two millennia. The preacher prayerfully discerns, based largely on the fruits of her exegetical labor, what God is saying to her congregation in this particular time and place.

In this scenario the church's rich tradition of allegorical interpretation remains an invaluable homiletic resource. But the appropriateness of a given allegory must be judged by the preacher's nonallegorical exegesis. Recourse to allegory, in other words, should not short-circuit the exegetical enterprise any more than should recourse to a more amenable Gospel parallel. This allows the preacher to interpret each Gospel on its own terms, without the anxiety of having to arrive at, or defend, the Rule of Faith by strictly exegetical means. Today's preacher *inherits* the Rule, which grants her the freedom of exegetical play, along with the responsibility of proclaiming the truth of Christ. To return to the issue with which I opened this essay, the preacher may boldly explore how parallel episodes in the Gospels can in fact "mean" different things, provided the exegesis gives shape to a noncontradictory, orthodox sermon.

Honoring the Diversity in the Fourfold Gospel Canon

I began this essay by likening the four Gospels to four people gazing upon a single sculpture from four different angles. Students generally find this analogy useful in helping them appreciate the differences between the evangelists. What the analogy actually fails to explain, however, is why the exegete should interpret each Gospel on its own terms, without recourse to another Gospel. After all, isn't the point in gazing upon a sculpture precisely to view it from every possible angle? Do we not do Christ a great disservice in limiting ourselves to a single vantage point? Standing directly in front of Michelangelo's David, for instance, one cannot see the entire expression on his face, since his head is turned to the left. If we want to offer an interpretation of that expression, and thus of the sculpture as a whole, we would do well to walk over to David's left side and spend some time there too. There we will see more clearly a face that is surprisingly distraught. Yet, from David's left side, we will lose sight of his very strong right arm, which stands somewhat in tension with the facial expression. Each angle contributes to our understanding of the whole, yet each is limited in what it reveals. We need every angle to understand the sculpture.

A perceptive student will soon detect the limits of the sculpture analogy in defending the exegesis of each Gospel on its own terms. In fact, the analogy intends only to illustrate the logic of *canonization*, that is, the logic of the church as it discerned the appropriateness of a fourfold Gospel canon, as opposed to a single narrative or harmonization. My own *exegetical* point is better illustrated on the analogy first made by Irenaeus, who famously likened the fourfold Gospel canon to the four-faced creature of Ezekiel 1:10, with each face corresponding to an evangelist (lion, ox, human, and eagle).[10] Here there is no confusing the four faces—I do not better understand the lion face by turning my gaze to the eagle face. In fact, understanding the lion face requires giving it some amount of *separate* attention. Yet I do not forget that it is only one of four faces belonging to the same creature. In this analogy the distinctiveness of each of the four Gospels is better retained, but without compromising their underlying unity. Each of the Gospels represents a *distinctive* face of the one Lord.

Of course, in his own context, Irenaeus is trying to defend only the appropriateness of the number four and not a particular exegetical method. So I am pushing the analogy somewhat beyond his intention. My point is simply that each Gospel narrative exhibits its own narrative coherence, its own inner logic, and that one's exegesis of a given Gospel requires attention to that distinctive logic, especially if the goal is preaching. This is not to deny the predominant coherence of the Gospels, much less the Rule of Faith to which they all point. It is, rather, to insist that preachers ground their sermons in the exegesis of a particular Gospel text—indeed, the *entire* Gospel text. Every Gospel passage, in other words, falls within a larger narrative context that helps determine its meaning for that particular evangelist. To preach a text from Matthew demands intimate knowledge of the entire Gospel of Matthew. To preach a text from Mark demands intimate knowledge of the entire Gospel of Mark. And so on. In homiletic terms, *extracting a passage from its narrative context precludes that Gospel's distinctive voice, thus placing limits on what it can say to a congregation.*

Interpreting Peter's Messianic Confession

An exegetical example will go some way toward illustrating my point. The Gospel of Mark narrates a well-known scene, also used by Matthew and Luke, in which Peter first acknowledges that Jesus is the Christ or "anointed one" of God (Matt. 16:13-28; Mark 8:27—9:1; Luke 9:18-27).[11] In all three accounts Jesus initiates the conversation by asking the disciples about whom people perceive him to be. They respond by telling him that people view him as some kind of prophet. Jesus then inquires as to the disciples' own view. Peter answers on behalf of the group in identifying Jesus as the Christ, a royal title designating Jesus as the anointed king of Israel ("Messiah," as derived from the Hebrew). In all three accounts Jesus commands the disciples to silence, tacitly acknowledging the truth of Peter's claim. He then proceeds to prophesy his impending passion for the first time and to explain the demands of discipleship in christological terms: denying one's self, taking up one's cross, and losing one's life.

The three accounts obviously share some fundamental themes. Most notably, there is the contrast between the "people" (Matt. 16:13; Mark 8:27) or "crowds" (Luke 9:22) on the one hand, and the followers of Jesus on the other hand. Unlike the rest of the world, the disciples are called to recognize Jesus for who he really is, not merely one prophet in a long line of prophets but the one and only Christ. Likewise, the disciples are called to understand the necessity (δεῖ) of Jesus' passion, a violent consequence of his messianic authority and ministry meeting the resistance of those wielding worldly power. Finally, they are called to follow Jesus in a way that mirrors his passion, giving themselves—entirely—to Jesus and his mission for the world. In short, Christology defines discipleship. Who Jesus is determines who his followers are.

Yet despite these basic parallels one still finds tension stemming from distinctive modes of discourse. This is especially the case in the juxtaposition of Matthew and Mark. Matthew (unlike Luke) retains from his Markan source Peter's protest against Jesus' passion prediction, to which Jesus responds by more clearly aligning that passion with "the things of God" (τὰ τοῦ θεοῦ; Matt. 16:23; Mark 8:33). However, in Matthew the logic of Peter's protest is more praiseworthy. Moreover, Matthew adds a positive response from Jesus to Peter's initial messianic confession. The key Matthean additions can be seen in bold below.

Mark 8:29-33	Matthew 16:16-23
[29]Peter answered him, "You are the Messiah."	[16]Simon Peter answered, "You are the Messiah, the Son of the living God." [17]And Jesus answered him, **"Blessed are you, Simon son of Jonah! For flesh and blood has not revealed this to you, but my Father in heaven. [18]And I tell you, you are Peter, and on this rock I will build my church, and the gates of Hades will not prevail against it. [19]I will give you the keys of the kingdom of heaven, and whatever you bind on earth will be bound in heaven, and whatever you loose on earth will be loosed in heaven."** [20]Then
[30]And he sternly ordered them not to tell anyone about him. [31]Then he began to teach them that the Son of Man must undergo great suffering, and be rejected by the elders, the	he sternly ordered the disciples not to tell anyone that he was the Messiah. [21]From that time on, Jesus began to show his disciples that he must go to Jerusalem and undergo great

chief priests, and the scribes, and be killed, and after three days rise again. [32]He said all this quite openly. And Peter took him aside and began to rebuke him. [33]But turning and looking at his disciples, he rebuked Peter and said, "Get behind me, Satan! For you are setting your mind not on divine things but on human things."

suffering at the hands of the elders and chief priests and scribes, and be killed, and on the third day be raised. [22]And Peter took him aside and began to rebuke him, saying, **"God forbid it, Lord! This must never happen to you."** [23]But he turned and said to Peter, "Get behind me, Satan! You are a stumbling block to me; for you are setting your mind not on divine things but on human things."

At first glance it might appear that Matthew has simply removed the ambiguity from Mark's account. He seems to have clarified the source of Peter's confession (a revelation from God) and the reason behind Peter's resistance to the passion (he does not want Jesus to suffer). Consistent with these positive details, he adds the promise of Peter's role as the apostolic foundation of Jesus' church. Students are generally prone to explain the differences in precisely this way, not as real tensions but as one evangelist clarifying another. In fact, when faced only with the passage from Mark, students often supply such Matthean details subconsciously, having encountered them at some point in the past.[12]

Attention to narrative context, however, reveals that these differences are real tensions. In Mark's narrative, for instance, subsequent episodes show that the disciples resist Jesus' passion out of *self*-preservation, not out of concern for Jesus' well-being. It is true that Peter's "rebuke" of Jesus in Mark 8:32 is ambiguous—and perhaps intentionally so—but by the end of the Markan narrative it becomes painfully clear that the disciples simply do not follow the path of discipleship modeled on a crucified Messiah. In fact, Mark 8:27—9:1 is only the first of three episodes in the Gospel's crucial middle section (Mark 8:22—10:52) in which the disciples fail to take in Jesus' passion prediction, respond with self-serving, glory-seeking concerns, and elicit from Jesus a bold corrective teaching on the true nature of discipleship (Mark 9:30-37, 10:32-45). Each episode follows precisely this threefold sequence, with no sign of Jesus' teaching actually sinking in.

This is all part of a larger dynamic in Mark (and unique to Mark) according to which *no one* in the narrative exhibits a right understanding of the Christ before his death. The original ending of Mark's Gospel

(16:8) does not even include a resurrection appearance from Jesus and the expected restoration of the disciples who had abandoned him. The evangelist promises this reunion (Mark 14:28, 16:7), just as he promises the disciples' proclamation of the gospel to the nations (13:9-13); but he does not actually narrate either one. The effect of these omissions is to accentuate the magnitude of Jesus' suffering and death as the climax of the story and as the very thing that blinds characters to his messianic authority. The passion, in other words, so violates traditional expectations for a power-wielding Messiah that it can only elicit misunderstanding, abandonment, and, in the case of Jesus' opponents, mockery. So it is no wonder that Peter rebukes Jesus after his first passion prediction: it does not square with the messianic title he has just accepted. Nor does it square with the disciples' understanding of their own status as the Messiah's trusted companions. In Peter's view, then, Jesus does not understand who he really is! In reality, however, it is Peter who misunderstands. He is using the right word ("Christ") but resisting Jesus' radical redefinition.

Of course, one need only read Matthew's own passion account to see that he retains many of these themes. He upholds the connection between Jesus' messianic authority on the one hand, and his suffering and death on the other hand. Related to this, he keeps the account of the disciples abandoning Jesus upon his arrest (Matt. 26:56; omitted by Luke), so that there is still a sense in which Jesus' suffering and death scandalizes even his followers. The fundamental connection between Christology and discipleship is no less Matthean than Markan, as Jesus' teaching in Matthew 16:24-28 makes clear (see also Matt. 18:1-5, 20:25-28). However, Matthew does not go as far as Mark in depicting wholesale misunderstanding of Jesus' messianic identity prior to his death. Indeed, the messianic confession of the Matthean Peter is hardly misguided. Rather, it stems directly from divine revelation: "Blessed are you, Simon son of Jonah! For flesh and blood has not revealed this to you, but my Father in heaven" (Matt. 16:17).

Moreover, Matthew's redaction of Mark 8:22—10:52 includes the softening of key moments of the disciples' misunderstanding. The disciples no longer respond to Jesus' second passion prediction by "arguing with each other" (πρὸς ἀλλήλους γὰρ διελέχθησαν; Mark 9:34) about who is the greatest. Rather, they simply ask Jesus, "Who is the greatest in the kingdom of heaven?" (Matt. 18:1). Jesus' answer is the same in both accounts: it is the child. But the initial question is significantly different. While the Markan disciples debate their own greatness quite apart from Jesus' wisdom, the Matthean disciples seek Jesus' wisdom on "greatness" without any apparent self-interest. Similarly, after Jesus' third passion prediction, it is no longer James and John who request seats of honor in Jesus' coming glory (Mark 10:35-37) but, rather, their mother who requests it on their behalf (Matt. 20:20-21). Again, the response is the same: disciples are called "to serve" like Jesus (διακονῆσαι; Matt. 20:28; Mark 10:45) rather than to "lord it over" others like Gentiles (κατακυριεύουσιν; Matt. 20:25; Mark 10:42). But the initial question carries a different significance coming from a different character. It allows Matthew to again safeguard a greater continuity between the teachings of Jesus and the actions of the disciples. For Matthew's own pastoral purposes, it is important to emphasize the obedience of the church's apostolic foundation (see also Matt. 10:2-4; 14:28-29; 16:16-19; 18:18, 21-22; 19:28).

Nowhere is this concern for an apostolic foundation more apparent than in Matthew's account of Peter's messianic confession. Not only does the confession stem from divine revelation (Matt. 16:17); it is an indication of Peter's future as "the rock" (ἡ πέτρα) upon which Jesus builds his church, "and the gates of Hades will not prevail against it" (Matt. 16:18). The authority to bind and loose (Matt. 16:19), which Peter shares with the other apostles (Matt. 18:18), points to Matthew's larger concern for the well-being and longevity of an increasingly institutionalized "church," a concern that scholars generally attribute to the late-first-century rivalry between Pharisaic Judaism on the one hand, and Jewish Christianity (or Christian Judaism) on the other hand.[13] Given these ecclesial priorities, Matthew makes sure to depict Peter's rebuke of Jesus as one of concern for *Jesus'* well-being. There is still misunderstanding; and Jesus still attributes the misunderstanding to Satanic influence (Matt. 16:23; Mark 8:33). But the fundamental disagreement shifts from self-concern to genuine concern: "God forbid it, Lord! This must never happen to you" (Matt. 20:22).

Preaching Peter's Messianic Confession

What difference does it make for the preacher to heed these tensions between Matthew 16:13-28 and Mark 8:27—9:1? What difference does it make, in other words, to read each Gospel on its own terms, honoring its distinct narrative coherence? To begin, it should reinforce for the preacher the extent to which each evangelist intends to offer a *theological interpretation* of Jesus, as opposed to a strictly historical-factual chronicle of his life. To be sure, each tells the story of the same flesh-and-blood figure, and their oral and written traditions originate, for the most part, in the words and deeds of that historical figure. But the purpose in collecting those traditions is not primarily to record them, unaltered, for the sake of posterity, as if each evangelist were creating a kind of literary time capsule. The purpose is, rather, to shape the faith of early Christian communities, moving beyond the bare facts of Jesus to illustrate his true significance as the Christ and to help believers live into their calling as his disciples.[14]

This means that the preacher, faced with tensions between the Gospels, should not get caught up in the question of "what really happened," at least not to the point that she becomes an historian of Jesus rather than a proclaimer of Jesus. Of course, any historical information that sheds light on the meaning of a text will prove helpful. But her vocation as preacher is more analogous to that of the evangelists themselves, insofar as she is called to build up the church in its love for the Lord and to clarify its collective purpose in the world. The obvious difference is that she is retelling and interpreting the Gospels rather than writing them. But her fundamental vocation is the same: to bring to Christians the good news of Jesus Christ in all his significance.

Nor should we assume that Mark is any more historically accurate than Matthew, or that Matthew is any more theologically driven than Mark. The fact that Mark precedes Matthew, and that Matthew reshapes Mark, has no bearing on our assessment of their overall purpose (in fact, Mark has reshaped his oral sources just as much as Matthew has reshaped Mark, and the oral sources were already reshaping previous traditions). At the end of the day, then, we cannot know exactly what words were exchanged between Peter and Jesus concerning Jesus' messianic identity. If we were to approach the subject as strict historians, we might deduce from the evidence that there *was* a conversation between them; but we could not move much beyond that. Obviously this kind of approach does nothing to build up Christ's church; it does not make for a meaningful sermon. Fortunately, however, the evangelists are not asking us to read their narratives as strict historians but, rather, as disciples of Jesus open to having our faith shaped by their written testimony. This gives us the freedom to hear each Gospel on its own terms, to be shaped by each testimony in accordance with its own distinct logic. Stated simply, all four evangelists share the same vocation of interpreting Jesus' theological significance, but they carry out that vocation in their own ways.

To get right to the point, then, a sermon on Mark 8:27—9:1 should be grounded in exegetical work that has not imposed its Matthean (or Lukan) parallel onto the text, while a sermon on Matthew 16:13-28 should be grounded in exegetical work that has not imposed its Markan (or Lukan) parallel onto the text. In my view this rule applies to any sermon that is focused primarily on a Gospel text, and it includes passages without obvious parallels in other Gospels.[15] The point, in other words, is to keep one's exegetical focus firmly upon the particular Gospel at issue. To restate an earlier claim, every Gospel passage falls within a larger narrative context that helps determine its meaning for that particular evangelist. To draw from a different narrative context, then, is to risk losing sight of an evangelist's distinct angle on Jesus.

Consider, for instance, how the larger narrative context of Mark helps us explain Peter's rebuke of Jesus in terms of Peter's own self-preserving impulse. Peter does not understand the full import of his own "messianic confession," and in fact stands strongly at odds with Jesus over the nature of Jesus' messianic vocation. But what would happen if the preacher went to Matthew 16:13-28, either consciously or subconsciously, for assistance in her exegetical work of Mark 8:27—9:1? She would likely lose sight of a major point (if not *the* point) of the conversation in Mark's Gospel, which is to accentuate the scandal posed by a crucified Messiah *even to the Messiah's own followers.* This is not to say that the preacher could not ultimately preach something biblically or scripturally "true." But in losing sight of Mark's distinctive logic she does, at the very least, do a great disservice to the Gospel text from which she purports to preach. Stated simply, she has not allowed *Mark* to shape her sermon. She has missed an opportunity to confront her congregation with the manifold ways it resists Jesus' crucifixion out of concern for its own survival in the world.

Likewise, what would happen if the preacher went to Mark 8:27—9:1, either consciously or subconsciously, for assistance in her exegetical work on Matthew 16:13-28? This is somewhat less likely since Mark is the more ambiguous of the two. However, it is not going too far to imagine that some preachers, somewhat put off by the concept of a "Petrine foundation," might find the Markan (or Lukan) parallel more suitable to their homiletic ambitions. I do not mean to endorse any particular ecclesial manifestation of that foundation but, rather, to insist again that the preacher should strive to hear the Gospel on its own terms. Matthew has a particular stake in Jesus building (οἰκοδομήσω; Matt. 16:18) the church upon Peter specifically (even if Peter shares the responsibility of binding and loosing with the other apostles), and it is precisely through his messianic confession that Peter is revealed to be that foundation. This Petrine claim must be understood and engaged and not simply dismissed. Here again the preacher does the Gospel a great disservice in losing sight of, or avoiding, its distinctive narrative logic. She has not allowed *Matthew* to shape her sermon.

Final Clarifications

It is worth repeating that this entire discussion has focused on the task of scriptural exegesis, which I take to be different from the process of *sermon writing*. While the preacher can never forget or entirely bracket her concerns as pastor, ideally she will not allow those concerns simply to dictate the message of her sermon. Ideally the preacher will attempt to have her exegesis of the scriptural text inform and direct her sermon to some degree. Her concerns as pastor help her discern what "in" the text merits special attention and homiletic reflection; but her prayerful exegesis first helps her see what is "in" the text. While this is a grossly oversimplified depiction of the interpretive process—at least as far as philosophical hermeneutics is concerned—it is a helpful way for preachers to imagine their vocation as heralds of God's word.

Of course, when it comes to the Gospels, a preacher can always find a way to honor an evangelist's distinctive logic in her exegetical preparation while in her actual preaching still avoiding the things she does not like. A pastorally honest and responsible preacher will, however, be more likely to wrestle with such challenging issues in her sermon if her initial exegesis has at least brought them to her attention. At the same time, there is nothing wrong with taking from one's exegesis a message that is not distinctive to the particular Gospel in question. I have already noted, for instance, how the Synoptic accounts of Peter's messianic confession share important themes related to Jesus' authority as Messiah, his future as suffering Messiah, and the implications for following a suffering Messiah. The task of Gospel exegesis is not strictly a matter of isolating an evangelist's distinctive logic; it is a matter of discerning *everything* that an evangelist might be saying to the church. The point is simply that this "everything" includes what is distinctive, and that what is distinctive is just as important as what is shared. Exegesis that treats each Gospel on its own terms will inevitably uncover both, while confusing Gospel narratives will likely preclude uncovering what is distinctive. At stake, then, is the degree to which the preacher opens herself up to *the full range of homiletic possibilities* that an evangelist provides. This, in a nutshell, is why the preacher honors, rather than harmonizes, the tensions between the Gospels.

Finally, there is the issue of the preacher's use of the lectionary. In no way do I mean to suggest that a sermon must be "based on" a single lectionary text, Gospel or otherwise. The lectionary, after all, reflects the church's belief in the underlying unity of Scripture: all the canonical documents, despite their divergent historical circumstances, point to the one story of salvation. Because of this the preacher is free (though in my view never obligated) to incorporate the full range of lectionary texts into her sermon. It is often appropriate even to draw from passages outside the lectionary. It will depend on what emerges from the intersection of exegesis and pastoral context.

However, the lectionary is not a license to bypass sound academic exegesis and the discernment of an evangelist's (or any biblical writer's) distinctive voice. If the preacher opts to emphasize a particular aspect of a Lukan text, for instance, because it coincides with something in the accompanying Exodus text, then she should be cognizant of the homiletic possibilities that this decision leaves behind. Again, it is a matter of opening oneself up to the full range of homiletic possibilities that an evangelist provides. Because one does not want to close the door on a surprising and challenging scriptural message, one honors the diversity of the fourfold Gospel canon.

From the Gospels to the Sermon 5

The Presence of the Church in Text and Proclamation

AGNETA ENERMALM TSIPARIS

Underlying this essay is a concern for bridging the gap between texts chosen from the Synoptic Gospels and the sermon based on them. The gap I perceive is at times the result of a lack of exegesis, but more commonly it exists because of a lack of appreciation for the realities of the church reflected in those texts. This is explicable with the shift in biblical scholarship away from attention to the functions of the Jesus traditions within the life of the early church as in form criticism, and away from attention to the theology of the authors and their communities as in early redaction criticism. Instead, much current biblical research gives major or exclusive importance to literary features of the texts or their relationship to sociocultural issues of their time. While such emphases are all valid and worthwhile, for preaching it is detrimental if the theological content of the texts, their nature as faith documents, is neglected in favor of other concerns. This essay will focus on the realities of the church as one can discern them in New Testament texts, predominantly chosen from the Synoptic Gospels.

Another gap that I will address regards the reception of the sermon. Due to deficient knowledge of and appreciation for the Bible, the listeners may not perceive the connection between the text they have heard and its exposition in the sermon. Among the listeners whose relation to the church is more remote, misconceptions about the Bible are rampant. In Europe,[1] biblical texts are interpreted in the name of private religiosity, neglecting both the findings of biblical scholarship and the interpretive traditions of the church. Appreciation for the Bible is limited to its role as a component of the European literary and cultural heritage. It follows, then, that interpretation of biblical texts is restricted to historicizing, psychologizing, or aesthetical points of view.[2] Such perspectives of interpretation do not pay attention to the link of biblical texts to living communities of faith. If knowledge of the Bible and its world will facilitate reception, so will awareness of being a worshiping community of faith, in the midst of whom and for whom preaching occurs. In this essay, then, I am concerned about two frames of reference that ought to be shared between preacher and listeners: that of the biblical world and that of being a worshiping community. Within the biblical texts themselves the presence of worshiping communities can often be discerned. Once the preacher and the listeners have begun to see that presence, the distance between the biblical text and its use in today's worship may be diminished.

After these statements of introduction I will proceed as follows. A passage from 1 Peter will be the point of departure for an exposition on how "church" was defined early in the history of our Christian faith. I have chosen to start with the passage from 1 Peter 2:9-10 because it is a very full description of the church, apt to stimulate our thinking. With the recent *Evangelical Lutheran Worship*[3] also as our guide, I will then analyze the Community Discourse in Matthew 18, where the word ἐκκλησία (*church*) actually appears (v. 17; also in 16:18), this without any parallels in the other Synoptic Gospels. The focus is on Jesus' promise in 18:20, "I am there among them." A brief discussion of the church understood as "people of God" in the Gospel according to Luke will follow. I will then explore the Gospel according to Mark for elements of ecclesiology. Under the separate heading "The Gospels and Worship" I will search for connections between the Synoptic Gospels and a developing early Christian liturgy. For this purpose, I will again investigate the Gospels according to Mark, Luke, and Matthew, in this order, with most attention paid to Matthew. A brief conclusion will complete my essay.

What Is the Church According to the Synoptic Gospels?

What we can call a capsule version is found in 1 Peter 2:9-10:

> But you are a chosen race, a royal priesthood, a holy nation, God's own people, in order that you may proclaim the mighty acts of him who called you out of darkness into his marvelous light. Once you were not a people, but now you are God's people; once you had not received mercy, but now you have received mercy.

When Christians gather for worship, they express who they are: a royal priesthood, a fellowship of priests. They know that the life they live in private or public arenas is vertically oriented—toward God, the King of the universe. The dignity of standing close to God is a privilege given by God to this fellowship of priests who represent the Gentiles, to whom God's mercy now extends.[4] Furthermore, those who have been called together by God to be the church have a common origin (γένος, "race"). The preceding context shows that their origin is in Christ, the cornerstone. On this cornerstone they are being built up as a church, the house of the Lord (2:4-7).[5] The church is also a "holy nation," which means that its people have the same customs or ways of life (ἔθνος, "nation"). They are called to a distinctive way of life as they, "citizens" of this nation, live out their vocation in the societies of which they are a part. In so doing, they are pursuing a common goal as those who through God's mercy have been made God's own people (λαός) for the purpose of mission, to make known the "mighty acts of God."[6] We note in this Petrine passage a plethora of corporate definitions of the church. The richness of description should remind us of the many images for "church" in the New Testament,[7] out of which a few will be discussed below. For now, we can paraphrase the *précis* of 1 Peter 2:9-10 in the following short statements: Christ is the basis for the church's existence; worship is its essential mark; human society is where the vocation of its members is lived out, in reverence for God.

In the guide to worship that *Evangelical Lutheran Worship* provides, we learn that Christ as the Word of God is encountered in the liturgy in several ways. Among them is the bodily presence of the Christian community.[8] This very biblical statement is worthy of our attention. The apostle Paul speaks extensively about the church as the body of Christ. The Gospel according to Matthew does not reach the Pauline (or Petrine) precision in its understanding of ἐκκλησία, the church as assembly. After all, it is a narrative and not an arguing letter. Nevertheless, in this Gospel we hear of a particular closeness between Christ and the community of faith. Such an understanding permeates the entirety of Matthew 18. This chapter, called the Community Discourse, contains a multiplicity of topics. All of them gravitate toward two concerns: (1) care for the "little ones"; and (2) practice of forgiveness. In 18:20, the promise of Christ's presence with the ἐκκλησία, the assembly, resounds: "For where two or three are gathered in my name, I am there among them." The key expression "I am among them" is a manifestation of a prevalent biblical theme. It is also a christological motif that plays a key role in the Gospel according to Matthew, from the name Immanuel in 1:23 with its Greek translation "God with us," to the repetition at the very end of the Gospel (28:20), where the risen Jesus says, "And remember, I am with you always, to the end of the age." This repetition, or inclusion, conveys that the presence of the exalted Lord with his church[9] establishes him as Immanuel, that is, as "God with us."[10] That the risen Jesus is Lord is clear from verse 18: "All authority in heaven and on earth has been given to me." The prepositional phrase in 1:23, 18:20, and 28:20—"with us," "among them," and "with you [plural]" respectively—connects this high Christology (that is, an evaluation of Jesus that includes an aspect of divinity) closely with ecclesiology.

The declaration of God's being with a person, a group, or the people of Israel is frequent in the Hebrew Bible. It often occurs as promise to those who are journeying into the unknown, reassuring them of God's protection and blessing, for example, Genesis 28:15 (Jacob) or Exodus 3:12 (Moses). The history of the Davidic period, beyond the time of the ancestors or of Moses, is another crucial point for the use of this promise (cf. Isa. 7:14, quoted in Matt. 1:23). In a survey of "God's being with" in the Old Testament, Hobst D. Preuss highlights this declaration's firm connection with history. Even though we find the phrase used in postexilic texts as a greeting, it never becomes cultically determined.[11]

What about Matthew 18:20, where the immediate context for "I am there among them" is one of prayer (v. 19)? Does this connection between prayer and the declaration by Jesus limit the presence of the resurrected Christ to the worship services of the assembly (ἐκκλησία, v. 17)—that is, is the phrase after all cultically determined here? A closer reading of 18:20 in its context (v. 19) reveals that Christ's presence is assured to those who *agree* in what they are praying for (two or three is the minimum number of persons who can agree or disagree about anything). What they ask for in unity of will and mind will be done for them "by my Father in heaven" (v. 19). For those who gather (ἐκκλησία, "assembly"; 18:17) in the name of Jesus—that is, for the sake of Jesus[12]—to worship or take action together, there is the promise that the risen Lord will be in their midst. We can conclude, then, that for 18:20 the background is not liturgical nor is Christ's presence understood to be limited to worship.[13] To rightly understand the ecclesiological significance of Jesus' promise, we need to respect the context, particularly the concern for the little ones and the emphasis on the practice of forgiveness. John P. Meier concludes:

> When they act decisively, Jesus-Emmanuel, the divine presence in human form, acts with them. Rather than puffing the community up with pride, this realization should move them to even greater mercy [author's note: see 18:23-35]. The mercy Jesus has shown them has made them the church. The survival of the church depends on their extending what they have received: mercy without measure.[14]

In verse 6 of the same chapter 18, we hear of Christ's compassionate closeness to "the little ones who believe in me." Christ's presence with these, most vulnerable to the "scandals" of the church caused by people who offend and destroy community life, is affirmed and given admonitory force: give attention to those who easily get neglected within a community of believers. Christ's own closeness to them is expressed in protection, his being on their side. The little ones are those who have dared to become low (18:1-5) and with that mind-set and attitude are especially apt to live in community.[15] Jesus' utmost concern for the little ones is a concern for the health, in the deepest sense, of the community of believers. Jesus' taking side with the little ones is akin to God's partiality for the poor as attested in the Psalms and elsewhere in Scripture. The Sermon on the Mount with its "Blessed are the poor in spirit" is never far from the horizon of Jesus' teaching in Matthew.

Matthew 18 also makes it clear that there is no equation between the church and the kingdom of God (cf. 13:24-30). Rather, the "Kingdom of Heaven is the reality for which the church exists,"[16] and of which it may be a sign, allowing the kingdom to be tangible reality. The biblical kingdom of God has a social dimension. It is about people and people restored.[17] Accordingly, Bishop Jackalén of Lund, former professor at the Lutheran School of Theology in Chicago, when interviewed about her view on the role of the Church of Sweden, said that it must be a church in critical solidarity with the society.

In the Gospel according to Matthew, the story of the church can be said to be written into the story of Jesus.[18] Luke, however, chose to present these stories as two separate narratives, although with multiple connections between them. Because of the importance of the book of Acts for delineating a Lukan understanding of the church, I will not discuss the Gospel according to Luke much at this juncture. I will treat this Gospel again under the heading "The Gospels and Worship." Here, I will make a few remarks on the concept of the people of God, λαός, and its ecclesiological significance for the Gospel.[19] The first two chapters are particularly telling. In the annunciation given to the priest Zechariah, while an assembly of people are praying outside the sanctuary where he is serving on their behalf, we find this description of the task assigned to the prophet soon to be born: John is to make ready a prepared *people* for the Lord (1:17). The term λαός ("people") offers an important bridge of continuity between the old and the new: the new begins with the proclamation of the kingdom of God. John the Baptist, called to minister to the people as a whole, is the threshold figure (16:16). The church originates *within* Israel, and its longtime history offers important elements of self-understanding. The grand figures presented in the first two chapters of Luke's Gospel echo the traditions of the ancestors (for example, Abraham and Sarah) as well as prophetic traditions. Israel's experience under the guidance of Moses is reflected in the framing of the Sermon on the Plain. As did Moses, so Jesus addresses a multitude of people (λαός) down on a plain (cf. Exod. 19:25). He descends from the mountain where, after solitary prayer, he has elected the twelve apostles, representing the tribes of Israel (6:12-16). That the sermon is broadly directed to the people of Israel is underlined at the end: "After Jesus had finished all his sayings *in the hearing of the people*, he entered Capernaum" (7:1). Another panorama serves as background to the Lukan Travel Narrative, 9:51—19:44. Here we find reminiscences of Israel's wanderings with Moses toward the land promised to them. During this journey the disciples learn from experience, guided by Jesus' teaching. They witness God's acts of salvation, examples of God's gracious "visitation" or favorable regard for the people of Israel (1:68, 19:44). Individuals are restored to health and are incorporated, as when the bent-over woman is healed and called "Abraham's daughter" (13:6). A whole society is being healed when Zacchaeus (19:1-10) is led to act with justice toward the poor. The horizon is broadened when someone asks Jesus whether only a few will be saved (13:22-23). Jesus answers that "people will come from east and west, from north and south, and will eat in the kingdom of God" (13:29). In line with this widening of horizon is the emphasis on mission. While the journey toward Jerusalem is first of all Jesus' personal journey, it is also a journey prefiguring the formation of the church through the proclamation of the gospel far and wide and through a sharing of hospitality—that is, through encounters, people with people.

Mark's story is more restrictively a story about Jesus than the other Synoptic Gospels. This does not exclude that on occasion the time of the church is reflected in the text, and with that an understanding of what the church is about. So in Mark 13:10 and 14:9 we find the church engaged in *proclaiming* the gospel of Jesus' death and resurrection. For 13:10, "and the good news [εὐαγγέλιον] must first be proclaimed to *all nations*," the perspective of the resurrection predominates. Chapter 13 is firmly oriented toward the future: the Son of Man is coming in glory (v. 27). Read in the context of the entire Gospel, "glory" presupposes the resurrection and Jesus as the Son of Man. Comparable to Mark 13:10 is the command of Jesus, the risen Lord, to "make disciples of *all nations*" in Matthew 28:19. Likewise, in Luke, the scriptural witness about a coming proclamation to *all nations* cited by Jesus figures in a post-resurrection context (24:47). Mark 14:9 is part of the story about the woman who lavishly anointed Jesus for his burial. Here, as in 13:10, Jesus refers to the good news later to be widely announced: "Truly I tell you, wherever the good news [εὐαγγέλιον] is proclaimed in the whole world, what she has done will be told in remembrance of her." The focus this time is on Jesus' redemptive death (10:45, 14:24). What makes the woman's act exemplary is her service of honoring Jesus, whose shameful suffering and death is at hand (14:10). Among the followers of Jesus, service and voluntary lowliness are the characteristics of communal life. The reason for this rule stated by Jesus (10:43b-44) is precisely Jesus' giving of his life as "ransom for many" (10:45).[20] The act the woman performs also equals a confession. She demonstrated that she was not ashamed of him who was to die such a shameful death (cf. 8:38).[21]

Beyond these references to the time of the church, we find in the Gospel according to Mark certain turns of phrases, scenes, and regular settings that allude to the evolving church. In the explanation to the Parable of the Sower (4:13-20), the repeated phrase, "those who hear the word," assumes continuous proclamation. This, together with the mini-list of vices in verse 19 (cf. Gal. 5:16-21), reflects the reality of the church. In 3:31-35 we find Jesus surrounded by a circle of disciples and declaring with reference to them that all who do the will of God are his family, "my brother and sister and mother" (v. 35). The new family sketched in this scene is an image of the church. The newness of the family comes across in their relationship to God, their Father, implied in the text through the signal constituted by the absence of "father" in verse 35. This interpretation is confirmed by 10:28-31, since verse 30 lacks mention of a father, whereas in verse 29 a father *is* mentioned.[22] The text reads:

> Peter began to say to him, "Look, we have left everything, and followed you." Jesus said, "Truly I tell you, there is no one who has left house or brothers or sisters or mother or father or children or fields, for my sake and for the sake of the good news [εὐαγγέλιον], who will not receive a hundredfold now in this age—houses, brothers and sisters, mothers and children, and fields, with persecutions—and in the age to come eternal life. But many who are first will be last, and the last will be first.

Among the regular settings for the stories about Jesus in Mark is "the house." We often find Jesus with his disciples teaching in a house (9:28-29). The earliest churches, as we well know, were not separate buildings but ordinary houses. The first Christians regularly met in someone's home, big enough to accommodate a group of people. They met for worship and teaching in connection with it. The circle of Jesus with disciples in a house thus has ecclesial connotations. Of course, the disciples themselves as presented by Mark, in their frail but also recurrently renewed loyalty to Jesus, are emblematic of the church, although in Mark less obviously so than in Matthew or Luke (where the first Christians are called "disciples"). Any person of faith is called to an evolving personal relationship with Jesus; for us today through baptism, and at the time of Jesus, through a call physically to follow Jesus or to sit around and listen to him.

Although there isn't much reflection of an existing church in Mark, we can learn from this Gospel what it is that creates the church: its existence presupposes the action of the word of God calling people together. The prologue of Mark (1:1-13) delineates such a beginning (ἀρχή, 1:1) with God's coming, triumphantly making the way to restoration and redemption. The phrase "the way of the Lord" in the prologue of Mark (1:3a) is not so much the way that people are supposed to walk; rather, it is the Lord's *own* way. In the context of Isaiah, the main source text for the quote in Mark 1:2-3, the way signifies God's leading the people back from the exile. That is no less than a manifestation of God's saving power. "The way," often considered a *leitmotif* in Mark, is announced in the prologue and amplified in the central section of the Gospel (8:27—10:52). The central section shows that "the way" is, above all, a path to suffering and death in Jerusalem. This, in Mark, is the true way to redemption (10:45).[23]

God's word in action is where the story starts in the Gospel according to Mark. Although the phrase introducing the scriptural quote in 1:2-3 uses the verb *written* (γέγραπται), the oracle of the citation comes across as direct and dynamic address: "See, I am sending my messenger ahead of you, who will *prepare* your *way*." Next, God's own word reverberates in the messenger crying out, "*Prepare* the *way* of the Lord" (1:3a). The oracle is a mighty word indeed. Abruptly, the oracle breaks the silence; there is complete lack of preparatory narrative for its in-breaking. The oracle announces that important events are about to occur. The events, narrated after the quote, are nothing less than groundbreaking events: the baptism of a multitude of people who repent (that is, turn to God with their heart, mind, and whole way of being); and then the baptism of Jesus with the divine declaration as to who he is—God's representative in will and action. These events signify that God is coming to God's people to create new conditions of life.

The ending of Mark is also abrupt, even more so. The women fled from the tomb, "for terror and amazement had seized them, and they said nothing to anyone, for they were afraid" (16:8). But at the end there is again a voice: the voice of a divine messenger robed in white who refers to the saying of Jesus, the one raised by God, that "he is going ahead [προάγει] of you to Galilee; there you will see him, just as he has told you" (16:7). With this the angel refers to the *promise* by Jesus to his disciples, "I will go before [προάξω] you to Galilee" (14:28). The women fail to report, but what is reliable is the angel-Jesus chain of words. The quoted promise from Jesus also gains in reliability when seen in relation to the three passion predictions by Jesus (chaps. 8, 9, and 10) and their fulfillment in the passion narrative. And so Mark's Gospel can end abruptly on the note that a way is prepared for a beginning by Jesus, the one raised by God, as the disciples gather again in Galilee, the ones who had previously scattered in fear and confusion (14:7 and 50). A new phase has begun, the phase of the church.

We will return to the first chapter of Mark: "The time is fulfilled, and the kingdom of God has come near; repent, and believe in the good news" (1:14-15). This passage is a so-called summary, a general outline of what is to follow in narrative detail. More than presenting a table of contents, the verses give a perspective from which the following story about Jesus is to be read and without which it will not be understood. The passage calls to the reader's attention that the kingdom of God is coming through the ministry of Jesus. As the narrative sequence shows, the actual ministry of Jesus does not start until *after* the calling of the first four disciples (1:16-18), the embryo of the church. The communities of faith who read or hear Mark's Gospel are thus invited to see that the ministry of Jesus not only happened in the past, but involves them, as they now act upon God's word in their place, pointing to the kingdom that God brings about.

The Gospels and Worship

While all the Synoptic Gospels show connections to early Christian liturgy, the Gospel according to Mark does so more indirectly. Petr Pokorný explains this with reference to Mark's desire to rehabilitate underappreciated traditions while respecting the well-functioning forms of oral tradition. Mark does not quote the Lord's Prayer (though there are possible echoes of the prayer in 11:25 and 14:36), nor does the author of the Gospel include much material of ethical teaching.[24] While it is a bit chancy to suggest to what material the community of Mark had access, I think it is a point well taken to see the earliest Gospel as a complement to traditions regularly used and well established within the community they address. Also, the abrupt ending of Mark, with no appearance reported of the risen Jesus, can be seen in this light— the gospel of the resurrection was certainly preached and celebrated in many ways. As we have said, the statements of Mark 13:10 and 14:9 have an aim beyond the narrative in which they are inserted, pointing to the present reality of the church engaged in proclaiming the gospel of Jesus' death and resurrection.

Luke underlines the importance of prayer for the church through the examples of Jesus himself and the disciples. It is in this Gospel that the Lord's Prayer is introduced by a disciple who observes Jesus absorbed in prayer and asks, "Lord, teach us to pray, as John taught his disciples" (11:1). Luke also integrates several hymns with the infancy narrative, hymns that, although they are attributed to certain characters in the story, have a strong communal flavor. This Gospel begins and ends with people immersed in prayer in the Temple (1:10, 24:53). Jesus himself begins his ministry in the context of worship, in the synagogue of Nazareth (4:16-30). But Luke also includes many stories about Jesus visiting with people in their homes, where they experience forgiveness of sins (7:36-50) and receive the blessing of peace (7:50; cf. 10:5) and salvation (19:9). These visits of Jesus in people's homes prepare for the book of Acts where conversion happens in and to the house(hold) and where Christians regularly gather in homes for prayer and breaking of the bread (2:42-47). At the end of the book, Paul is presented as proclaiming the kingdom of God and teaching about the Lord Jesus Christ in a "house," a rented apartment in Rome. Of liturgical activities, praise is commonly mentioned in Luke and expressed in all places, notably outdoors. Those witnessing Jesus' powerful act of raising the widow's son from death (7:16) express their reaction to the immensity of the event in words of praise as they recognize God's hand and activity in Jesus: "[T]hey glorified God, saying, 'A great prophet has risen among us!' and 'God has looked favorably on his people!'" Liturgy, as F. Cromphout has put it, is "to confess and to sing, in the presence of God, that there is salvation."[25]

While in the Gospel according to Luke prayer as practiced by Jesus and his disciples has a modeling function for the recipients of the Gospel, in Matthew the prayer and confession of the church are reflected in ways integral to the narrative. A telling example is the stilling of the storm in Matthew 8:23-27. When compared with the Markan source text, it appears that the story is given an ecclesial character already in its introduction. Whereas in Mark the disciples take Jesus along, in Matthew the disciples follow Jesus. The drama the disciples experience in the storm-tossed boat becomes a paradigm for how the endangered church is protected by its Lord. In Matthew, Jesus addresses the disciples *before* calming the storm (cf. Mark 4:39-40). Furthermore, the disciples here as always address Jesus as Lord (cf. Mark 4:38, "Teacher") and their cry for help is conveyed through the words of prayer, "Lord, save us." In this prayer, the community's liturgical experience is reflected, thus connecting the story with their own life.[26] With miracle stories in general in Matthew, we notice the increase of dialogue in comparison with Mark, reflective of a shift in the purpose of the stories to become paradigms of faith.

The means through which the confession of the Matthean community expresses itself within the Jesus story are at times subtle but visible to anyone studying Scripture with the tool of comparison. I will briefly cite two examples. In the infancy narrative, the virgin birth is announced in 1:23, as we have said above, through a quote from Isaiah 7:14. The quoted text closely follows the Septuagint except for the form of the verb *call*. "You [singular] will call" in the Greek translation of Isaiah appears in Matthew as "*they* will call him Immanuel." The plural form of the verb in Matthew may well be a reference to the community of believers, the church, the genesis of which can be seen as included in Jesus' birth and infancy narrative. The second example relates to the death of Jesus. When Jesus has died and upon the rending of the Temple curtain, in Mark a Roman officer confesses Jesus as the Son of God. In Matthew we find that the officer makes the corresponding confession *together with* the guards (27:54). Not only for the Matthean community but particularly for the Gentiles within it, the moment of Jesus' death is in this way made into a foundational moment for their understanding of Jesus.[27]

I will end my treatment of the Gospel according to Matthew by discussing the importance given to forgiveness (cf. above on chapter 18). Forgiveness has both a christological and an ecclesiological focus. To highlight the prerogative of Jesus to forgive, Matthew has "moved" the forgiveness of sins from the stated purpose of the activity of John the Baptist in the source text to the Lord's Supper where the institutional words of Jesus include: "This is my blood of the covenant, which is poured out for many for the forgiveness of sins" (26:28). For the second focus, we note that it is precisely on the issue of interpersonal forgiveness that the Lord's Prayer connects with the ensuing warning of the Sermon on the Mount (6:14). Another example of the importance of forgiveness for the life of the community is the story about the healing and forgiving of the paralytic man. It ends: "When the crowds saw it, they were filled with awe, and they glorified God, who had given such authority to human beings" (9:8). To the church ("human beings," plural) God has entrusted the authority to forgive. Its developed liturgy from early on includes confession of sins and assurance of forgiveness (*Didache* 4:14; 1 John 1:9).

Conclusion

In this essay I have wanted to use the experience of worship as a way of entering into the biblical world, particularly that of the Synoptic Gospels. In these texts, we hear people pray for rescue and protection. We encounter both individuals and communities who express their loyalty and adherence to Jesus in acts of confession. Not least, we rediscover people who experience forgiveness and restoration, for which they praise God and in consequence of which they express mercy toward others.

In this essay I have also looked at the Synoptic Gospels in order to explore their connections with communities of faith, not in the interest of locating these historically or sociologically, but rather to give justice to the Gospels as faith documents. The Gospels are foundational not because they tell of people's faith then, but because they witness to Jesus Christ, who invites us now to a life in faith, in community. The Gospels, even as documents of the first century, connect us with communities of faith, their worship and their beliefs, including their self-understanding as such communities. We learn from the Gospels to see ourselves as a people of longtime history with God, as in Luke. We learn to regard ourselves as called together (ἐκκλησία) by the Lord Immanuel ("God with us"), even to a place where "heaven and earth meet" (Matt. 18:18-19). We learn to trust the living dynamic speech of God, creator of new conditions of life as in Mark. Having heard the witness of all three, we acknowledge that as the church, we do not exist for ourselves alone but for the kingdom of God, to promote justice and peace, in a spirit of reconciliation. Anchored in such self-understanding, the task of preaching continues "with boldness" (Acts 28:31).

Gospel Happenings

6

Pauline Proclamation and Exhortation

BRIAN K. PETERSON

Paul understood his call, first and foremost, as a call to preach (1 Cor. 1:17; Gal. 1:15-16). Both Paul and his opponents recognized that his letters were not to be simply equated with his preaching in person (Gal. 4:20; 2 Cor. 2:1-4, 10:10). However, these letters are also arguably the closest equivalent in the New Testament to actual apostolic preaching. Here, an apostle addresses specific communities who will gather together for worship, share the meal, and hear the word of the Lord. Moreover, Paul's letters retain their basically oral nature, despite their written form. They were probably all dictated aloud (cf. Rom. 16:22; 1 Cor. 16:21; Gal. 6:11), and were intended to be read aloud to the recipients (1 Thess. 5:27; cf. Col. 4:16). Paul's letters contain statements like "I say" about twice as often as "I write."[1] Paul not only understands these letters as in some fundamental way "oral," but he describes them in terms that are similar to his own preaching: through the letters he is "appealing" to his hearers (παρακαλοῦμεν in 1 Thess. 4:1, 10; 5:14; NRSV = "urge"), just as his initial preaching to them is described as "appeal" (παράκλησις, 1 Thess. 2:3). Paul's letters are an extension of his apostolic proclamation.

It is at this junction of gospel proclamation and exhortation that contemporary preaching so often goes off the track. On the one hand, preachers may find themselves convinced that proclamation of the gospel and sermonic exhortation are mutually exclusive; the result is a gospel that doesn't actually change anything in the world or the life of the congregation, and a preacher who is compelled to dismiss a good deal of the biblical witness, including much of the Pauline letters, because it is exhortation and thus does not find a place within the preacher's theological framework. On the other hand, preachers may focus on the exhortation, including that contained in the Pauline letters, in a way that has nothing to do with the gospel of what God has done in Christ, and thus makes the gospel superfluous and the message simply obligation without the power of the gospel to bring about the needed transformation.

I contend in this essay that a careful look at the Pauline proclamation contained in the letters may help us find our way to more faithful proclamation. Paul's letters are always addressed to specific assemblies of believers; he does not preach or write into an abstract vacuum, but to real communities. To respect that incarnate specificity of his proclamation, this essay will not be a survey of all that Paul says about the gospel and exhortation, but will focus on what Paul says in 1 Thessalonians about his understanding and practice of proclamation. Among Paul's letters, this may seem like an odd choice. In this letter, Paul never quotes the Old Testament explicitly, and he never mentions justification or righteousness. However, since in 1 Thessalonians Paul is not engaged in a heated defense of his ministry, but instead is addressing a community that maintains positive and supportive loyalty to Paul, this letter may provide a useful place to start. Here, in a congregation birthed and nurtured through Paul's proclamation, we may be able to hear the tones of the apostle's proclamation without some of the polemical noise that is a part of other Pauline letters.

First Happenings First

As Paul opens this letter, he begins by reflecting on his initial preaching of the gospel in Thessalonica. In 1 Thessalonians 1:5, Paul describes the gospel not as an object or a teaching, but as an event: the gospel "happened" (ἐγενήθη NRSV = "came") to them.[2] Note that immediately after "the gospel happened," Paul says that he "became" something (1:5b) and that the Thessalonian church "became" something (1:6); all three of these claims use the same verb (γίνεσθαι). Though it may not be possible to maintain this verbal connection in English translation, it is vital for understanding 1 Thessalonians and for the argument of this essay that we not miss the verbal link that Paul has forged here: the gospel "happens" or "becomes active" in Thessalonica, and from that foundational event both Paul and the Thessalonian church "become" something new. The gospel is something that happens, and that word of God continues to be "at work" (ἐνεργεῖται) among the Thessalonians (2:13).

The crucial result of this event is that the Thessalonians "turned to God from idols, to serve a living and true God, and to wait for his Son from heaven, whom he raised from the dead—Jesus, who rescues us from the wrath that is coming" (1 Thess. 1:9-10). The gospel has some particular and necessary content. It is not simply a general message that "you're okay." It has to do with God raising Jesus from the dead. Not only does the focus on Christ crucified and raised appear here at the end of the thanksgiving section, but returns again in what may arguably be the central concern of Paul in this letter, 4:13-18.

The message Paul preaches is "the gospel of God" (2:2, 8, 9). The gospel is about God and God's activity in the world. However, the preaching of the gospel is more than a transfer of information. The "word of God" that the hearers receive is nothing less than God speaking through the preachers (2:13). Paul speaks in similar terms elsewhere. In 2 Corinthians 5:20, Paul uses the image of an ambassador to illustrate how God is the one making the appeal through apostolic proclamation. The NRSV translation of Romans 10:14b says, "How are they to believe in one *of whom* they have never heard?" However, the Greek text does not indicate that Jesus is the one *about* whom these people need to hear (NRSV translates as though the text says περὶ οὗ οὐκ ἤκουσαν, but περὶ ["about"] is not part of the Greek text); rather, Jesus himself is the one who must be heard: "How can they believe in one whom they have never heard?" The issue in Romans 10:14 is not about information, but about hearing the Lord speak.[3] It is that speaking that happens through the apostolic proclamation of the gospel. At the center of that proclamation is not just information, but Jesus Christ crucified, raised, and calling.

Paul's focus on this as the gospel may be a particularly apt reminder for us that when we preach, we are not forced to come up with something new and clever to say each week. This is not an excuse for either sloppy or unimaginative preaching, but is a reminder that in our culture, where we are glutted with stories, the preacher's task is to tell one story over and over again: "The point is not to tell bunches of substitute stories for their inspirational value or to recount meaningful experiences that are vaguely analogous to divine truths but to tell one story as creatively and powerfully as possible and to allow that one story to probe our world."[4] In 1 Thessalonians, Paul repeatedly reminds the Thessalonians about what they already know. Paul reminds them of his initial preaching and their reception (1:9-10), and he reminds them of how he worked and preached among them (2:1-10; note "you know" in 2:1, 5, and 11; "you remember" in 2:9; "you are witnesses" in 2:10).

> The appeal to the memory will connect the community with its foundational story, reaffirm the liturgical expression by which the community responds to God, and recall the community's moral norms. Paul's preaching, therefore, demonstrates that preachers should not have an aversion to stating what has been said before.[5]

Paul's opening summary of his preaching in 1:9-10 also strikes an unmistakably apocalyptic note. The Jesus whom God raised from the dead is the same one that we now await from heaven, the one who rescues us from the coming wrath. The reminder of Jesus' coming also appears in 3:11-13 and in 5:23, key moments in this letter. The apocalyptic scene of Jesus' return is the center of Paul's discussion about those believers who have died and those who are left alive in 4:13-18. But this apocalyptic shape of the gospel is not a form of escapism, a way of rejecting the world in favor of some sweet by-and-by or an eagerness to abandon this world through the *deus ex machina* of "the rapture." This apocalyptic message is more akin to the African American spirituals, which sing of God's deliverance and God's heaven as a form of resistance and protest to the workings of sin in this world.[6] The apocalyptic message is one that disrupts the "normal" workings of the world by declaring not the wonders of progress and human possibility, but by declaring what God will do, and by reading the present in the light of God's future. Such apocalyptic waiting is not passive, but declares that the future is not ultimately in our hands to win or to lose; it is in God's hands—as are we. It is God who will accomplish salvation. That radical declaration is what enables the church to face the open grave, and the brutality of oppression and injustice, and to declare, "This will not be the last word, because Jesus has been raised from the dead, and he will leave none of his people behind." Such an apocalyptic edge is necessary if our preaching is to be faithful and hopeful.

As the church waits for that coming, God is already at work, invading the present and creating a colony of the new age here on the shores of the old. Paul describes how the people of the church at Thessalonica have become "people of the day and of the light" (5:5), and distinctly different from those who say "peace and security" (5:3). That final phrase reflects the political-religious claims of the Roman Empire, which declared *pax* and *securitas* as the divine gifts given to the world through the Roman system. We should note how politically loaded many of Paul's favorite terms were: gospel, kingdom, Lord, salvation, peace, and righteousness all were claimed by Rome as the benefits of empire.[7] Paul declares that God will not let such deceptions stand. It is by no means safe or easy to talk about "wrath and destruction" among those who claim "peace and security," particularly in a Roman provincial capital like Thessalonica. The proclamation of the gospel directly challenged the claims of Rome. In our setting, proclaiming the gospel may also mean renouncing the other things that are too often equated with the good news—common sense, peace of mind, prosperity, competition, status, democracy, "family values," militarism, patriotism, positive thinking.[8]

Preacher Happenings

It is not only the gospel that "happens" or "becomes" among the Thessalonians. Paul describes himself and his partners using the same verb: they "happen" or "become" something among the Thessalonians (ἐγενήθημεν in 2:5, 7, 10, inconsistently translated by NRSV). The event of the gospel that "happened" in Thessalonica is connected verbally with something that happens to and through Paul, or with something that he "becomes" among them. That apostolic "becoming" has two facets: a "becoming" related to the method of Paul's preaching, and a "becoming" related to his relationship with the Thessalonians.

In 1:5 and 2:5, 10, Paul reflects on the mode of his apostolic preaching. He did not "come" (1:5b; ἐγενήθημεν = "proved to be" in NRSV, but this misses the connection with how the gospel "came" to them [ἐγενήθη] in 1:5a) with flattery or greed. Paul is contrasting himself to other philosopher-preachers, who were commonly criticized as acting out of such motives. Paul, unlike such charlatans, does not act out of deceit or trickery (2:3).

Paul describes his preaching as "being bold" (ἐπαρρησιασάμεθα, 2:2), a characteristic often claimed as central to the work of hellenistic philosophers. But the fact that Paul's boldness is "in God" has unavoidable consequences for the manner of his proclamation. His message will not come in the guise of flattery, a common trap in both the Roman world and in ours. "To be bold to speak the gospel" means not necessarily adopting whatever methods are popular, comfortable, or "successful." Paul will be faithful to what has been entrusted to him (2:4), even when the results are shame and suffering (2:2). Paul refuses to treat the gospel as merchandise, or to substitute for the gospel something more culturally acceptable. Modern Western culture is focused to a large degree on entertainment, and our TV culture may convince people (even preachers) that "successful" sermons must above all be entertaining. Enjoyable style and the production of good feelings then replaces depth of content as the primary goal and measure of "success," and language is used not to declare the truth but to manipulate.[9] Preachers are tempted, and perhaps attracted, by those trappings and techniques that our culture values so highly as signs of power. From such a perspective, what could be more foolish than actually preaching? Preparing sermons, doing careful exegesis of the texts and careful interpretation of the community, seems ludicrously inefficient and ineffective. It seems to many that it is better by far to download a generic sermon or to rely on flash and dazzle to look powerful, knowledgeable, and cutting edge. Such things are the equivalent of the first-century rhetorical eloquence that Paul rejected as unfit to communicate the gospel of God. For the sake of the gospel's integrity, Paul's preaching will not be conformed to what is admired and valued by the culture around him.

Paul describes his proclamation as the activity of a herald (ἐκηρύξαμεν, 2:9). Paul is an announcer for the ruler of the world. As such, for Paul to proclaim the gospel does not mean that Paul came talking about what might be, or that Paul came to make a suggestion or an offer, or to give instructions. Rather, a herald comes to declare what is: "Jesus is Lord!" (2 Cor 4:5, with κηρύσσω again).[10] Thus, Paul came announcing the inaugurated reign of the Lord Jesus. We expose our misunderstandings and our faithless fears when we replace such declarations of what already is the reality because of Jesus with strategies for self-help or offers couched in conditional language, aimed at religious consumers from whom we hope to elicit a response by appealing to their self-interest, whether temporal or eternal.

Besides shaping his proclamation, Paul's "becoming" also determines his relationship to the Thessalonians themselves. The proclamation of the gospel cannot be separated from the preacher's life and conduct. Like it or not, the preacher becomes an example and a display of the image of Christ. Paul repeatedly notes how his congregations have imitated him by their obedience to the gospel, or he calls for such imitation (1 Thess. 1:6; 1 Cor. 4:6, 11:1). Paul's description of his ministry in 1 Thessalonians 2:1-12 is not a self-defense in the face of criticism, but is a reminder of what kind of life the gospel has led Paul to live with the Thessalonians, so that they in turn will be able to see what the gospel accomplishes among them. Paul did not act out of impurity (2:3), as the Thessalonians are reminded that they are not called to impurity (4:7). Paul loves them (2:8), just as they are to abound in love for one another and for all (3:12). Paul labored so as not to be a burden, just as they are to work with their own hands and so not be in debt to another (4:11-12). Paul was blameless in his conduct among them, just as the Thessalonians will be kept blameless by God at the coming of Jesus (5:23). Paul exhorted them (2:12), just as they now should exhort one another (4:18, 5:11).[11]

The gospel is not a timeless myth; it declares that God was active in real time and space in Christ, and that God continues to be active in time and space through the proclamation of the gospel. "The preacher is, therefore, the personal, living voice of the gospel."[12] We may at times lament the kind of "double standard" that is applied to the lives of pastors, and we may rebel against the fishbowl existence. Paul would remind us that the messenger must conform to the message. Paul brings the good news of Christ crucified and raised, and he is sure that the Spirit is working in his life to conform him to the death of Jesus. His congregations never saw Jesus, but they have seen Paul, and Paul insists that they can see the gospel enfleshed in his own life. We cannot evade responsibility by asking congregations to settle for less than that from those who would proclaim the gospel among them. The gospel and the preacher become wrapped up and visible together.[13]

Paul shares himself when he shares the gospel (2:8). Whether 2:7 says "we became gentle" or "we became infants," it speaks of a startling vulnerability on Paul's part. The preaching of the gospel creates ties and relationships that cannot be casually broken or discarded. Paul is connected to this congregation such that the shape and the conduct of his ministry is reformed by his concern for them: he cannot simply move on to fruitful fields, but must stop in Athens to send Timothy back for a report about them (3:1-2, 6; see 2 Cor. 2:12-13).

I do not think that such gospel connections mean that pastors should never move on to another congregation, nor that pastors should continue close connections to parishes from which they have resigned. But it does, I believe, challenge the ways in which congregations and pastors often treat pastoral ministry as a simple business relationship: congregations measuring pastoral ministry according to business models and treating pastors as hired hands, and pastors for their part longing and even competing for the "plum" congregations, as though climbing up some ecclesiastical-corporate ladder.

Reflecting on what it means for Paul that he proclaims the gospel may also warn us about some false assumptions regarding evangelism. The gospel not only transforms the hearers; it also transforms the messenger. Paul becomes vulnerable in this relationship; that is part of what it means to be conformed to the dying of Jesus. Paul's ministry has come to depend on the very life and faith of the Thessalonians (1:8). His confidence before God at the *parousia* of Jesus depends on their faithfulness (2:19). His life depends on their continuing to stand firm (3:8). One cannot treat the gospel as something that can be left safely on the doorstep, or hurled at people from a safe distance. To share the gospel will change you because it will form relationships that can only be conveyed in the deepest human terms: father (2:11), mother/nurse (2:7), child (2:7, perhaps), and even "orphan" longing for the parent (2:17). Any model of evangelism that leaves the "proclaimer" (whether an individual preacher or the evangelizing community) unchanged is not truly "good news."

Community Happenings

The primary result of the gospel's happening in Thessalonica is God's election of this community (1:4). Through the preaching of the gospel

God calls the community into existence (2:12, 4:7, 5:24). The call of God is not private, silent, or hidden; it means a call into a specific concrete community. Paul probably never envisioned that his letters would be read by individuals; they are intended as messages to the gathered community (5:27). First Thessalonians has forty-three second-person verbs, and all of them are plural. The letter also has eighty-two second-person personal pronouns, and again all of them are plural. We may miss Paul's communal emphasis because English has no second plural forms,[14] though I doubt that our deafness to this aspect is that simple. The church in our culture has largely succumbed to the illusion that the congregation is simply a gathering of individual religious consumers looking for the "deal" or the "package" that meets their needs and desires the best (and usually at the lowest cost). Paul's proclamation is aimed at forming and nurturing a community. Sermons in our context tend to be treated differently. The question we bring seems to be, "What did I get out of that sermon? How did it address MY needs, MY questions, MY experiences, MY life? What can I take from that sermon to use in the rest of MY life?" That is, we seem to expect sermons to meet our individual needs and desires as religious consumers looking for personal peace and self-fulfillment. Paul's proclamation should remind us of a different sort of question: "What is God calling *us* to be and to do as a community of faith?" In Paul's ministry, the sermon is not a cheap form of individual therapy. Rather, to preach is by its very nature "to act ecclesially, to build on the supposition that this body of listeners intends to believe and to *act as a community*."[15]

What God continues to do within the community is an integral part of the ongoing happening of the gospel. The new life and transformation of the Thessalonians has become part of the gospel's proclamation, and so the Thessalonians have "become" an example to all those in Achaia and Macedonia (1:7-8). Note that here, Paul is not saying that the Thessalonians are sending out preachers themselves. Rather, their life together has become a divinely inspired proclamation of the gospel.

The faith of the Thessalonian church is also good news, of course, to Paul. When Timothy returns to Paul and reports on the Thessalonian congregation, Paul says that Timothy "proclaims the good news about your faith and love" (3:6). As the gospel forms and reforms the

Thessalonian church, their life together becomes a proclamation of the gospel to Paul.[16] Just as Paul's preaching to them was παράκλησις (2:3) and just as he sent Timothy to them to continue that gospel activity (παρακαλέσαι, 3:2), so now their continuing faithfulness has encouraged/comforted (παρεκλήθημεν, 3:7) Paul.

This is the reason, often overlooked, that approximately half of the material we have from Paul consists of "exhortation." That exhortation material is often identified as "parenesis" (παραίνεσις), a Greek word often used by Roman rhetoricians that means "exhortation" and that, importantly, never appears in Paul's letters. We should perhaps follow Peter Stuhlmacher's suggestion[17] and retain Paul's term of *paraklesis* for this material. Paul's church-creating proclamation, the comfort and encouragement given and received within the community, and the ongoing exhortation to live out the new life given in Christ are all described by Paul with this same word, and the various meanings of the term form an inseparable whole for Paul. The exhortations and instructions given to the community are not "what happens after the gospel," but are part and parcel of that gospel's work within the community of faith. The gospel is the declaration of Jesus' sovereignty over this world, already begun and coming to completion at the *parousia*, but embodied already in the Spirit-led life of the church. In Paul's letters, *paraklesis* as urging to obedience is inseparably tied to, rooted in, and made possible through *paraklesis* as the proclamation of the gospel of God. Perhaps we don't often hear, appreciate, or live out the connection between Paul's *paraklesis* as declaration and his *paraklesis* as exhortation because we think and talk as though the gospel means proclaiming that Jesus is our friend and helper, instead of proclaiming that Jesus is Lord.

The church is being formed into the image of Christ (cf. 2 Cor. 3:18). Paul says that they "became" imitators of the Lord Jesus in 1 Thessalonians 1:6, but such "becoming" remains God's activity and not simply human choice. The fact that the Thessalonians became imitators of the Lord does not result in congratulations to them, but thanks to the God who is at work among them. God's will for the Thessalonians is their "sanctification" (5:23), but Paul is clear that this sanctification is God's accomplishment among them (5:24). This means that moralistic sermons are possible only by ignoring the theological context of the story that Paul is telling. Preaching the gospel means to expose how

God is already at work within the community of the faithful. Such a reminder might help us avoid the error of thinking that salvation is accomplished by our response. We should also notice that Paul spends no time on those "effects" with which our churches seem so preoccupied: membership rolls, square feet of building space, and growing budgets. God is at work conforming the church to Christ crucified, and not to any other criterion or standard.[18] The church is being made into a cross-cultural community.

We have often defined the mission of the church too narrowly. Paul apparently understood that a part of his apostolic mission included the nurture and maturation of his congregations, and so he leads, urges, and invites them into deeper obedience and deeper conformity to Christ. If we see the mission of the church only in terms of getting new members, or if we cannot see that the way in which we live with each other is part of the church's mission, then we have failed to grasp the radically new way of life brought by the gospel, and Paul's exhortations will seem to us either pointless or a threat to the gospel itself. God is conforming the church to Christ, and Paul insists that this transformation is a vital part of the good news. "There is no meaningful distinction between theology and ethics in Paul's thought, because Paul's theology is fundamentally an account of God's work of transforming people into the image of Christ."[19]

Although 1 Thessalonians lacks the language of "justification/righteousness," it does contain the important Pauline language of being "in Christ." The church exists "in God the Father and the Lord Jesus Christ" (1:1); the church stands firm "in the Lord" (3:8); Paul's exhortation is given "in the Lord Jesus" (4:1); the will of God for the church is found "in Christ Jesus" (5:18). William Wrede, Albert Scheitzer, and more recently E. P. Sanders have claimed that Paul's pervasive use of such language shows that the center of Paul's theology was not forensic justification, but rather was found in Paul's participatory understanding of "being in Christ." The reaction of some, supposing to defend both Luther and Paul from such a reading, has been to insist that justification was in fact the heart of the matter for Paul, and that this justification must be understood in strictly juridical terms. At times the proponents of this have insisted (and perhaps even rejoiced) that nothing actually changes in the person so justified.[20]

These suggestions on both sides, however, set up a false dichotomy and a misunderstanding of Paul. For Paul, "to be justified" always means to be changed; it means to be graciously, divinely moved from the realm of sin and death into the realm of righteousness and life. Luther understood this more clearly than some of his defenders or detractors:

> Faith is a work of God in us, which changes us and brings us to birth anew from God . . . . It kills the Old Adam, makes us completely different people in heart, mind, senses, and all our powers, and brings the Holy Spirit with it. What a living, creative, active powerful thing is faith! It is impossible that faith ever stops doing good. Faith doesn't ask whether good works are to be done, but, before it is asked, it has done them. It is always active.[21]

Recent work on Luther's theology has argued that "participation in Christ" was more important for Luther, and that he was less focused exclusively on justification as judicial verdict, than has often been recognized.[22] For Paul (and it seems for Luther as well), "righteousness by faith and participation in Christ ultimately amount to the same thing."[23] To be "crucified with Christ" (Gal. 2:19), to be "buried with Christ" (Rom. 6:4), to be "conformed to Christ" (Phil. 3:10), and thus to be "in Christ" are precisely what justification means.[24] Paul's letters are an antidote to any version of "cheap justification," because Paul everywhere assumes that justification is accompanied by actual transformation in the believers: already begun, ongoing, and to be completed at the *parousia* of the Lord Jesus (Rom. 8:4; 1 Cor. 6:9-11; 1 Thess. 5:23-24). Both individually and as a unified, holy community (1 Thess. 4:1-12, 5:12-22), the church is being transformed, by its union with Jesus, into the faith and love of Christ (Gal. 5:6), that is, into conformity to the death of Jesus (Phil. 3:10-11). If our preaching is going to avoid the Scylla of ignoring biblical exhortations as inimical to the gospel on the one hand, and the Charybdis of an exhortation that forgets and clouds the fundamental gracious action of God in, with, and under the whole life of faith on the other hand, we will need to keep together in our preaching what Paul in his letters kept together: justification and God's ongoing action of conforming the church to the Son. Paul's exhortations are understood and faithfully proclaimed only within that context, and as a part of that story.

Conclusion

Paul's letters are a proclamation of what God continues to do within the community. The same God who raised Jesus from the dead continues to work through the gospel within the community of the church (1 Thess. 5:24), calling them to new life in Christ, and creating within them that new life. Paul's proclamation is more than just information. Through his declaration of the gospel (again), and through his exhortation toward living out the new life in Christ, Paul's preaching becomes the means by which God is at work to create this new reality. First Thessalonians begins and ends with mention of the Lord Jesus and of God's grace (1:1, 5:28).[25] That double reference frames all that is happening in the church, and provides the context for παράκλησις as proclamation, as comfort, and as exhortation. As such, this letter is a particularly fitting example of what Pauline proclamation of the gospel is about and what it is for.

Preaching the Gospel and the Law in the First Testament

7

LAMONTTE M. LUKER

Your word is a lamp to my feet and a light to my path.—*Psalm 119:105*

The title of this essay is a conscious reversal of the common and perhaps more comfortable phrase, *law and gospel*, which, sanctified and correct as it is as a summary of the contents of the Bible, can lead to the portrayal of the Old Testament[1] as simply "rules and regulations," followed by the gospel in the New Testament. By the term *gospel* I mean the good news of the God of freedom. By the term *law* I mean the helpful boundaries and teachings, commonly referred to as the first and third uses of the law, and the inevitable judgment on human behavior, what Luther called the second use of the law. The two thrusts of my argument are to encourage the preacher to (1) hear the gospel in the Hebrew Bible, as well as its law, and (2) to appreciate how the Hebrew Bible reflects real life as part of its value in preaching.

The Hebrew Scriptures are essentially a message of good news. On the first page of Genesis God creates our world for us and it is good. God promises Abraham and Sarah that they will become a great people through whom the whole world might embrace the freedom and joy of monotheism (Gen. 12:1-3). In the exodus event, God, reticent to give God's name, demonstrates the divine identity as one who liberates from bondage, from all that would enslave us (Exodus 3; 20:2). God establishes the "office" of messiah, fully human with fully divine attributes, to lead the kingdom of God (2 Samuel 7; Psalms 2, 45, 72). The prophets consistently present the vision of this hope, and in Chronicles, the last book of the Bible according to the Hebrew canon, the people of God are portrayed as a joyful worshiping community whose leaders (the Levites) embody the prophetic spirit (2 Chron. 20:5-22). Along the way comes the realization that this world (*ha'olam hazeh*) is not all there is, but the reign of God conquers even death, and the consummation of life with God is in the world to come (*ha'olam haba'*; Isaiah 25–26; Daniel 12).

And yet, as Gerhard von Rad pointed out long ago, the Hebrew Bible commences with a theology of law as well as gospel (Gen. 3:1—12:3).[2] Adam and Eve attempt to usurp God's role as Creator by eating from the Tree of Divine Knowledge, so they are cast from the garden of Eden; yet God sews for them leather garments to protect them in the "fallen" world. Cain is sent away from his family because he killed his brother Abel, but God gives him a protective mark. The world must be cleansed by a flood because of its sinful nature, but God saves Noah and his family. And when this family multiplies to repeat the sin of the world's first parents, God must multiply human languages and scatter them over the earth, but calls Abraham to be the agent of universal salvation. The rest of the Bible is the working out of this salvation.

The Hebrew Bible takes very seriously the existence of evil, as should the twenty-first-century preacher. Hence, there are passages that condemn evil in no uncertain terms. When the exegete meets such a passage, it is helpful, rather than following the modern tendency to discount it outright because it offends current codes of nicety, to ask, What is the evil that the passage illuminates and condemns? Hosea is a tough read, but he is confronting the deification of sex. Amos offends, but he offended the Israelites as well.

Because the Hebrew Bible recognizes the reality of sin and evil, it offers words of guidance and sometimes even condemnation. The same is true of the teachings of Jesus and the New Testament. But its core message is of a God who loved the world into being and, despite God's creatures' rebellion, nurtures it as a parent, forgiving sin and loving the sinner, while condemning evil behavior that undermines God's good creation and gracious rule.

What ever happened to the Ten Commandments? For years when I gave a quiz in my introductory Old Testament class on the book of Exodus, I included what I thought was a giveaway question: List the Ten Commandments. To my surprise, most seminarians were unable to do so. Both temporally (it is the oldest of the law codes, I think dating to Moses himself) and literarily (in both Exodus 20 and Deuteronomy 5 it introduces all the others), the Decalogue is both the summary and mother of all Hebrew law. It adorns every synagogue and has been viewed as the essence of God's will throughout the Christian centuries. This is truly the first use of the law, a curb for society. Perhaps this issue is more catechetical than homiletical, but I think the two are intimately linked. If the preacher's audience knows and has been imbued by the Ten Commandments, their ears will be tuned for further instruction in Torah (see below).

When or how is the third use of the law, as a guide or rule or canon of ethics, a valid hermeneutic for the Hebrew Bible? This is a sticky wicket because nascent Christianity decided that Gentiles do not need to keep Torah, but went on to declare certain guidelines in the spirit of Torah (see Acts 15 and the Epistles *passim*). My own hermeneutic is to honor and implement the spirit of Torah as it proceeds consistently from page after page and is affirmed by Jesus and the New Testament; for example, issues of justice, especially for the oppressed, love of human beings at all levels of society, and stewardship of the earth. Extracting a specific law, such as "You shall not wear clothes made of wool and linen woven together" (Deut. 22:11), can be problematic and not in the spirit of Paul or, for that matter, Jesus.

When interpreting the First Testament it is important to keep in mind the context. The Hebrew Bible is a witness of God's activity among the Hebrews in a polytheistic, idolatrous, and pagan world. The exegete needs to ask, "What is new here?" not, "Does this measure up to the church's interpretation and implementation of Jesus' teaching?" So, for instance, when the Covenant Code legislates that a man who passes a concubine to a son has no more conjugal rights to her but, rather, she gains all the rights of a daughter-in-law (Exod. 21:7-11), this is in stark contrast to the rights of women in the Code of Hammurabi, which states that if a wife is accused of adultery but found innocent she will nonetheless drown herself for her husband's sake.[3] Neither Ruth nor Esther are Gloria Steinem, but they could be called "feminists" of their day in that they were women in a man's world who by their courageous individualism made a tremendous difference to their society.[4] Similarly, the Hebrew Bible allows slavery but only if granting slaves copious rights not received in the rest of the ancient Near East, including the release of debtor slaves in seven years (see Exod. 21:2-6; Deut. 15:12-18). The rest of the society, including resident aliens, was largely egalitarian, in stark contrast to, for example, Babylonian society where the Code of Hammurabi legislates three different degrees of justice based on the three social classes. God is doing a new thing in the First Testament but has not yet done the final thing.

Torah is not to be confused with law. The Hebrew root of torah is *yarah*, "teach." Torah is God's good word of instruction to help us live in God's kingdom. The latter, as Norman Perrin[5] has pointed out, is really a verb, the reigning of God, and is never a place but always an activity. "The Torah," the Five Books of Moses, contains many stories, myths, legends, fables, historical narratives, songs, poems, sermons, theophanies, genealogies, architectural plans, liturgies, and yes, some laws—all of which instruct the hearer about the way of life in the kingdom of God. As a written collection, "the Torah" is a rather late development from the early Second Temple period and is celebrated in such psalms as 1, 19, and 119. In the book of Proverbs, torah simply means the instruction of the sages in the way of wisdom (their term for the kingdom of God; see Prov. 1:8, 3:1, 4:2, *passim*). The best summary of prophetic theology in the entire Bible, Micah 6:6-8, has often been called "priestly torah," and the words of the prophets are their own form of instruction. For this reason, the word *torah* in Psalm 119 of *Evangelical Lutheran Worship* is translated "teaching," because its canonical connotation is much broader than law or even the Torah.[6] For the Christian, the teachings of Jesus are torah, instruction for the kingdom of God. Consider Matthew's Jesus who emerges from Egypt after a slaughter of young boys and then ascends a mountain to deliver, as the new Moses, a new torah (Matthew 5–7; cf. the book of Exodus).

This should establish that the worst mistake a preacher can make is to assume that the Old Testament is law and the New Testament is gospel. A similar misstep is to think that the Old Testament presents a God of judgment and the New Testament undoes this by introducing the God of grace. Jesus can say, "Woe to you" (for example, Matt.

11:20-24, 23:13-36; Luke 6:24-26) and "unless you repent, you will all perish as they did" (Luke 13:1-5). Acts recounts the story of a couple struck dead for failure to turn in their stewardship pledge (5:1-11), and Revelation describes a Jesus with a sword of judgment in his mouth (1:16, echoing Isa. 11:4; cf. Dan. 7:13). The Torah tells of a God who will save a sinful city if only ten righteous persons are found there (and the implication is, if Abraham had pressed God, for the sake of only one God would have saved the city, Gen. 18:22-33). The Prophets envision a time when death will be destroyed and God will wipe away every tear from human eyes (Isa. 25:6-9). And the Writings include a book declaring that God is love (Song of Songs; cf. Hosea; 1 John 4:7-8).[7]

One reason for preachers' misunderstanding of the First Testament is their failure to recall the long period of development and composition involved compared to the Second Testament. The latter was completed within two centuries; the former over two millennia. Hence, the New Testament is going to be much more succinct and unified and, if you will, "orthodox" in its presentation. The Old Testament will, rather, witness to the Spirit's work with her people to bring them from henotheism to monotheism to a unique definition of what the latter means, that is, who this unique God is. Recall we are awaiting the full answer until this God's incarnation in the man Jesus Christ—so we should not expect to find the fullness of truth in every page of the Hebrew Bible, but by the same token we cannot miss the revealed truth inscribed on these pages even be it viewed through a mirror dimly. The first heresy of the church was the Marcionite heresy (that is, denial that the Hebrew Bible is Scripture for the church), and so it is a given that every book of the First Testament has something to teach us that cannot be ignored and that may, in its own way, supplement or even complete and explain and ground the Second Testament.

A second difference from the New Testament is the very varied circumstances that the Old Testament addresses and out of which it grew. To be sure, the New Testament addresses varied circumstances, but it is unified in that it all concerns God's act in Jesus Christ. The literature of the First Testament deals with the world before God's name (*Hashem*) was revealed, with God before there was an Israel, with national governance, history, and liturgy, as well as with human philosophy. In other words, it is the national literature of Israel, such as if Americans would have a book comprising Beowulf, Shakespeare,

Goethe, Native American legend, *Pilgrim's Progress*, Augustine's *Confessions*, Aquinas, Kant, and *Evangelical Lutheran Worship*. Too many exegetes fail to appreciate the *literature* of the First Testament—viewing it too narrowly as "religious scripture" and thereby missing its profound artistry, depth of quest, and unique angle on Truth.

The Old Testament is full of great stories. To paraphrase Paul Tillich, never say it is only a story; say it is nothing less than a Story! To become an excellent preacher one should spend as much time reading poetry and good novels and viewing artful film as he or she spends in exegesis. Use everything you learned in high school, college, and seminary about literary criticism to unpack the beauty of the story and let it speak. The modern tendency to read the Bible as a history book also diminishes the appreciation of its literature, but the question of empirical history is a very recent one, unasked by the ancients. See the fine book by Hans Frei, *The Eclipse of Biblical Narrative*, in which he argues that the minute one asks the modern question, "Did it happen?" the story has lost its power.[8] The works of Frank Honeycutt, himself a parish pastor who preaches every Sunday, are helpful in recovering the power of narrative for biblical preaching.[9] The Gospels are full of great stories; so be sure to search for the links between the First Lesson and the Gospel for the day, when they exist. Often that can reveal to the preacher the key for the sermon and to the congregation a theme for the lessons of the day.

When we approach the First Testament in this fashion, it becomes clear that not all of it is prescriptive. Some of it merely voices the human heart and thereby gives permission for such a voice in the context of faith. Fourth-century bishop Athanasius explained sagely that while much of the Bible speaks *to* us, the psalms speak *for* us. Hence, we have the imprecatory psalms uttered in honesty by the righteous sufferer. And would Christianity be richer without the voices of Job and Kohelet? Does the preacher's audience really want a candy-coated religion without honest reflection?

Which leads to our last point, related to the above but somewhat different. The Old Testament is wed to "real life." What originally attracted me in graduate school to the study of the Hebrew Bible is its earthiness. Even its Hebrew language is guttural, visceral as it describes stories of Noah's drunkenness, Abraham's cowardice, David's concupiscence, Job's blasphemy, and Kohelet's agnosticism. To be sure, the New

Testament has its share of shoddy characters, but it deals with a unified story of salvation that is admirably lofty. The Old Testament meets us where we are, in the muck of life, and that in many ways is its beauty and its profundity.

It is also its intimate connection with the New Testament. That the ultimate theophany would be a pooping baby born among stable animals to a pregnant virgin and growing up in a godforsaken Galilean village (Isa. 9:1-7; John 1:46) to become an itinerant rabbi outside the rabbinic establishment (that is, the pairs of rabbis descending from the Great Synagogue of Ezra) in order to clear up the foggy mirror by being condemned to die a naked criminal on a cross and rising to affirm Isaiah's claim of victory over death *is* the ultimate affirmation of the First Testament. So preacher, when you meet there an odd word, a troubling word, a word that does not fit expectations, know that this is the word of God. Wrestle with it and preach it (Gen. 32:22-32).

So where is Jesus in the Old Testament? Clearly the historical incarnation did not occur until the first century C.E. But as noted at the beginning of this essay, there is persistent expectation throughout the First Testament for a messiah who will bring the kingdom of God. These passages can and should be preached on. It is then up to the preacher to persuade the listener that Jesus is this Messiah.[10]

Does the preacher have to mention Jesus in a sermon on the Old Testament text? Probably usually; see above on linking the First Lesson with the Gospel reading. But I think the preacher must assume the context of the liturgy through which Jesus is proclaimed and in which his holy supper, the messianic banquet, is celebrated by the baptized. Jumping to Jesus too quickly in a sermon may actually be a disservice to the text, leading to a failure to plumb its depth of meaning, diversity, and challenge in terms of all that we have discussed in this chapter.

Some years ago I preached the Reformation sermon, using as my texts Jeremiah 31:31-34 (new covenant), Ezekiel 36:25-27 (new heart from sprinkled waters), and Deuteronomy 30:6 (circumcised heart; cf. Deut. 6:4, the *Shema*). Not necessarily by design but in the spirit of the gospel, I did not mention Jesus by name in the sermon. Afterward, an elderly woman approached me and said to me most authentically, "Pastor, I have never heard the gospel so clearly, and you didn't even mention Jesus!" This is the ultimate job of the Christian preacher: that the listener might hear the gospel, perhaps for the first time, even from the First Testament.

PART THREE

Gospel Proclamation and Context

Sermonic Song   8

The Legacy of Luther's Reformation Hymnody

ROBERT D. HAWKINS

The sixteenth-century continental reformers were in absolute agreement concerning one issue: the fundamental crisis the church faced was a systematic lack of engagement with the biblical word by the ordained and laity alike. Luther himself thought the crisis was twofold. Clergy, insufficiently schooled in the Bible, were incapable of preaching with integrity: "When God's Word had been silenced such a host of un-Christian fables and lies, in legends, hymns, and sermons were introduced that it is horrible to see."[1] The laity, thus deprived of a thorough schooling in Scripture, were incapable of praising God with any degree of understanding, and instead were simply distracted and misled by often questionable practices, legends, and teaching.

Luther's reforming treatises on worship focused on the utter necessity of renewed engagement with the word, particularly in the formation of the young and immature "who must be trained and educated in the Scripture and God's Word daily so that they may become familiar with the Bible, grounded, well versed, and skilled in it, ready to defend their faith and in due time to teach others and to increase the kingdom of Christ. For such, one must read, sing, preach, write, and compose."[2]

Always the pragmatist, Luther considered the various parish contexts that informed and shaped his musical and liturgical reforms in order to bring renewed focus to the Word: (1) court chapels and principal municipal churches, (2) smaller city parishes, (3) rural parishes with few resources, and finally, (4) gatherings of committed Christians willing to live out the implications of God's radical call in Christ.[3] These diverse parish contexts demanded careful discernment of the needs and educational levels of parishioners as well as the resources each context afforded for worship. The first category was marked by a complement of professional vocal and instrumental musicians as well as a number of leading composers. Parochial school children received thorough musical training and formed choirs for the daily prayer liturgies. Such musical forces continued the best of the Western polyphonic tradition. The second category, still under the musical supervision of capable cantors, supported more modest but still credible musical programs. The third category, often overlooked in the official histories of church music,[4] were also the most needy. Such rural parishes could not sustain the livelihood or interest of gifted musicians. The rich musical diet afforded by composer-cantors and musicians such as the Lutheran "proto-cantor," Johann Walter (1496–25 March 1570), simply was inaccessible to many parishes. Thus, at first for those with few resources and then for the entire church, Luther turned to hymnody.

Luther and a good number of his colleagues became hymn writers out of pastoral necessity. Evangelical preaching clearly was understood to be the primary way of immersing the faithful in God's Word: ". . . when God's Word is not preached, one had better neither sing nor read, or even come together."[5] However, it was certainly not the only way of proclaiming the Gospel. Luther remarks in the original, brief preface to the 1529 Large Catechism:

> For you should not assume that the young people will learn and retain this teaching from sermons alone. When these parts have been well learned, one may assign them also some psalms or hymns, based on these subjects, to supplement and confirm their knowledge. Thus young people will be led into the Scriptures and make progress every day.[6]

It is clear that Luther envisioned a hymnody intimately connected to the lectionary and able to "supplement and confirm" as well as "interpret" and contextualize Scripture in the life of the church, his brief working definition of biblical preaching.[7] At the same time he encountered parochial reluctance to learn the growing corpus of evangelical hymnody. In a less than charitable moment from the pulpit of the Wittenberg city church, Luther excoriated his congregation:

> I know of your laziness and that you have not learned the hymns that we use which you have heard the pupils singing for almost two years now. You do not make the least effort but rather pay more attention to the latest hit songs. Those of you who are heads of households must take it upon yourselves to teach these hymns to your families, for such hymns are a Bible for the untrained and even for the educated.[8]

Luther's concern was not prompted by entrenched conflicts in musical taste. Indeed, stylistic differences between sacred and secular music, "classical" and "popular," were not nearly as pronounced as now. Rather, Luther's frustration centered on congregational laxity in learning new hymns ". . . so that God's Word and Christian teaching might be instilled and implanted in many ways."[9]

> We have put this music on the living and holy Word of God in order to sing, praise, and honor it. We want the beautiful art of music to be properly used to serve her dear Creator and his Christians. He is thereby praised and honored and we are made better and stronger in faith when his holy Word is impressed on our hearts by sweet music.[10]

Nevertheless, "psalms, hymns, and spiritual songs" remain a battleground for present-day worship wars among Lutherans and others, despite Luther's helpful insights regarding the content and purpose of viable congregational song. "Praise music" and its context, "contemporary worship" or "praise services," propose to speak to disenfranchised seekers for whom more traditional forms of worship and song are inaccessible and off-putting. The missional concern is obvious and laudable even though it is suggested that proponents have scuttled the ecumenical, liturgical consensus of the church catholic. Others, couched as traditionalists, sometimes "high-church" types, are, in fact, nurtured and sustained by the Western church's venerable treasury of liturgical song and point as well to its ability to attract and sustain young and old of surprisingly divergent backgrounds. Despite the claims, the same traditions have had to contend with serious attrition in numbers. Still others, desiring neither the burden of the historic repertoire nor the perceived pop-performance style of praise music, long for a body of hymns ambiguously named "the old hymns." The frustrations and acrimonious tone of much of the discussion reflect more of stylistic and performance stalemates than solutions that contribute substantially to the upbuilding of the body. As parishes advertise veritable smorgasbords of worship styles, which hopefully assuage the spiritual hunger pangs of the faithful, we do not seem to have gotten much beyond "You say tomato; I say tomahto."

About fifty years ago a related debate appeared in the German theological literature. Unlike the present rancor fueled by disagreements over style and performance technique, the earlier debate raised serious issues regarding the content and purpose of congregational song. Reformed theologian Götz Harbsmeier and Lutheran musicologist Walter Blankenburg invoked a central Reformation-era question: Can congregational song be both proclamation and response, or is it only response?[11] Harbsmeier asserted that congregational song theologically is purely response; Blankenburg argued that it is both proclamation and response. While the debate might seem a rarefied exchange between professors, their discussion echoes earlier disputes of Luther, Calvin, Zwingli, Cranmer, and the medieval church during the turbulence of the Reformation. Moreover, the way in which the Reformation-era disputes and their continental revival in the 1950s addressed the controversy provides helpful insights concerning the present musical and liturgical skirmishes. Importantly, the willingness of earlier theologians and musicologists to enter sustained and probing discussions also commends itself to the present dilemma.

A brief summary of historical positions is helpful[12]: officially the Western catholic tradition accorded Gregorian chant official status and embraced as well the closely related Renaissance polyphony. While a lively folk and congregational hymnody was known, it was understood as paraliturgical until the impact of the Second Vatican Council.[13]

Archbishop Thomas Cranmer, not known as a particularly adept poet or musician, was content to continue the inherited choral tradition in his prayerbook reforms for the English church. The Reformed presence in Great Britain eventually introduced metrical psalmody, but Anglican composers themselves did not turn to hymnody to any significant degree until the eighteenth century.

The sixteenth-century continental reformers all shared a common concern: the Bible and the lively proclamation of the word must have central place in the worship of the church. Many of the liturgical reforms on which the reformers embarked were undertaken to achieve a clearer scriptural engagement in worship. Their solutions, however, varied greatly.

The Genevan and related reforming movements embraced congregational song, but restricted texts to the psalter, particularly the popular metrical versions of a number of authors. Calvin, Knox, and others understood the Spirit's work in such compositions as the God-given response and praise to the proclaimed word, the heart of public worship.

Zwingli, perhaps the most gifted reformer musically, was thoroughly trained as a humanist. His familiarity with philosophical concerns regarding the arts' ability not only to inspire but to beguile had direct impact on the Zürich reform. The arts, including music, were banned from public worship as distractions from the word of God. Congregations recited biblical psalms and canticles antiphonally as the fitting response to proclamation.

Luther stands in contradistinction to the other reformers. In the preface to the 1524 *Wittenberg Hymnal*, he stated that he was not ". . . of the opinion that the gospel should destroy and blight all the arts, as some of the pseudo-religious claim."[14] This position, consistent throughout his career and the impetus for the venerable Lutheran musical tradition spanning the centuries, had far-reaching ramifications. Unlike Cranmer, Luther was a gifted musician, preacher, and poet. Unlike Calvin and Knox, Luther did not find biblical warrant for concluding that the Holy Spirit inspired only the authors of the psalms. While aware of the arts' ability to beguile and distract,[15] he nevertheless found them fitting embodiments of the gospel. Finally, unlike the medieval church's exclusion of congregational hymnody from the liturgy, he found the need for such hymns to be crucial.

Turning to the more than thirty hymns the reformer penned during the course of his career, a consistent pattern of proclamation and response to the word can be identified, veritable sermons in song. Luther pairs preaching and hymnody, music and theology, as the most appropriate medium for proclamation. Frequently he employs "rhyme pairs," a popular German linguistic device, not only in his preaching and writings but in the growing corpus of hymns. *Singen und sagen*—"to sing and to say"—captures the inherent connection between proclamation and song.

> After all, the gift of language combined with the gift of song was only given to [humankind] to let them know that they should praise God with both word and music, namely, by proclaiming [the Word of God] through music and by providing sweet melodies with words.[16]

The Hymnic Pattern of Proclamation

The most significant characteristic of song, Luther suggests, is its ability to wed the human voice musically to God's own word. For such a wondrous gift, the fitting response is to praise God's gracious favor, true even when one is in torment and despair. Such praise leads logically into a recounting of salvation history, in short, to proclamation. However, preaching does not remain merely an objective recounting of the biblical text but seeks to anchor the living word in the lives of the faithful. Preaching for Luther, whether from the pulpit or the hymnal, is the honest confrontation with our dire need for God's saving presence in our lives. Preaching is the carefully crafted announcement of what God in Christ by the power of the Spirit is still accomplishing, ". . . beginning with Moses and the prophets," that is, "the whole Christ." Preaching announces that humankind, indeed, all creation, was not created to struggle independently or in isolation—such futile efforts are the ravages of sin—but to live forever in relationship with God, the original intent and the goal of God's saving work. God is to be known as God-for-us, God-with-us.

Luther developed a clear sermonic structure for his hymns that in time was emulated by other poets. Evidence of this structure became the gauge for Luther's and others' adopting, critiquing, as well as rejecting the myriad hymns being written. Lutheran provinces saw in his hymnic pattern of proclamation and response the hallmark of authentic evangelical hymnody.

While "A Mighty Fortress" remains the most familiar of Luther's hymns, the 1524 "Dear Christians, One and All, Rejoice" presents the initial and comprehensive pattern of Luther's sermonic hymn treatment of the gospel. The hymnic pattern is easily outlined:

- [Prologue exhorting the faithful to doxological praise]
- [Dramatic flashback of the human to sinful isolation, the absence of God/lament]
- Announcement of God's [or the Father's] sorrow about creation's plight and righteous anger that such must be the case
- The Father's sending of the incarnate Son to accomplish the reestablishment of relationship as well as to place death and the devil in captivity
- The Son's cosmic battle with the devil; the extent of God's sacrifice "for us and for our salvation"
- The Son's mission completed, the Spirit is sent both to comfort and to guide into all truth, believing, and importantly, the active, sanctified life
- [Restatement of doxological praise]

This and other hymns by Luther and his colleagues constitute careful biblical and theological constructs; it is foolhardy even to attempt to abridge them. While few of the myriad hymns of the Reformation present the full pattern, it is easily demonstrated that the whole is implied even in the partial treatment. Never is confronting the costliness of God's grace avoided or downplayed; neither do the hymn writers avoid addressing the consequences of sinful behavior. Praise, conversely, is exuberant, and fidelity to the proclamation of God's mighty act in Christ is clear.

Throughout his career, Luther and others referenced these hymns in sermons, the very texts the congregation sang during a given liturgy, as readily as the appointed pericopes, so closely were the two aligned. The gradual development of the Lutheran *Liedpredigt* ("song sermon") demonstrates the absolutely central place chorale texts have played in Lutheran preaching and the liturgy from the Reformation to the present.[17] By 1587 a complete set of hymns related to the Sunday and Festival cycle of propers was in place, a tradition emulated to this day in various "hymn of the day" cycles.

Dear Christians, One and All, Rejoice![18]

1. Dear Christians, one and all, rejoice, with exultation springing,
And, with united heart and voice and holy rapture singing,
Proclaim the wonders God has done, how his right arm the vict'ry won,
What price our ransom cost him!

10. "What I on earth have done and taught guide all your life and teaching;
So shall the kingdom's work be wrought and honored in your preaching.
But watch lest foes with base alloy the heav'nly treasure should destroy;
This final word I leave you."

Stanzas one and ten constitute an ecstatic framing of the hymn, although the translation blunts the praise of the final stanza. The faithful are exhorted to rejoice in united voice, to spring with exultation, to sing and proclaim ("to sing and to say") both the saving works of God and the radical cost of such loving action. For Luther, this is the reality of the baptized people of God and the source of his unwavering hope— "But I am baptized!" The final stanza again gives voice to unbounded praise as the way God's kingdom is made manifest by the faith community's teaching and action. The English translation opts somewhat passively for a conceptual orthodoxy ("life and teaching," "wrought and honored in your preaching"), appropriate "teachings" and sermons *about* the Christian life. Luther's German, however, encourages orthopraxis (*das solt du thun unnd leeren*—"that you should *do* and teach"), the active "doing" of faith, the "good works" of Ephesians 2 understood as the fitting consequence of God's creative work in our lives.

2. Fast bound in Satan's chains I lay, death brooded darkly o'er me,
Sin was my torment night and day; in sin my mother bore me.
But daily deeper still I fell; my life became a living hell,
So firmly sin possessed me.

3. My own good works all came to naught, no grace or merit gaining;
Free will against God's judgment fought, dead to all good remaining.
My fears increased till sheer despair left only death to be my share;
The pangs of hell I suffered.

Stanzas two and three comprise a dramatic flashback couched entirely in the past tense, a perspective often overlooked. Luther struggles to present a bracing description of "once you were no people; now you are my people," a baptized people now simultaneously saints and sinners. Again, while not specifically mentioned, the now-transformed reality of the baptized is the context, thus Luther's initial exhortation to rejoice. Human despair and isolation is graphically described. The past tense of the flashback preserves the tension with the new reality of the baptized life of God's saintly sinners. Although the baptized continue to "fall short of the glory," the consequences of God's act of baptism are mightier than the consequences of sin. Christians might continue to imagine that they are at times in "chains of death," but the bondage to sin, death, and the devil has been destroyed by the compassionate God.

4. But God had seen my wretched state before the world's foundation,
And, mindful of his mercies great, he planned for my salvation.
He turned to me a father's heart; he did not choose the easy part,
But gave his dearest treasure.

5. God said to his beloved Son: " 'Tis time to have compassion.
Then go, bright jewel of my crown, and bring to all salvation;
From sin and sorrow set them free; slay bitter death for them that they
May live with you forever."

6. The Son obeyed his Father's will, was born of virgin mother;
And, God's good pleasure to fulfill, he came to be my brother.
His royal pow'r disguised he bore, a servant's form, like mine, he wore,
To lead the devil captive.

Stanza four guides the singer into the heart of the Reformation theme of the justifying work of God in Christ by the Spirit's power, not as cerebral formulation but as a dramatic and graphic presentation of intra-trinitarian relationships. Also evident is the complementary doctrine of sanctification, otherwise understood in the Lutheran confessions as the appropriation of and living thereafter in the context of God's justifying act. Luther's concern is to describe the economy of salvation as clearly and concisely as possible. Anticipating the Large Catechism discussion of the Creed, the Father is identified as the compassionate God who sacrifices everything for the sake of a dying creation in order to restore creation to its rightful relationship with God. The Son is revealed as the incarnate "mirror of the Father's heart," whose self-emptying act (cf. Philippians 2) is both obedience to the Father and the divine reckoning with sin, death, and mortality.

7. To me he said: "Stay close to me, I am your rock and castle.
Your ransom I myself will be; for you I strive and wrestle;
For I am yours, and you are mine, and where I am you may remain;
The foe shall not divide us.

8. "Though he will shed my precious blood, of life me thus bereaving,
All this I suffer for your good; be steadfast and believing.
Life will from death the vict'ry win; my innocence shall bear your sin;
And you are blest forever.

Crucial to Luther's portrayal of God's justifying work in Christ is the image of cosmic battle between Christ and the devil, an image which appears in a number of his hymns, particularly "Dear Christians," "A Mighty Fortress," "Lord, Keep Us Steadfast," "Out of the Depths," "God the Father Be Our Stay," "To Jordan Came the Christ," and "Christ Lay in Bonds of Death." Gustaf Aulén's classic study of the doctrine of atonement, *Christus Victor*, argues that Luther's hymns recover the patristic treatment of atonement and reject the cerebral, speculative theology of Scholastic authors.[19] Significant, too, is Luther's reliance on relational language: Christ invites the faithful into saving relationship, defends them to the death, and is revealed as God-for-us who sends the Spirit to comfort, enlighten, and enliven the redeemed for life in the kingdom already breaking in. It is about this for which Luther's dear Christians have good reason to rejoice.

9. "Now to my Father I depart, from earth to heav'n ascending,
And, heav'nly wisdom to impart, the Holy Spirit sending;
In trouble he will comfort you and teach you always to be true
And into truth shall guide you.

10. "What I on earth have done and taught guide all your life and teaching;
So shall the kingdom's work be wrought and honored in your preaching.
But watch lest foes with base alloy the heav'nly treasure should destroy;
This final word I leave you."

While Lutheran ecumenical partners have had on occasion good reason to wonder whether Lutherans are theologically able to move beyond justification, Luther himself was quick to address the sanctified life as an unfolding reality (he frequently employs another rhyme pair, *hie und da* ["here and there"]), not merely an eventuality. The closing stanzas of the hymn address our embodiment of God's justifying work, namely the sanctified life of faith. Stanza eight concludes, "you are blessed forever." Somewhat ambiguous in English, the German makes it abundantly clear: *du bist selig worden* (". . . you have become [been made] blessed/holy"). Luther invokes language that is commended by the Lutheran confessions to address the sanctified life even when the documents assiduously avoid the word *sanctification* (*Heiligung*) itself in their struggle to describe and defend the evangelical doctrine of justification. Such implications have been more recently explored by Finnish theologians and presented in *Union with Christ*.[20] As the Large Catechism reminds us, sanctification appropriately is addressed in preaching, catechizing, prayers, and particularly in hymns since it explicates how God's saving work in Christ is appropriated and embraced by the church. It is the stuff of the Christian life that is given expression in the liturgy.[21] Although the English translation of stanzas nine and ten couches the sanctified life in passive, conceptual terms, the German text describes for the singer an active life of "doing, teaching, and praising," "establishing God's kingdom to God's glory and praise." And this, Luther notes in conclusion, is God's and his "last word" for us.

Recovering Sermonic Song as Articulate Response

Luther's Reformation hymnody clearly was intended to serve as the word's fitting and articulate "handmaid," the liturgical counterpoint to biblical preaching and proclaimer of God's saving story in rhyme, thereby "impressing it upon the hearts" of those who sing and hear. Moreover, Luther's hymns in particular illustrate how intimately the proclamation of salvation history and human response to God's saving work are connected.

At the heart of Judeo-Christian practice is the fundamental belief that proclamation and human response to the divine word constitute an indivisible whole. For example, the *Berakah* pattern of Jewish prayer is simultaneously prayer, praise, and proclamation: "Blessed are you, O Lord our God, King of the Universe, for in your goodness you have . . . !" Recounted thereafter *in* prayer *as* praise, God's mighty and creative deeds great and small are proclaimed.[22] One need only review the psalms to discover that lament, too, is part of the fabric of salvation history, moving ultimately to praise.

My God, my God, why have you forsaken me? . . .
But as for me, I am a worm and not human, scorned by all and despised
   by the people.
. . . Yet you are the one who drew me forth from the womb . . .
I will declare your name to my people; in the midst of the assembly I
   will praise you . . .
(Ps. 22:1, 6, 9, 22)

Such a unity of purpose brings significant resolution to some of the
Reformation-era disputes regarding proclamation, the Reformed–
Lutheran disagreement of a half-century ago, and present-day bicker-
ing over "praise music" versus "other music."

While Reformed and Lutheran theologians have been careful to
insist that the word is always addressed *extra nos* (outside ourselves),
nonetheless, it must be embodied in order to be heard and integrated.
Whether this embodiment occurs when the ordained read and preach
the word of God, the sacraments are celebrated, or as Luther insisted,
hymns are sung, the necessity of embodiment is inescapable. The
word is always a mediated word. The conservative Reformed position simply struggled to preserve the integrity of the preaching
office as well as the unique place of the scriptural word in the life
of the church. By insisting that congregational song was exclusively
response, the Genevan Reformed tradition adopted a highly restric-
tive understanding of the acceptable mode of proclamation, namely
the preaching office. A psalm chosen as the appointed preaching text
would be understood as proclamation; were the same psalm sung by
the congregation, it was response. The only difference was the mode
of embodiment.

Zwingli, the humanist, pushes present-day Christians nearer to the
source of the dilemma. His awareness of the power of the arts both
to inspire and to distract focuses attention on the *modes* of embodiment, not to the actual content of the word itself. Zwingli's own reform
merely brought such an understanding to its logical conclusion: *all*
forms of embodiment other than the *spoken* word of the preacher were
considered suspect because of the potential of distraction.

Present-day controversies fixate primarily on performance modes
but differ substantially from earlier discussions and debates on one point.
Rhetoric regarding "authentic" or "appropriate" music for public worship, whether praise music or more traditional forms of congregational

song, has often sundered proclamation, praise, and lament as if they comprise discrete and unconnected realities. Luther's hymns remind the church that proclamation, praise, and lament are of one fabric; if separated they are seriously compromised.

The inherent biblical connection between proclamation, lament, and praise provides the church with helpful, even healing, guidance about the choices we make regarding congregational song as well as the purpose and function of such music in the church's liturgies. Moreover, this fundamental biblical connection affords some appropriate correctives regarding the liturgy itself.

1. Praise and lament are fundamental responses to life as it is experienced and perceived. Introspective and reflective, they address how we feel or what we believe our life situation to be: past, present, and future. From the heart, from the most dire straits to mountain-top moments, they are the signs that we are alive, whether we feel we are dying, drunk with love, or in the grasp of ecstatic vision. Praise and lament are the experiential, emotive counterpoint to that which forms us, shapes us, or is addressed to us.

Important, however, is the ability to discern that which is *extra nos*, the formative realities confronting us, vital when the formative reality is the Word of God. To grow, to learn, to be transformed, to be more fully human—in short, to become the people God calls us to be—we learn to articulate accurately these formative realities as well as honestly to express our responses to such actions and forces.

Thus, "praise music" as well as lament, if they are to serve the "upbuilding of the body," must be intimately connected to and informed by salvation history, even when the text of a particular song is simply "Praise the Lord!" The Gregorian *jubilus*, the extended melismatic conclusion sung on the final syllable of "Alleluia," expressed ecstatic praise as pure melody beyond words. It, however, was paired with the Easter proclamation. Augustine, discussing the *jubilus*, notes that it "is a melody which conveys that the heart is in travail over something it cannot bring forth in words. And to whom does that jubilation rightly ascend, if not to God the ineffable?"[23] Likewise, in a poignant prefatory remark to the frenzied organ work "Litanies," composer Jehan Alain echoes Augustine's insight: "When the Christian soul in great distress is no longer able to find new words to implore the mercies of God, the person with fervent faith repeats without ceasing the same invocation. Reason has reached its limit; only faith is able to ascend."[24]

Authentic praise and lament acknowledge their object, the God of salvation history who both triumphs and shows profound compassion, not merely our own enthusiasm or response to divine favor. Rhetoric that points solely or even primarily to music's ability to uplift, engage, or express human emotion subtly moves the assembly into spiritual narcissism. Such rhetoric also skews the discussion by focusing on performance-mode preferences rather than the word itself. The word may well comfort, inspire, and delight, but it equally has the power to unsettle, admonish, correct, convict, and even become a stumbling block.

2. Conversely, traditional forms of congregational hymnody and liturgy that have served the church's lively proclamation over the centuries run the risk of being domesticated by the very people who value the church's musical and liturgical heritage. The focus can be as readily skewed by unreflected defense of traditional genres and instrumentation. Neither chorales and organs, liturgical orders and ceremonial[25] are intended to serve as orthodox counterweight to "praise music" or "spirited worship," thought solely the stuff of seekers' services. Appropriate critique is leveled when the church values controlled order and suppressed emotion while excluding the potentially surprising and unexpected power of the word to make an impact on lives, thereby eliciting human response. God's "frozen chosen" are not named completely without reason. Often ignored or left uncelebrated are the church's forms of "praise music," past and present, as well as profound lament. "Christ Is Arisen," the 1533 recasting of a twelfth-century hymn, is a Reformation-era example of praise music, particularly its third section. "Ah, Holy Jesus" as well as "Calvary: Every Time I Think about Jesus" remain two better-known yet strikingly different forms of lament, although hymnals and song collections include few such works. The *Ausbund* of the Anabaptist Amish, the "hymns of the martyrs" and the oldest hymnal in continual use, remains the notable exception.

"Praise music" champions themselves need to be challenged to expand their understanding of response to God's Word. It might as readily prompt contrition and remorse; it might well invoke hushed and prolonged silence. Christian worship, if it is authentic, must give voice to the full range of human experience, including the myriad ways that response may be embodied. The improvisational tour de force of inspired musicians, the clangor or solemn tolling of tower bells, the technicolor explosion of processions, paintings, drama, dance, and billowing clouds of incense too often are rejected as foreign to the Lutheran tradition or dismissed as "incidental" to the word, yet all may serve as significant, embodied responses to God's presence in our midst. Thus would Luther remark that "places, times, persons, and the entire outward order of worship have therefore been instituted and appointed in order that God's Word may exert its power publicly."[26] To the stony-faced faithful who would cast "Soul, Adorn Yourself with Gladness" as a dirge, Luther might well observe: "This is precisely the sin that used to be numbered among the mortal sins and was called *acedia*—that is, laziness or weariness—a malignant, pernicious plague with which the devil bewitches and deceives many hearts so that he may take us by surprise and stealthily take the Word of God away again."[27]

3. Proclamation is of necessity wedded both to praise and lament. The ecstatic nature of both praise and lament, on the one hand, serves as the appropriate sign that the word has engaged the hearer. Such responses may constitute only short acclamations or be "beyond words," but never are they divorced from the word. Proclamation, on the other hand, can run the risk of becoming pedantic recitation of disconnected scriptural texts if little or no place is given to response. Authentic worship does, in fact, hold proclamation and response not so much in tension as in creative counterpoint. The liturgy is impoverished if either is lacking.

4. Once the complementary nature of proclamation and response is perceived, then one finally can turn to musical style and modes of performance. This need not devolve into stymied discussions about taste, but rather affords a necessary broadening of categories regarding faithful proclamation and response.

The Lutheran confessions insist that the Spirit did not cease to inspire, among others, poets and composers once the psalter was completed.[28] By extension, one may rightly conclude that the Spirit has remained active after Luther, Bach, and F. Melius Christiansen, too. Lutherans have made significant contributions to the church catholic's reception of the word, although not of exclusive importance. For example, African American spirituals have little connection to Western catholic liturgical tradition nor to much of its musical heritage. Drawing on African traditions of song and dance as well as the evangelical hymnody of nineteenth-century America, spirituals emerged as songs of enslaved people exiled from home who discovered meaning in the exodus account. Spirituals are laments about enslavement, the struggle and journey out of bondage, and ecstatic praise for and trust in the God who delivered Israel and would deliver them as well. Thus, spirituals find a surprising yet fitting home in the liturgies of the Triduum, giving voice in particular to the entire sweep of the Vigil Office of Readings.

Hard questions must be asked of congregational song. Insofar as it is proclamation, does it present the "whole Christ" as part of the saving biblical record "beginning with Moses and the prophets"? Whatever the congregational song, will the faithful over time come to know the whole saving story recounted in song? Insofar as the song is praise or lament, is it simply preoccupied with emotive expression, or does it connect fully the congregation's response to the living Word, the One who actually brings life to the dying and joy to the despairing? Whatever music, whatever style, whatever medium—do they serve the Word's unfolding for a particular people in a particular place at a particular time? Without apology, this will be difficult to answer, for evangelical hymnody and preaching as faithful, lively proclamation *and* response demand absolute honesty and a willingness first to listen to the ever-searching Spirit of God.

"The Sound of the Gospel"

9

Historical Perspectives and Contemporary Reflections on Lutheran Theological Education and Preaching

SUSAN WILDS MCARVER

At the end of an April day in 1863, forty-four-year-old Rachel Muller Bernhard, a widow who had recently lost her only son to disease in a Confederate hospital, sat down to compose her thoughts. For a period of at least ten years, she had been keeping a religious journal, quietly recording every worship service she attended, the name of the pastor whom she had heard preach that day, the scriptural text, an outline of the sermon, and a brief reflective response. The death of her only child had shaken her, but she clung to the assurance of her pastor's words. "What a privilege to sit under the sound of the gospel," she wrote that Sabbath evening, "as it is explained by this holy servant of God. Nothing but the word of God can convince us of sin and bring us to true repentance. . . . Oh my father I thank thee for the privileges of this day."[1] For Rachel Bernhard, the "sound of the gospel" served as a powerful moment when the sermon of her pastor delivered to her the word of God.

Pastors today deliver that same word of God in a vastly different universe from that inhabited by Rachel Bernhard. But in at least one way, Bernhard's experience reflects a reality increasingly found in our own. Bernhard had been raised in a Lutheran household, had married a Lutheran pastor, and stood as a devout member of her rural southern Lutheran congregation. But in Bernhard's nineteenth-century world, Lutherans found themselves faced with more congregations hungry for that word than they had pastors who could provide it. Bernhard's small parish had to share its pastor with at least two other churches, and Bernhard often had to attend the churches of other denominations in order to hear regular Sunday preaching. In the twenty-first century, in ways similar to Bernhard's experience in the nineteenth, many congregations today also experience a shortage of adequate numbers of clergy to fill their pulpits. Many denominations are currently considering a variety of options and attempting a number of different methods to fulfill the need for theologically prepared men and women to serve as ordained pastors. In the Evangelical Lutheran Church in America, leaders are exploring a number of possibilities for addressing this need, including programs that allow persons to serve in Word and Sacrament ministries in specific contexts and settings through alternatives to a full, four-year seminary education.

Clergy shortages and the search for creative ways to provide pastors stand as nothing new within the history of Lutheranism in North America. Indeed, the lack of highly trained and seminary-educated clergy plagued Lutherans from the earliest days of colonial settlement in this country, as the journals of early pastors such as Henry Melchior Muhlenberg, the private writings of laypeople such as Rachel Bernhard, and others often attest.

In the nineteenth century, two systems of theological education emerged side by side in the southeastern United States in response to these same needs. On the one hand, classical seminary education, the norm for clergy preparation in Europe, still stood as the ideal, but it did not really become a possibility in this country until the late 1820s. In its place, an alternative developed: training programs that relied on mentors, synodical oversight, and what we today might call independent study.

The concern of this essay is to examine the ultimate impact these two ways of forming pastors had on the *preaching* heard in Lutheran congregations in the southeastern United States. This chapter examines the ways in which antebellum southern Lutherans addressed their need for qualified clergy, the impact their training had on the preaching heard in their nineteenth-century congregations, and finally, the implications these experiences might hold for ongoing church life and clergy formation in the twenty-first century. The study finds that at times, these two nineteenth-century approaches to theological education created pastors who preached their sermons in very different ways. But at other times, theological preparation for preaching had less *substantive* impact than one might have imagined, and the content of preaching heard in southern Lutheran congregations often showed far more similarities than differences. These two quite dissimilar approaches to the formation of pastors, therefore, produced clergy who sometimes differed in significant ways, and yet at other times, differed hardly at all.

To examine these questions, this essay considers (1) the pattern of mentored theological education as it emerged in response to the needs of the nineteenth century and the preaching that resulted from it; (2) the development of seminary education as it emerged later in the South and the preaching styles of seminary graduates; (3) themes found within the sermons of both types of pastors; and (4) possible implications for ongoing church life today.

The Emerging Need: The Formation of Pastors Through Mentoring

Lutherans began to arrive in the Southeast in significant numbers by the early 1730s through the ports of Charleston and Savannah and by overland travel from Pennsylvania through the Shenandoah Valley of Virginia and into central North Carolina. Most Lutherans who settled in America in the colonial period did not bring their own clergy with them, and no Lutheran seminaries existed in North America for the first several decades of Lutheran settlement. Thus, congregations generally had to rely on one of two sources for their clergy: university-trained pastors sent from Europe (desirable, but extremely rare) or pastors who served in other German-speaking denominations, such as the Moravians or German Reformed (helpful, but not entirely satisfactory).

As the eighteenth century rolled into the nineteenth, however, even these two sources of clergy grew increasingly inadequate. Pious laymen who felt the call to study for the ministry found travel back to Europe impractical, but local seminaries did not yet exist. A new educational approach therefore emerged to address this clergy shortage: a mentoring system to produce "homegrown" pastors who could serve local congregations. Local pastors served as mentors, guides, and teachers to those who studied with them, allowing the candidates to read their theological books and learn their profession through observation and participation. In effect, many southern Lutheran pastors sought out formation for their ministry in the same manner as those entering the fields of law and medicine: through apprenticeship to local practitioners.

The emerging synods decided to grant yearly licenses to these apprentice pastors and required them to report annually to the Ministerium for evaluation. If students had made sufficient progress since their last meeting with the Ministerium, the synod could grant relicensure each year until they judged the students ready for ordination.

In central South Carolina between 1824 and 1835, several men "of mature age" felt the call "to preach the Word" and presented themselves to the synod for licensure under these rubrics. By and large, these men came to the synod as unlettered farmers, while one was a former sheriff. They stood as men "of very limited book-learning, and knew not how to convince themselves or others of the truth by process of reasoning—that is to say, by logic." Their sole qualifications for the office of the ministry appeared to have been their "sound judgment" and their ability to "[stand] up to show the people their transgressions and the only way of escape from the consequences of them."[2] They each began to preach under a license from the synod and to read theological books independently under the direction of a supervising pastor.

Herman Aull (d. 1852) provides a good example of this type of aspiring pastor. Born sometime before 1800 into a German-speaking home, he apprenticed at a young age as a carpenter. Aull reportedly exhibited some "wild, frolicsome habits" in his youth, but apparently at some point in his thirties, he became profoundly aware of the error of his ways, perhaps through attendance at a nearby revival, and in 1831, he applied to the synod for a license to preach. His life had given him little opportunity for formal education, and in common with many of his generation on the Carolina frontier, he struggled to make the transition from German to English, a slow but inevitable process in the new nation. Not wishing to stand as a burden to his people, he remained primarily a farmer as well as a carpenter, even after the synod granted him license to preach: "he endeavored to instruct [his people] in the way of salvation," a parishioner noted, and "wrought with labor and travail that he might not be chargeable to any of them."[3] H. George Anderson has noted, in fact, that many of these Lutheran pastors into the late nineteenth century "should be seen as preaching farmers rather than farming preachers."[4] Such "secular" employment alongside of their service as pastor may have made ministerial labors more difficult, but it did keep southern Lutheran pastors closely linked to the everyday lives of the parishioners among whom they lived and worked.

Not all of these men were completely "unlettered," however. Like Herman Aull, Joseph Fesperman (1841–1917) never had the opportunity to attend formal school. He grew up on a farm in Rowan County, North Carolina, but a farming accident when he was thirteen confined him to bed for weeks. While there, he "carefully read the Bible, *Book of Martyrs, Pilgrim's Progress, Alleine's Alarm, Pollock's Course of Time,* and the *Life of Whitfield* and that of Wesley."[5]

Reading books of theology confirmed in Fesperman an already insatiable desire to preach: "My desire to preach became intensified. I retired to bed thinking about preaching, I dreamed of it, talked in my sleep concerning it, and when I awoke it was the first thought to enter my mind. . . . I could not refrain from preaching." He reported that "the boys of the neighborhood erected for me a pulpit, with steps attached and a bookboard on it, and I preached to them in the woods almost every Sunday noon. This was not child's play. We had our Bibles and Hymn Books, and we sang, prayed and behaved ourselves."[6] Throughout his young adulthood, Fesperman "endeavored . . . carefully, faithfully, patiently, unwaveringly, [to do] the best I could in whatever circumstances I was placed, and at the same time direct . . . all the powers of mind and body toward the desired object,—preaching."[7]

This remarkably determined young man persevered toward his goal through adversity that would have stopped many a lesser candidate. He was twenty when the Civil War broke out, and he wrote that once "entrance into the army became unavoidable," he packed "Schmucker's *Popular Theology,* Gregory's *Evidences of Christianity,* Porter's *Homiletics,* the *Lives of the Ancient Philosophers,* my Bible and Hymn Book into my knapsack, and went into the service of the Confederacy against all my inclinations."[8] Between battles, "I gave my whole time to theological studies," he wrote, going often to a college professor of ancient languages who served as regimental chaplain "if I did not comprehend a point in theology, or did not know the correct pronunciation of a word." Although Fesperman's conscience troubled him that he had not yet obtained formal permission from the synod to preach, "license or no license, I intended to preach," a practice he maintained even as a prisoner of war following his capture during the Battle of Chancellorsville and a second capture during Stoneman's Raid in North Carolina.[9] Against all odds, he survived the entire conflict and was finally officially licensed by the North Carolina Synod in December of 1865. Even so, it was yet another six years before he was at long last ordained.[10]

Like Fesperman and Aull, Alfred J. Fox (1817–1884) of North Carolina received very little formal education, receiving all he ever had "at the common schools of his neighborhood." One of the first sermons he ever preached came as he appeared for approval for ordination as a deacon before his synod. The results were not promising. "Young, diffident, and speaking in a poorly lighted room, he did not succeed well, and many persons thought he had mistaken his calling. His examination on the following day, however, gave promise of better things."[11] Recovering from this near fiasco, Fox worked hard to redeem himself and "secured without aid a knowledge of Latin and Greek" and a "remarkable vocabulary of English words." Like Fesperman, Fox's erudition came through "extensive reading until late hours at night," and he became legendary for his ability to read on horseback: "Sometimes when riding his interest in reading was so intense that he did not perceive the passing of persons until looking back he saw them going in an opposite direction." In theology, he read "chiefly German works, studying Reinhardt, and the *Book of Concord* especially" under the direction of his uncle, the Reverend Daniel Moser.[12]

Despite these impressive individual efforts, the various southeastern synods recognized that such idiosyncratic preparation for formal call to ordained ministry could produce decidedly mixed results. Some students, such as Fesperman and Fox, obviously proved exceptional and excelled despite their lack of a formal theological education. Others, however, did not succeed nearly as well. In 1831, therefore, the South Carolina Synod passed a resolution requiring that those who were licensed to preach but not yet ordained keep "a journal of their studies and proceedings during the year, and that they compose at least one sermon annually to be submitted to the inspection of the Ministerium."[13]

At the next year's examination of three licensed young men, licentiate George Haltiwanger (1793–1849) reported that during the previous year, he had maintained his required journal, preached fifty-nine times, and attended fourteen funerals, including two under the supervision of ordained pastors. His studies had been "confined to Church history and the Bible with the assistance of Horne's *Introduction to the Critical Study of Theology* & Clark's *Commentary*."[14] During the same time period, however, Herman Aull could not report such sterling progress. Aull found himself chagrined to report to the synod that "I have not been able to attend to my Study as constant as I wished in consequence of having a large Family to provide for."[15] Nevertheless, after review, the Ministerium renewed the licenses of both Haltiwanger and Aull, as well as that of a third candidate, no doubt at least in part due to the extreme shortage of available pastors.[16]

The Preaching of Mentored Pastors

A letter of call sent to Daniel Efird from Godfrey Dreher in 1851 indicated that his multiple congregations expected to hear preaching each week "when your health & the weather will admit of it," and "also [on] the Holy days, & the days preparatory to administering the sacrament of the Lord's Supper."[17] Since most pastors, including Efird, served multiple congregations, this could add up to a great deal of preaching.

An examination of the few surviving pastors' journals of this era indicates that pastors' chosen texts did not follow a lectionary. Instead, each pastor chose the weekly text on which he would preach based on his own interests, the context of the congregation, and the needs of the community, as he perceived them. Unlike much of contemporary Lutheran preaching, texts came as often from the Old Testament as they did from the New. Often, the sermon text comprised only one to three verses; it was not unusual for an entire sermon to be based exclusively upon a single verse.

Surviving texts of sermons from these mentored pastors are rare. Such preachers often prized their ability to speak "extemporaneously," that is, without a written sermon text before them, thus creating sermons that are by definition almost totally unrecoverable. Rachel Bernhard (1819–1882) listened to many of these sermons. Left alone at age twenty-four after the premature death of her husband, she moved back into the home of her parents to raise her son and devoutly attended worship services in her local Lutheran congregation, recording her spiritual reflections on the weekly worship she attended in her journal.

But often, the sermons of pastors who had received their education through mentoring received little more in her journal than a brief notation of the text upon which they had preached. One Sunday in July of 1855, for example, she experienced a "Sabbath of privileges. Thrice was I permitted to hear God's blessed word expounded." She listened to mentored pastor George Haigler preach on both 1 John 2:1 ("My little children, these things write I unto you, that ye sin not . . .") and also on Hebrews 3:7-12 ("Today, if ye will hear his voice harden not your hearts"), but she did not record the content of either sermon. Similarly, she recorded only the scriptural text for a sermon she heard by Jacob Crim in December 1857 (Rom. 6:23, "For the wages of sin is death"). For a sermon by Elias Hort that same year, she did no more than record the date and the pastor's name.[18]

Still, surviving accounts give us at least some indication of the style and content of this preaching. After accepting the call outlined in Godfrey Dreher's letter above, for example, Daniel Efird preached in central South Carolina between 1851 and 1881 and

> used very brief notes, if any at all. His style was animated; he spoke with spirit and rapidity and his supply of language was free and ready. His sermons were seldom embellished or explained by anecdote or narrative, but were of the old school Lutheran type. Biblical doctrine being explained, sustained or modified as occasion required by quotations from the Bible itself. His voice was naturally strong, and in speaking he raised it almost to its highest key, which made him easily heard in every portion of a large building.[19]

The style of the Rev. A. J. Fox of the Tennessee Synod, on the other hand, was reportedly "chiefly conversational." Even his admirers confessed, "Dr. Fox was not what the world commonly styles a great preacher. If even his natural endowments, with proper culture, had fitted him for such a distinction, and he had aspired to it, the circumstances under which he began his ministry and prosecuted it through life, were, to say the least, all unfavorable to this." But "his object was not self-aggrandizement," it was "the glory of God and the good of man. He preached not himself, but Christ Jesus, the Lord."

Despite his limitations, Fox "was particularly apt and happy in his illustrations and enforcement of religious truth by comparisons drawn from nature, science and art; and he knew how to take advantage of the common incidents of everyday life, and remarkable occurrences in the country with which his hearers were familiar, and in which they were interested." He often "preached without manuscript, and for many years without even notes. He had before his mind his plan clearly marked out and he needed no reminders." Fox's slightly nerve-wracking method of sermon preparation was to select his text early in the given week and ponder it as he went about his pastoral visits. "On Sunday morning before he rose from bed he would fix definitely his plan, think out the order of the more important arguments in their relation to each, and if he had his usual clearness he was ready." Fox used humor in his sermons, but his witticisms "never breathed the air of vulgarity."[20]

Farmer preacher Herman Aull's style in the pulpit was decidedly more austere and mixed "sternness with pity." His parishioner Dr. O. B. Mayer remembered "the pensive emotion excited by the tender persuasiveness [his] *'Broken English'* gave to his sermons." Picturing Aull behind the raised, central pulpit of St. John's, Pomaria, South Carolina, Mayer wrote:

> he was small of stature, and quick in his movements. His hair was black and strait, and his eyes were brown and bright. In the pulpit he would frequently depress his chin upon his breast, and glancing his gaze from under his eye-brows . . . the hymn he gave out at that time was one which I believe must have been his favorite— his song of repentance. . . . I felt sure from the slow movement of his head to the right and to the left. . . . that the third and fourth stanzas affected him with sorrow: *This is the way I long have sought And mourned because I found it not; My grief a burden long has been, Because I could not cease from sin. The more I strove against its power I sinned and stumbled but the more; 'Til late I heard my Saviour say, Come hither, soul, for I am the way.*"[21]

In the end, synods and congregations found that preaching could vary widely under this individualistic approach to theological education. The 1833 "Report of the Committee on the Sermons and Journals of the Students of Divinity," appointed by the South Carolina Synod to review the quality of sermons preached by its licensed candidates, illustrated the shortcomings inherent in such a system. The committee reported that the synod's students had been "active and zealous" and demonstrated "a manifest improvement in penmanship and composition," but the committee also noted that it "would kindly suggest to the young Brethren the propriety of attending strictly to composition, to make a free use of the dictionary, and labour to produce compositions as original as possible."[22]

Seminary Education in the Nineteenth Century

Lutheran seminaries finally began to appear in the eastern United States by the early 1800s with the chartering of Hartwick Seminary in New York State in 1797, Gettysburg Seminary in Pennsylvania in 1826, and in 1830, "The Theological Seminary at Lexington" in South Carolina (the present-day Southern Seminary).[23] Though some resistance to the formation of seminaries existed, two factors began to push toward their ultimate creation: the unevenness of the mentoring system, and a general rise in the educational standards of all of the professions, including those of medicine and law.

After a brief initial sojourn in rural Pomaria, South Carolina, southeastern Lutherans moved their seminary in Lexington, a small community a few miles from the state capital of Columbia, located in the central portion of the state. According to its students, Lexington stood as "one continued piney, monotonous, saharan-like level" in an environment containing "more grog-shops and bars than churches" and marked by "every species of idleness and sloth,"[24] but its head, Ernest Lewis Hazelius (1777–1853), stood as a scholar of impeccable character. A friend and warm supporter of both Samuel Simon Schmucker at Gettysburg Seminary and the national church body Schmucker helped establish, the General Synod, Hazelius was a former Moravian and a professor who had already served at both Gettysburg and Hartwick seminaries before his arrival in Lexington. Hazelius was a man with "a deep and unaffected humility, an implicit confidence in God, a lover of all mankind, a detester of polemical disputes, and a promoter of Christian fellowship and union." A student noted that he bestowed upon his students "all the advantages of an experienced teacher, a faithful councellor (sic) and a kind parent, sweetly blended,"[25] and he was, observed non-Lutheran

Edwin Scott, the only German he ever knew who could "neither sing nor smoke."[26]

Hazelius needed all of these gifts, because his duties proved enormous. As the only professor of the seminary for years, he taught the entire curriculum, including Greek and Hebrew philology, Sacred Geography, Sacred Chronology, Biblical and Profane History Connected, Jewish Antiquities, Philosophy of the Mind, Evidences of Christianity, Biblical Criticism, Exegesis, Biblical and Systematic Divinity, Ecclesiastical History, Polemic Theology, Church Government, and Pastoral Theology.[27]

Hazelius considered the spiritual formation of his students, however, to be as important as their academic development. He constructed a strict "rule" for seminary life, expecting seminary students to "spend a portion of time every day in devout meditation, self-examination and prayer, and in reading the holy Scriptures, solely for the purpose of practical application to himself." In addition, noted Hazelius, "The whole of the Lord's day should be spent in devotional exercises, either social or secret."[28]

Despite these strictures, seminary students found ways to loosen their bonds, at least a bit. Student Thaddeus Boinest (1827–1871) recorded with delight the events of one Sunday: "I attended to prayer meeting, after which the Dr. [Hazelius] preached and the communion was administered and a collection taken up. About 4 o'clock went over to see Hopkins and found a house full of ladies, walked with them up to Aunt Caty's and sat a while."[29] Student William Houck (1826–1874) found that "my solitary condition gives me ample scope for reflection & study," which he promptly filled by writing entertaining and vivid courtship letters to his future wife.[30]

The Preaching of Seminary Students

At Southern Seminary, Hazelius's carefully crafted curriculum included no specifically assigned textbook for preaching. Instead, members of the Junior and Middle Class (first and second year students) took "composition," which was taught by "verbal Instruction." Not until the Senior year (third year) did students take specific "Exercises in pronouncing and delivering of sermons,"[31] and not until the constitutional revision of 1850 did any explicit reference to "homiletics" (sic) itself appear in the course list.[32]

The lack of a stated textbook, however, hardly indicated a haphazard approach to the subject of preaching. Hazelius's method of instruction followed traditional nineteenth-century (and earlier) forms of pedagogy in teaching all of his subjects. Students dutifully copied down lessons taught by the professor word for word, usually in a question-and-answer format, memorized their notes, and then recited them back to their professor at assigned times to demonstrate mastery of the material.

Even by nineteenth-century standards, such instruction could prove exceedingly dull, and students, it is to be feared, apparently did not always treat their professor with the respect he was surely due. The monotonous nature of the routine led Boinest to sketch doodles in his otherwise pristine copybook, thereby violating injunctions against "levity or inattention to practical religion."[33] John Phillips Margart (1816–1901) clearly suffered from spring fever in March, 1838, when he "passed through the day (with rather too much feeling of indifference to my Prof. during the hours of recitation)" and recorded on the next that "the day passed on as usual except my swinish temper had in one or two instances in some manner got the better of me, viz.; In recitation room I was rather spiteful towards my teacher."[34]

While neither Hazelius's own lecture notes on homiletics nor his students' seminary copybooks have apparently survived, students clearly imbibed from him a strict, formulaic style of preaching well known and in use in many nineteenth-century traditions that had become standardized since the Protestant Reformation. Martin Luther had rejected the traditional fourfold interpretation of Scripture (literal, allegorical, moral, and anagogical)[35] in favor of concentrating instead on a text's "literal, ordinary [and] natural sense."[36] "In my preaching," Luther reportedly stated, "I take pains to treat a verse [of Scripture], to stick to it, and so to instruct the people that they can say, 'That's what the sermon was about.'"[37]

Protestant preachers following his example in subsequent centuries developed an emphasis on the "plain sense" of Scripture. Sermons were "plain" in two ways: "plain" enough to be understood by the simplest hearer, and "plain" in their "strict adherence to accepted homiletical order," consisting of exposition, doctrine, and application. By the time of the Puritan revolution, "every sermon began with a reading of the text, followed by the opening, or exegesis, of the text, the extraction from the text of the doctrine to be propounded, the discussion of reasons for and refutation of objections against the doctrine, and finally the application of the doctrine to the lives of the listeners."[38]

This method favored an *expository* approach to preaching rather than a topical one: such sermons concentrated heavily on the background, exegesis, and elucidation of a particular biblical text, and then made application of that text to present conditions in the life of the Christian, usually in a point by point fashion.[39] Unlike their mentored counterparts, then, seminarians were taught a method of preaching that aimed precisely "to convince themselves or others of the truth by process of reasoning—that is to say, by logic."[40]

This formal preaching style did not lend itself to the "extemporaneous" approach of mentored pastors. Virginian Josiah Smeltzer much preferred the formal written method he had learned from Samuel Schmucker at Gettysburg Seminary, but his congregation apparently preferred something freer. He recorded one Sunday, "Sabbath. Preached in Newberry. Extempore. Hard work. Wish I could write every sermon; yet I doubt not the Cong[regation] [p]refer an extempore address." Smeltzer struggled when forced to "Preach from a sketch,"[41] and for many classically trained pastors like himself, such studied informality could prove difficult to obtain.

It would be a mistake, however, to assume from the description of this rather spare framework that such highly structured "logical" preaching contained no emotion. Hazelius regarded it the duty of seminary professors to "promote genuine piety and true devotion . . . by warning their pupils against cold formality on the one hand and fanaticism on the other."[42] George Haltiwanger Jr. (1811–1862), who studied at the seminary under Hazelius in the late 1830s, articulated the goal of a preaching style he had been taught there that united head and heart:

> If we preach entirely to the intellect, and never awaken the passions we will fail to enlist man's sympathies in the cause of God. [But] if we play entirely upon the passions of his nature, while there maybe much show for the time being, it will soon pass away. Both should move harmoniously together—the intellect leading, and the passions of man's nature urging him on to follow the leadings of an enlightened mind.[43]

Many of the sermons Rachel Bernhard heard in the 1850s and
1860s given by seminary-educated clergy reflected this pattern. Unlike
the spare notes she recorded upon hearing the sermons of mentored
pastors, she filled her journal with extensive descriptions of the sermons she heard by those who had attended seminary. In response to an
1854 sermon by Rev. Lewis Eichelberger (1803–1859) on Genesis 1:1,
for example, Bernhard recorded that he "first explained what is meant
by creation, and what was created . . . secondly [what] we are to learn
from this; the absurdity of denying the existence of God; the absurdity
of denying the power of God; the absurdity of denying the Sovereignty
of God." William Berly's (1810–1873) sermon on Revelation 8:13 "first
showed who were meant by those who had washed their robes and
made them white in the blood of the Lamb and secondly that we must
through much tribulation enter into the kingdom of God." Berly then
"described the happiness of the Christian in the eternal world."[44]

In other ways, however, the preaching of seminary graduates did
prove similar to that of mentored candidates. In common with mentored pastors, seminary-educated pastors' chosen texts did not follow
a lectionary—each pastor chose the short text on his own. And like the
Scriptures chosen by mentored pastors, the texts chosen seldom stood
longer than three verses, with the Old Testament a popular choice for
preaching.

Common Themes in the Preaching of Both Mentored Students and Seminary Graduates

Despite the profound differences in education and style between those
pastors trained by apprenticeship and those trained in the seminaries,
however, certain common themes emerged in the preaching of almost
all southern Lutheran preaching throughout the nineteenth century.

1. *Pietism.* In theological substance, the preaching of both mentored
and seminary-educated southern Lutheran pastors agreed in one fundamental way: it all stood as deeply pietistic.

As some of the foregoing examples have suggested, Lutheran
preaching in the early to mid-nineteenth century often had an "evangelical" quality to it. With the important exception of the entirely
mentored pastors of the Tennessee Synod (discussed more fully below),

preaching in both the North and the South stood heavily influenced by the surrounding evangelicalism of the larger culture.

Lutheran pastors were quick to identify similarities between classic Lutheran pietism and the emphases developing in nineteenth-century evangelical Protestantism as a whole. Pastor John Margart's record of sermon titles hint at his preaching themes: Romans 8:6, "the carnal and spiritual minded contrasted"; Malachi 3:7, "Return unto me and I will return unto you"; Revelation 10:6, "First and last days"; Acts 17:30, "Repentance"; Luke 13:24, "Strive to enter in at the strait [sic] gate"; and finally, Philippians 3:13, 16, "Progressive religion essential to a satisfactory evidence of the existence of true piety in the heart at [sic] a comfortable hope of salvation."[45]

Rachel Bernhard gloried in such preaching. She often heard and recorded her appreciative impressions of such sermons, such as one by seminary-educated William Berly in 1853 on Isaiah 53:1, which stressed "the fall, natural depravity of man, and the plan of salvation through the gospel. 'It is necessary for man to feel and know his lost condition that he must come as a lost, ruined and undone sinner to the cross of Christ. . . .' How earnestly did he entreat believers," wrote Bernhard, "to live more holy, and exemplary lives, to exercise strong faith in God, and to leave all our concerns in his hand."[46]

Such pietistic emphases led inevitably to a growing emphasis on moralistic concerns. Southern Lutheran pastors who already leaned toward pietism demonstrated no reluctance to preach against what they saw as the great moral failings of the day. John Margart clearly reflected both his seminary professor's devout predilections as well as the beliefs of his own pious heart in his preaching and teaching. He recorded with obvious pleasure in his journal that an address at a "muster ground" on "the subject of Temperance" led to the conversion of three people to the cause, including one who was "a confirmed drunkard." He also preached "against fashionable amusements," on the "Obligations of Christians to a life of holiness" and on "the importance of family prayer and worship."[47] It is no wonder Rachel Bernhard often prayed, "Oh Lord deliver me from sin, let not Satan have dominion over me, help me to resist all temtation [sic], and to cleave unto thee with my whole heart."[48]

The funeral sermon provided a special opportunity to praise the worthy and warn the unfaithful. Both mentored and seminary-educated pastors filled their journals with the records of such sermons, which were often preached in the home (with burial taking place on family land), sometimes weeks after the actual death itself. The funeral sermon for the pious departed gave assurance to the living. Lewis Eichelberger used the occasion of the death of Joseph Wingard to preach on Revelation 14:13 and "first pointed out the blessedness of those that die in the Lord . . . secondly, that the Christian rests from all his labours, from all the cares, anxieties, turmoils and sufferings of this life—and thirdly that his works follow him."[49] Those who were "willing to die & died not fear[ing] death" could "warn the young" to be similarly prepared.[50]

The death of the evil, on the other hand, provided a different kind of opportunity. Alcoholism stood as a contributing factor to many a death recorded in the journal of Josiah Smeltzer, who learned from his own observations as a pastor of the damage alcoholism wrought on families and communities. Sometimes Smeltzer pitied the alcoholic dead—"Poor man, he was too fond of strong drink"—but more often, he clearly felt such sinners got what they deserved: "He had both legs cut off by the [train] cars at the bridge; died shortly afterwards drunk at the time; died cursing & swearing; aged about 53 years; left a widow & two children; was often warned." "An aged man," he wrote on another occasion. "No church member. Fond of stimulating drinks. Sick for some time. Few to mourn his loss. I endeavored faithfully to improve the occasion." Sometimes words simply failed Smeltzer: "supposed to be 79 years of age. Infidel in sentiment. What could a preacher say on such an occasion? He has gone to the bar of God."[51]

For all its emphasis on piety and morality, however, southern Lutheran preaching studiously avoided the gravest moral issue of the day—the institution of slavery. Southern Lutheran pastors regularly recorded in their journals the baptizing, catechizing, and marrying of both slaves and "free persons of color" throughout the antebellum period. Often, however, such acts did not list the full names (or any name at all) of those receiving baptism, confirmation, or Holy Communion. David Bernhard of South Carolina merely noted in 1838, for example, that he had baptized "Lucy," the slave of "C. Cotes," as well as "W. Keller's Siby," "G. Cote's Hetty," "Mrs. Wolf's Amy," and John Kennerly's "Sally & Coty," among many others.[52] The annual congregational statistics required by synods typically broke down membership categories and ministerial acts by race and reveal that African Americans made up a significant proportion of the southern Lutheran population in the years before the Civil War. By 1859, for example, up to a quarter of the Lutherans in South Carolina were African Americans, both slave and free.[53]

Significantly, however, no surviving sermons of the period after 1830, or even journal entries for that matter, question the morality of the institution of slavery itself. While at various times over the years the southern synods addressed the "duties" of congregations to their African American members, what was *not* questioned was the *existence* of slavery as an institution.

2. *Ecumenism.* A second similarity emerging in both mentored and seminary-educated preaching flowed logically from the pietism and morality these sermons emphasized: they all embraced a generous ecumenical quality.

Because of their theological commitments to Lutheran pietism, seminary professors such as Ernest Hazelius at Southern Seminary and Samuel Schmucker at Gettysburg found a congenial spiritual home within the growing evangelical emphases of many nineteenth-century Protestant denominations. This comfort found formal expression in the first constitution of Southern Seminary, which stood "open for the reception of Students of all Christian denominations."[54]

Seminary professors and their students could make an argument in favor of such ecumenism on the theological basis of Lutheran pietism, but mentor-trained pastors and many laypeople often arrived at an easygoing "folk ecumenism" on their own. Indeed, the historical context of the antebellum eastern Lutheran experience had made such a position almost a necessity. In the absence of their own pastors in the frontier days, eighteenth-century Lutherans had accepted with gratitude the ministrations of pastors of other German-speaking denominations. As the clergy shortage continued, however, and as they transitioned from a German-speaking to an English-speaking population, isolated Lutheran parishioners eager to receive the word of God often began to seek out the gospel wherever they could find it.

Even with the heroic efforts of pastors who traveled a circuit and preached in multiple congregations, most southerners of all denominations in the rural South did not have access to preaching services in their own congregations every week. Religious southerners therefore most often simply attended whatever church held preaching on a given day. Many, in fact, like Rachel Bernhard, went to the services of one denomination in the morning and to another in the afternoon or evening.[55] As scholar Ted Ownby has noted, the fact that many southern rural churchgoers regularly "rotated their church attendance" helped create a common morality and value system among southerners in which they saw "in each other far more similarities than differences."[56]

Parishioners were not the only ones who "rotated" their church attendance. Ecumenical generosity also found expression in the open pulpit exchanges of Lutheran pastors with pastors of other denominations. Whether seminary trained or mentored, southern Lutheran pastors preached freely and often from the pulpits of neighboring denominations. Most pastors' journals record preaching in Presbyterian, Methodist, Episcopalian, and Baptist pulpits, while Thaddeus Boinest even preached in the "Quaker Church" for "some months."[57] Josiah Smeltzer preached in three denominations in the same day on more than one occasion, yet he seemed genuinely surprised when other denominations recruited him for their own: "[I am] asked again & again to become a Pres[byterian], Baptist & even an Episcopalian. I cannot see why they wish me to change my ecclesiastical relations."[58]

In the end, in an America still largely rural and frontier, it seemed to many good Lutherans—seminary professors, pastors, laymen, and laywomen—that it was far more important for Lutherans, Methodists, Presbyterians, and Baptists to all work together as Christians in a land where church attendance was still phenomenally low and infidelity alarmingly high, than to accentuate the points of disagreement that divided them.

3. *Revivalism.* When Rachel Bernhard recorded hearing Rev. L. Eichleberger preach on Isaiah 55:3 in 1853, she noted that "this beloved servant of God . . . beautifully explained" Isaiah's meaning: "Free salvation is offered to all, it is the sinners [sic] own fault if he is lost and this will constitute one of the chief miseries of the damned, to think that salvation was offered to him and he refused to live."[59] In dramatic fashion, Eichleberger's sermon indicated the logical conclusion to the pietistic, moralistic, and evangelically ecumenical emphases developing among eastern Lutherans by the time of the Civil War—preaching at revivals.

Again, with the important exception of the mentored pastors of the Tennessee Synod, both seminary-educated and mentored southern Lutheran pastors participated in the evangelical revivals of the Second Great Awakening sweeping the entire United States in the early to mid-nineteenth century. Evangelical worship innovations such as "the anxious seat" or "mourners' bench," and "protracted meetings" encouraged participants to engage in rigid self-examination during what was often an exuberant outdoor worship service, ideally leading to an emotional and often wrenching moment of conversion. Following this cathartic moment, the new Christian sought to live a life of extreme holiness, self-discipline, and prayer.

Although in theory the overt "decision theology" of such revivals stood as antithetical to most Lutheran pastors, in practice the emphasis on right living and morality encouraged by the revivals appealed to their pietistic natures. Many Lutheran clergy from both the North and South therefore did not find this movement antithetical to their theological self-understandings, and they agreed that revivals in and of themselves were not necessarily suspect, provided they were conducted decently and in good order and were not considered a substitute for catechetical instruction.

Here, mentored and seminary-trained pastors differed mostly by degree. Mentor-trained pastors tended to embrace revivalism wholeheartedly. Pastor Joseph Fesperman, who had struggled for years to obtain his preaching license, described with enthusiasm the "days when the spirit of revivals existed in many portions of North Carolina," when the words of Lutheran pastors came on "fire with their themes and poured forth the living truth upon their auditory, and the voice of prayer and praise was heard in shops, and factories, and fields, and God and angels listened." Then, he recorded, "the people cried out, 'Men and brethren, what shall we do?' "[60]

Seminary-trained pastors, like their mentored counterparts, did not hesitate to participate in revivals or to embrace the ecumenical opportunities they provided. Seminary-trained John Margart particularly enjoyed protracted meetings—meetings that could extend for up to two weeks with preaching two or three times a day. In 1841, he conducted a three-day meeting at a rural South Carolina church, assisted by the local Presbyterian minister, a Methodist "exhorter," a Methodist pastor, his former seminary professor Hazelius (who "read the services preparatory to Communion after he had made a few preliminary remarks"), and a seminary classmate.[61] On another occasion, Margart reported the assistance of "two Baptist brethren" who "rendered us some assistance on Saturday evening, but went away on Sunday." The following year, he preached twice a day for five days at a "most glorious meeting" in 1842, when "an accession of 20 was made to the church," and at a "9 day meeting" in 1844 at "truly a reviving meeting" where "12 new members were received."[62]

Yet seminary graduates did prove somewhat more circumspect in their approach to these meetings. Lutheran pastors insisted that they could participate in such services without betraying Lutheran theological principles. A pastor later described a four-week series of revivals in 1865 as "good Lutheran services," not a "whooped up (miscalled) revival, with its disorder, and . . . unsound and dangerous teachings." The pastor's method was to preach the gospel simply, "No harrowing and blood-curdling anecdotes are necessary." The pastor urged the "awakened" to "come forward and occupy a front seat, sit or kneel, as they prefer. Then we announced and read the hymns, and had a few short prayers and instructed them more perfectly as to the way of life—giving it a very practical catechetical turn."[63] In a seven-day series of protracted meetings in Virginia, the Rev. Peter Miller wrote that he did not "preach," but read Scripture lessons and commented on them, exhorted, prayed, and led songs from the hymnbook. He did not "have any of the 'Hold the Fort' style in either words or tunes," and reported confronting skeptical rowdies in the back pews of the church on at least two occasions.[64]

But though they tried to maintain a distinction between "hold the fort" sermons and "good Lutheran services," eastern Lutheranism found itself on a slippery slope. Ernest Hazelius and Samuel Schmucker may have been able to make a nuanced argument on the basis of classical Lutheran pietism that properly conducted evangelical revivals held a rightful place within authentic Lutheran preaching and teaching, but whether their parishioners were able to maintain their fine distinctions is less certain.

Schmucker's former student Josiah Smeltzer in Virginia noted with disapproval: "For the last few days I have been attending a protracted meeting. . . . That people is curious. They are pleased with my preaching but think I am not severe enough on poor sinners. They believe it is the Province of a Pastor to pour down on poor sinners Rivers of

Hell & Damnation!" Smeltzer clearly recognized the danger of such a system: "They believe religion consists of a man walking to the mourner's bench & there experiencing a certain sensation & all is right." But then, he noted, the "poor souls, when they feel temptation's power, they believe they have lost all their religion. I have endeavored by the Grace of God to correct some of their erroneous notions. How far I have succeeded God only knows."[65]

The misgivings expressed by Smeltzer did not stand as his alone. No matter how carefully they tried to nuance their interpretation of revivals, such preaching came dangerously close to committing the unpardonable Lutheran sin—calling on people to do a good work (exercising their own "moral agency," as Daniel Bell puts it)[66] to earn their own salvation.

As early as 1803, some Lutherans in North Carolina expressed concern that such evangelical outpourings remained inconsistent with traditional Lutheran faith and practice and seemed examples of "'spiritual fanaticism' run wild."[67] While leaders such as Hazelius at Southern and Schmucker at Gettysburg argued for a freedom from the "literal sense" of the documents of the sixteenth-century Reformation, the ministerial members of the North Carolina Henkel family began to argue for precisely the opposite. Led by Paul Henkel (1754–1825) and more famously by his son David (1795–1831), these pastors attended no seminary and received no advanced theological degrees, yet they studied Latin and Greek, preached in English and German, and read the Augsburg Confession and *The Book of Concord* with a careful eye. In so doing, they came to quite different understandings of issues such as baptismal regeneration, the presence of Christ in the Lord's Supper, justification, and sanctification quite different from those embodied in the increasingly popular evangelical camp meetings.[68] The revivals, they found, had a tendency "to divert the mind from the regular Means of Grace as set forth in the Word of God, as well as from a reliance on the promises contained in Divine Revelation." Instead, the Henkels argued, the revivals led "to a dependence on the feelings or emotions . . . for salvation, thus disparaging, to a greater or less extent, the true doctrines of the Holy Scriptures, and leaving the Church in a state of distraction, in regard to some of the most vital features of sound Scriptural theology."[69] Eventually, their studies led the Henkels and their followers to stinging critiques not only of the revivals, but the existing synodical leadership, national synods, centralized authority of any type, and—interestingly—intermarriage between Lutherans and Presbyterians.

This "Augsburg Confession war," against the "so-called Lutheran preachers," as Paul Henkel termed it,[70] came to a head in 1820, when the Synod of North Carolina and Adjacent States split over the issue, forming a nongeographical "Tennessee Synod" that eventually claimed churches in Virginia, North Carolina, South Carolina, and Alabama (but ultimately not Tennessee). Forty years later, the same basic confessional issues lay behind the formation of a rival seminary to the one in Gettysburg (Philadelphia Seminary) and the formation of a new national church body to the General Synod (the General Council). The publishing empire of the Tennessee Synod, the Henkel Press based in New Market, Virginia, reintroduced a generation of southern Lutheran laypeople and clergy to the theological distinctiveness of Lutheranism through its translation into English of such works as the Augsburg Confession and *The Book of Concord*. But theological differences stood so deeply entangled with personal animosity, national and states-rights politics, and even economics, that the Tennessee Synod protest often took on the characteristics of a destructive holy war. The controversy sundered congregations, synods, and families in a bitter, divisive split not fully healed for over a century.

Implications for Ministry in the Twenty-First Century

Readers of this essay will have undoubtedly observed that the nineteenth-century Lutheran preaching reflected in this chapter hardly resembles the preaching discussed elsewhere in this book. In fact, one is almost tempted to conclude from the sermons presented here that perhaps this chapter can best serve as an example of how *not* to preach in our own day. This study does, however, raise a number of issues for consideration in the present.

First, a study of nineteenth-century preaching illustrates the obvious: context matters. For good and for ill, the context in which a sermon is preached powerfully shapes the theological message it propounds. Sermons, like church architecture, worship, or hymnody, reflect the surrounding milieu and changing times of which they are a part. Despite the concern of some that "contextual" preaching is somehow a modern denial of ancient truths, the reality is that preaching has *always* stood as "contextual." Brian Peterson has reminded us in his essay that even the earliest post-Jesus sermons were "addressed to specific assemblies of believers,"[71] and his point is worth repeating: preaching is incarnational. Just as the biblical narrative itself has a context, just as our very theology is embodied in the person of Jesus Christ, so the sermon itself exists in a particular time and a particular place. "The Word is always a mediated Word," as Robert Hawkins puts it.[72] Sermons thus reflect the themes, strengths, weaknesses, shortcomings, blindness, prejudices, tragedies, and glories of the particular era of which they are a part. Sometimes, then, sermons may tell us more about the preacher and the times in which the preacher lives than they do about the biblical text itself.

Evangelical revivalism was the rising tide of the nineteenth century, and all boats, whether originally in the water or not, could easily be carried away with it. Before we become too complacent in the judgments we pronounce on the nineteenth century, however, we should raise the question for our own: What waters are rising beneath us today that we may not even sense? How is the context of our own day shaping the sermon and its message in ways that will seem just as unlikely to our descendents a century from now as the revivalism of a past century now looks to us?

Second, by implication, an acceptance of the importance of context also implies that contexts change. In the early nineteenth century both the mentoring model and the seminary model emerged in response to the needs of the church when previous methods of providing pastors (obtaining them from Europe or from other German-speaking denominations) no longer could respond to the changing context of the new nation. Recognizing the historic reality that models have changed over time in response to changed needs can help inform the decisions we make for our own future.

Third, with the consistent exception of those who served in the Tennessee Synod, the chief differences between the sermons of those who were educated at seminary and those educated through a mentoring process may indeed have been differences of style, rather than substance. Mentored pastors may not have been able to argue their case as well through "logic" as did their seminary-trained colleagues, but essentially they argued theologically the same position: humanity is fallen, Christ has died for our sins, and some response is needed.

This does not mean, however, that "style" stood as unimportant. Rachel Bernhard sat at the feet of both types of pastor in the decades of the 1850s and 1860s and recorded what she heard in her journal. Time and again, the sermons of seminary-educated pastors received clear, lucid, point-for-point summaries in her journal. At the same time, the sermons of non-seminary-educated pastors received far less detailed treatment, often receiving little more than a notation of the text upon which the sermon was based. It is difficult to determine from this distance what this difference in notation meant. Did it reflect that the more "emotional," less "logical" sermons of mentor-trained pastors were simple enough that they did not require summary? Does it imply that a more "free-flowing" sermon structure was more difficult to follow and remember after the sermon was over? Or is it simply a reflection of "taste," delineating the type of preaching Bernhard preferred over that which she did not? While the answers to these questions are probably not recoverable, what is clear from the surviving record is that at their core, the theological points of the sermons stood as substantially similar to each other.

Fourth, while two tracks of theological education operated throughout the antebellum period, the lack of a seminary education did not "invalidate" the ministry of mentored pastors on at least two levels. On one level, many who went through the apprenticeship system proved to be voracious readers, students, and theologians. The fact that a pastor was not a graduate of the seminary did not mean that he was theologically incompetent and, in fact, sometimes meant exactly the opposite. While most mentored pastors adopted an evangelical position similar to that of the seminary-educated pastors of the day, for example, it is worth remembering that the most significant theological protest against the revivalistic flavor of much of southern Lutheran preaching and teaching in the antebellum era came *not*, as we have seen, from seminary-educated professors and clergy, but from the entirely mentored pastors of the Tennessee Synod who made an early and sustained theological critique of much of the theology of the day on the basis of the Augsburg Confession and *The Book of Concord*.

More importantly, pastors trained through apprenticeship provided meaningful ministry in the most basic—and the most important—way. While they might have differed in style, the sermons of both mentored and seminary-educated pastors often changed lives and enriched congregations. In the nineteenth-century context, piety mattered. It mattered even more, perhaps, than education. Rachel Bernhard, for example, may not have been able to reduce some of the mentored pastors' sermons point for point into her journal as easily as she was able to with the sermons of seminary-trained pastors, but these "beloved pastors" still fed her soul. European-trained physician Orlando Benedict Mayer long remembered the day in 1842 when he made a house call on South Carolina farmer preacher Herman Aull and "saw him coming from his field to greet me. His face was moist with the sweat of labor and his shirt-sleeves were rolled above his elbows. As I took his hand, and felt the palm hardened by contact with the plough-handles, I could not help admiring the old man."[73] In the end, Aull's piety and integrity, not his educational attainments (or lack thereof) mattered most in his ministry.

Finally, perhaps two differences not specifically related to preaching are worth noting for their implications for the present-day formation of pastors. In the early days of the southern synods, mentored pastors served in important leadership roles in the formation and establishment of those organizations. After about 1835, however, seminary-educated pastors began to move into a more active role in synodical life and leadership in their place. Over time, pastors who had been mentored for their education began to take less and less of a public leadership role in the southern synods and gravitated toward small, isolated, rural parishes where they tended to remain, while well-educated seminary graduates began to assume leadership at both the synodical and regional level.[74] Those students trained under the older mentoring system seem to have become increasingly isolated as their ministries progressed. Considering this historical experience, perhaps one might ask how such an eventuality could be avoided with present-day mentored pastors. How can mentored pastors in the present century be formed more intentionally in order to bring their gifts to the larger church and how, in turn, can the community of faith support them more effectively in their congregational life and ministry?

And lastly, the surviving record left behind by students of seminary education in the mid-nineteenth century demonstrates, in the words of the Auburn Study of Theological Education, the importance of "being there."[75] Community has its benefits. Students often complained about the tedium of life in rural Lexington, South Carolina, the unrealistic nature of seminary rules, and the dullness of their instruction while they doodled in their notebooks. But what also emerges in the surviving diaries, journals, and correspondence they left behind is the value these early students found in each other. Students debated each other, pushed each other, supported each other, preached for each other, commiserated with each other, visited "the ladies" with each other, and kept in touch with each other for the lifetimes of their ministries. Clearly, for these students, something more than "education" was taking place—today we would call it "formation."

Mentored students, on the other hand, did not have these opportunities. Isolated by their "secular employment" and their necessarily individualistic approach to their own education, these students did not have the opportunity to form communal bonds with others going through the same process. In our own day, this understanding might lead us to consider how the church might be more intentional in providing opportunities for similar formation and nurture among the candidates preparing for ministry through various "alternate routes."

Preaching in many nineteenth-century eastern Lutheran churches ultimately looked quite different from preaching in our twenty-first-century churches, demonstrating that whatever else preaching may be about, it is inevitably about speaking the word to a particular time and a particular place. The church still needs in every age to call forth men and women to preach—and to support them when they do. As we consider decisions about the formation and preparation of pastors in the future, perhaps a glance backwards to those who prepared for this work in previous generations can leave us better informed for the next ones.

Look and See

10

Text and Context in Preaching

NICHOLAS K. MAYS

Among the preaching aphorisms that were heard forty years ago—and still heard today—was this one: the preacher should preach with the Bible in one hand and the newspaper in the other. But who reads the newspaper when there is so much more information on the Internet? Regardless of the source, today's preacher is still admonished to connect the text with the context. For some, the inclusion of contextual matters in preaching seems intrusive. It is one thing to proclaim the gospel in a language that is easily accessible to the hearers, but newspapers and the Internet present a transient sort of truth. The truth of the gospel should be about some kind of universal truth, and not be coated with contemporary and cultural biases. Wasn't that Luther's idea in "The Babylonian Captivity of the Church"? For others, this notion of contextual preaching connects with new technologies and forms of communicating, and is long overdue. Forty years later, there still is concern for and anxiety over the relating of text and context in preaching. How does the preacher stay true to the text, while at the same time connect with a generation of hearers whose idea of history begins with the Reagan presidency—or even more recently?

But the matter of text and context is more complex than language, technology, or cultural wars. Simon Chan, a professor of systematic theology at Trinity College in Singapore, has been called "the world's most liturgically minded Pentecostal." In an interview in a 2007 issue of *Christianity Today*,[1] Professor Chan made the observation that "missional theology has not gone far enough. It hasn't asked, 'What is the mission of the Trinity?'" And the answer to that question, he maintains, is "communion." "Ultimately, all things are to be brought back into communion with the triune God. Communion is the ultimate end, not mission."[2] This observation echoes Paul's declaration that "in Christ God was reconciling the world to himself" (2 Cor. 5:19). It suggests that proclamation has a teleological purpose, that mission is more than the spread of Christianity, and that context is more than adaptation of language or techniques. Preaching is about what the creating, redeeming, and sanctifying God is doing to restore the created order in a broken world.

This means that the preacher has the daunting task of bringing text and context together into a moment of proclamation. Entering the pulpit or sauntering down the center aisle wearing a microphone headset, with a finger on the PowerPoint remote, the preacher brings deepened knowledge of the text to bear on discipleship in this segment of God's gathered people. As the preacher gazes into the faces of the hearers, a different and more intimate knowledge comes to the fore. It is the knowledge of the councilman whose wife has left him because he couldn't leave the bottle. It is the knowledge of the teenager who is worried about her appointment at the clinic tomorrow. It is the knowledge of the stewardship chairman who lost his job and the women's organization leader who just got promoted. The preacher in the South or West may see the faces of a flock of snowbirds who are seeking meaning to life after retirement. If the preacher is from the North or the Midwest, she might see the faces of the faithful looking around at all the empty pews and wondering about the viability of their congregation. It is the preacher's knowledge of the everyday lives of the hearers and the concerns of the community that are being addressed by this word. In this moment, the preacher is called upon to combine the exegesis of biblical scholar Walter Brueggemann and the visionary insight of ELCA pastor and author Michael Foss, to bring that to God's people, to proclaim that Christ has died, Christ has risen, and Christ will come again, and to help them to make sense of what that means in their lives of faithfulness and servanthood.[3]

Theologians Eric W. Gritsch and Robert W. Jenson have made the observation that preaching is at the heart of who the church is as well as what the church does. "The reality of the church is the hermeneutic event of the move from hearing to telling."[4] Hearing and telling have a specific content, what they refer to as "the special role of Scripture:"

> One set of documents stands out normatively from the tradition: the canonical books of Israel. . . . The apostles' message was a word spoken following the record in these writings. Our talk is hermeneutically the same as theirs only if it also submits to a text, and to this text.
>
> The function of the New Testament is quite different. [It] comprises the literary relics of the apostolic gospel . . . [and] is a substitute for the living voice of the apostles. . . . Our talk of Christ is gospel only if it is objectively about the same events as the witness recorded in the New Testament, and only if it opens our lives to the future in the same way as did that witness.[5]

By training then (and hopefully by inclination), the preacher turns to Scripture for models for this task of linking text and context. The accounts of Jesus' teaching in the Gospels of Matthew and Luke give a model for this linking. Matthew 11:2-5 and Luke 4:6-19 present concrete examples for interpreting Scripture contextually. Each story has to do with God's reign as being a time of the reversal of fortune for the lowly and the outcast. But the texts and the contexts differ. Jesus' hearers in the first text are the disciples of John, who are wondering if Jesus is the coming One, and if his advent marks the end of prophecy and the beginning of fulfillment—a rather standard early church interpretation of Isaiah 29, 35, and 61. In Luke's text, the hearers aren't identified as anybody's disciples, but as a sabbath gathering at the synagogue in Nazareth. This is a ritual reading from a book of prophecy, but it ends with a twist on the texts from Isaiah 61 and 58. The twist is that God has moved the prophecy from promise to fulfillment. But how do we know this? What gives authority to these texts? Jesus does not cite other authorities, nor does he proclaim this only by fiat. Instead, he invites his hearers to "look and see." Look around you and see what is going on. What is God doing right in front of you where you can see it, and behind your backs when you are not paying attention? These texts suggest that what you see God doing around you will give you insight into the kingdom to come, the One who ushers it in, and what discipleship in that kingdom will look like. This insight is like looking into a dim mirror, as Paul says, but the kingdom to come can be apprehended, even if it cannot be fully comprehended. So, Sunday after Sunday, preachers instinctively, intuitively, imaginatively, and intentionally invite hearers to look and see the new creation God has brought, is bringing, and will yet call into being. This proclamation is always both textual and contextual.

The Context and the Preacher

Let's look at how this proclamation has occurred in a specific context and with a specific preacher. The context is a split internship site committed to the formation of pastors in the Evangelical Lutheran Church in America (ELCA). At the time of this internship, this split site comprised an ecumenical congregation and a Lutheran care facility for the aged. The congregation is, in fact, three congregations (an Episcopal congregation, a Lutheran congregation, and a Presbyterian congregation), all of whom meet together for worship, outreach, and fellowship. The care facility provides a ministry of Word and Sacrament to a religiously diverse population whose physical, emotional, and spiritual needs range from those who live independently in community to those requiring full-time nursing care.

Let's take a closer look at the two components of the site. Smith Mountain Lake is a hydroelectric facility that was transformed into a retirement destination. The need for common facilities and a common mission led representatives from the Episcopal, Lutheran, and Presbyterian traditions to develop congregations that would come together in a covenant fellowship. This fellowship became Trinity Ecumenical Parish in 1991. There are about five hundred members, and another one hundred active nonmembers. There are around 325 worshipers on Sunday at two services. There is an early morning Eucharist service that uses an ecumenical liturgy, and a later service that uses liturgies of the three traditions rotating on a monthly basis. The supervisor is an ordained pastor in the Presbyterian Church-U.S.A. (PCUSA).

Brandon Oaks is sponsored by the Virginia Lutheran Home, Inc., and has a self-described "ministry of outreach and care for the elderly, providing a secure and comfortable environment." There are over three hundred residents with diverse needs for health care. A ministry of Word and Sacrament there means a daily chapel service and a weekly vespers service. The average attendance is seventy-eight. There are also Bible studies, prayer services, and one-on-one pastoral visitation. The chaplain supervisor is an ordained pastor in the ELCA.

The preacher was an endorsed candidate of the ELCA from the Southeastern Pennsylvania Synod who, at the time of her internship, was in her third year at Lutheran Theological Southern Seminary. She has selected the three sermons from her internship year in the site described above, and agreed to their use in this article on text and context in preaching. Each of the sermons deals with the concerns raised in Matthew 11 and Luke 4 about the kingdom that is dawning, the Messiah who ushers in the kingdom, and what discipleship in this kingdom might look like in a leisure community like Smith Mountain Lake and for those whose later years are being spent in an intentional community of care like Brandon Oaks in Roanoke, Virginia.

Sermon 1

> You and I—all those who gather weekly and those who walk through the doors as visitors—we are not always at the same place in our faith journey. . . . Some come wounded from other places. Some come with more questions than they have faith. Some still want to discover whether God's grace truly exists here, or whether there is room enough for them to worship and serve alongside others who are more certain of their faith than they. That is why community and gathering is so very important. We need each other. . . .

The text for this first sermon is from the Gospel lesson for the Second Sunday of Easter, John 20:19-31. It focuses on the encounter between the risen Jesus and "doubting Thomas." The sermon is about doubt and faith at a personal level. How do I know that God is taking care of me? This question has an obvious immediacy for those in the nursing center. Being up close and personal with too much suffering and too much dying deepens any discussion of doubt and faith. The sermon says simply and boldly to these hearers that Jesus has come into the midst of our suffering and our seeking. He comes with bloody hands and wounded side. Easter is precisely for those who are in pain and those who are dying. He is risen! He is risen indeed! Put your finger here; put your hand there. Touch and embrace, not a disembodied Jesus, but the crucified Jesus. The sermon also lifts the resurrection from the individualism of my faith and boldly asserts that the community holds others in the faith when they cannot see the risen Jesus.

The changes in this proclamation from one context to the next are subtle, but significant. Clearly, meeting the risen Jesus is a riper and richer possibility in the nursing home than in the suburban congregation. In the nursing home, discipleship is lived out in a profound waiting and anticipating. The kingdom is much closer. The suffering and the dying live next door, down the hall, or in the next bed. They have names and faces. In the congregation, discipleship is an active engagement with faith and community. Daily life for them is a rigorous rhythm of tasks and recreation. The congregational hearers might connect readily with the first part of the text, before Thomas appeared with his doubts, when Jesus appeared with a blessing of "peace," when he breathed the Spirit on them, when the disciples were glad, when there was rejoicing, when there were alleluias and family dinners. However, the preacher knows that the people of the congregation, who are so wrapped up in their daily living, also live in a culture of death: not just ordinary dying, but extraordinary dying, in warfare in the Middle East, and on college campuses, and on crowded highways. There are the poor and the poor in spirit in the suburbs, too. There are malnourished children and suicidal teenagers. Thomas's questions are as real here as they are in the nursing home. They just don't get asked as often, and are rarely asked out loud: How do I know God cares for me when my family is broken, when there is addiction, where there is helplessness? "My Lord and my God" is the affirmation for those whose hands and hearts are pierced. The proclamation to them also is "The risen Lord is the crucified One!"

This sermon counters a misunderstanding about the relationship between text and context in preaching. There is little change in this sermon from what was said in the nursing home context to what was said in the suburban congregation context. But this consistency of thought and emphasis reminds us that contextualizing a sermon isn't like ordering a hamburger your way at Burger King. You don't just adapt the text to the setting and substitute middle-class angst for dying when talking about doubt and faith. Contextualization may also be about seeing the symmetry of the human condition as much as seeing the differences in each of these contexts. Contextualization may be about drawing connections between the end of life and the middle of life. Because the intern moves regularly between the contexts, she is able to do this. She is able to remind the separate gatherings that the crucified and risen body of Jesus is good news for all. The difference is that however much the residents of the nursing home live with death daily, they do so expectantly. The congregation, however, lives in a culture of death that denies its reality, so its impact is often sudden, dramatic, and traumatic. In both contexts the good news of Easter is the proclamation that Jesus has won the victory over death.

Sermon 2

Jesus says, "My sheep hear my voice. . . ." There's an assumption in there—something being said without words, and that is that God is constantly talking to us. God's voice is always there. We are in a relationship with God where we are being spoken to. Even if we don't seem to hear, God is still speaking to us.

Jesus says, "I know them and they follow me." Jesus knows each one of us. Jesus has claimed us in baptism. We are known . . . and hear this voice of God guiding and directing us through the ups and downs and ins and outs of life.

We hear, "I give them eternal life and they will never perish. . . . No one will snatch them out of my hand." Sometimes it feels like we're being snatched. . . . It doesn't take much. . . . But there are no ifs, ands, or buts here. . . . God has spoken . . . and when we gather as a community we hear God speaking to us.

The second sermon has as its text John 10:22-30, the Gospel for the Fourth Sunday of Easter. In this text we hear the plaintive plea for clarity of communication. "If you are the Christ, tell us plainly." It is a text that reveals the contextual sensitivities of John who has "the Jews" (who are asking about Jesus) use a Greek expression *Christ* as a title for Messiah. Jesus shifts the language back to a more familiar Hebraic image: that of the shepherd. Using the shepherd metaphor, Jesus explores the ancient promises of Messiah, and does so with a language of incredible intimacy. The shepherd claims his own, and his own acknowledge him. This juxtaposition of a Lord who commands and a Lord who lives intimately with his disciples is at once startling and revealing, for the truth is that the shepherd does speak plainly to his sheep. Those who have to ask, "Are you the Christ, Messiah, Shepherd?" plainly are not of his fold.

This sermon, like the Easter sermon, again stresses the resurrection in both the nursing home setting and the congregational setting. But this time there is a notable shift. Eternal life is real, but so is abundant life. The upshot of having a Lord who lives in such an intimate relationship with his people is that the abundance of God's power and love surrounds them in their daily lives. Whereas the first sermon we looked at focused on the good news of the risen Jesus in the face of a culture of death, this sermon on Jesus the shepherd talks about an active, blessing Lord whose love and compassion create a culture of life and peace in the midst of our culture of death. Despite the daily headlines of illness, addiction, abuse, school shootings, and unending war, Jesus is alive and actively creating peace and order in the world for which he gave himself.

The sermon is the word of Jesus to his own in each context. Thus, though the sermon is strikingly similar in both contexts, there is a surprisingly different tone to this word of blessed assurance. Discipleship looks different when you are actively engaged in creating a climate of life in the face of death or when you are wrestling with the angel of death. This difference is most notable in the directions the preacher gives to help the faithful see where the active, risen Jesus is at work in their lives. For those in the nursing home, God's redeeming love can be seen in many ways: the Eucharist spread before them; the Word that is remembered, read, and proclaimed; in prayers spoken, silent, or groaned; and in acts of kindness, such as a timely visit from a friend or family member. These directions are present for those in the congregation as well, but the acts of kindness take on a deeper dimension for those in the congregation. Nothing less than the risen Jesus is at work when the body of Christ partners with others to feed the hungry or clothe the naked. The Jesus who prayed for the unity of the church is at work in the ecumenical dimensions of their joint life as an ecumenical parish, and in their joint prayers. A call to action is a part of the word of reassurance that Jesus is active in the community and ministry of the faithful in the congregation. The risen Jesus commands their hands as well as their hearts. The church's life together is a "foretaste of the feast to come."

In this sermon we encounter a significant aspect of the contextualization of preaching. What does faithful discipleship look like here? The preacher approaches this contextual concern *not* by predetermining what discipleship *should* look like here, and then passing judgment on the disciples' performance. Instead, she is content to describe what it *does* look like here. The differences in what discipleship looks like in each setting call for a different kind of pastoral admonition. The reassurance that Jesus knows his own is given to those in the nursing home who, like John Milton in *On His Blindness*, can "only stand and wait."[6] The same reassurance leads to a challenge to the congregants to take the good news into the world. In some ways, one can almost hear the preacher encouraging the elderly to stand like sentinels on the ramparts and watch for Jesus, while pointing the congregation to Luke 12 and challenging them with the words: "From everyone to whom much has been given, much will be required."

Sermon 3

> *To be honest, this sermon has been hard to write and it is hard to preach because I need to be sitting in the congregation.*
>
> *James and John wanted the honor and the prestige of being associated with the Messiah . . . the one whom they thought was bringing in the kingdom right then and there. . . . But I don't think James and John were alone in not understanding and in wanting to be linked with greatness, and I don't think I'm alone in that either.*
>
> *I may have gotten it wrong. James and John had got it wrong. Our king is the one who was rejected, suffered, and died . . . hanging on a tree between two criminals on a city trash dump with a crown of thorns. But this is the good news, that we don't have to reach and strive to be the best. . . . We get our value from our baptisms. There is freedom to "go in peace and serve the Lord." The Greatest has already given his life as a ransom for many.*

The text for the third sermon under review is the Gospel lesson for Pentecost 20. It is Mark's version of James and John's request to be on the right and left hands of Jesus in the coming kingdom (Mark 10:35-45).

The sermon takes pains to show the dullness of the disciples. Jesus had said he was going to Jerusalem to suffer, die, and rise. They had the whole kingdom idea wrong from the start. The text is about discipleship and presents a servant image for those who would exercise leadership in the kingdom. The Greek word δοῦλος presents a problem for a culture that has had slavery as part of its heritage, and has come to revere freedom as a much-preferred metaphor for discipleship. The preacher taps into this struggle as she gently chides the disciples in the nursing home and in the congregation to consider how much we are like James and John. Our struggle isn't just a matter of contrasting a disciple as a lord or as a servant, however. Our struggle is in our need to excel, to be the best, to be the best we can be. So if we're to be a servant, we struggle to be the best servant we can be.

The sermon explores faithful discipleship in each setting, and identifies a list of temptations that might lead to unfaithful discipleship in that setting. These temptations to unfaithful discipleship bear a remarkable resemblance to each other. The major difference between the two lists lies in the inclusion of things like clothes and cars for the congregational disciples. Apparently, consumer spending would have less attraction in the everyday life of those in nursing homes. But what the preacher is getting at isn't behavioral—it's theological. The temptation to unfaithful discipleship in any station or status in life is what bedeviled Paul and Luther in their times and places—the penchant for works-righteousness. The desire to win, place, or show based on our achievements is still a hallmark of our culture, and it affects and afflicts the young and the old, the rich and the poor, the healthy and the sick, the independent and the dependent alike. At this point the preacher is clear that discipleship is counter to culture, counter to every culture, including our own. The kingdom cannot be equated with any human design, so the disciples can only be servants of the One who transcends all cultures and all contexts.

For the preacher, discipleship is not about what we do or fail to do, but about what God has done to us and for us in Jesus. In both contexts, she points consistently and unwaveringly to the disciples' baptism. In this baptism there is unity. They were all baptized into Christ. In this baptism there is a shared life, death, and new life. They were all baptized into Jesus' life of suffering, dying, and rising. It is this new life in baptism that makes servant discipleship possible. In baptism there is a peace that passes all understanding. They are joined to Jesus. In baptism there is a freedom that empowers the servants to feed, clothe, and visit the least of these. In baptism the disciples are enabled to bear one another's burdens, knowing that what we are in the midst of is not worth comparing to the glory yet to be revealed.

Text and Context: Why It's Important

The words *text* and *context* often are used as opposite ends of a spectrum of church practices. If one is textual in church practice, one places the Scriptures, the confessions, and the liturgies of the church at the center of its acts of worship, preaching, teaching, and service. If one is contextual in church practice, one places the needs of the church, the people, and the community at the center of its worship, preaching, teaching, and service. Viewed as the opposite ends of a spectrum, it seems that the risk is having too much of a good thing. To be adamantly textual runs the risk of being right, but also becoming irrelevant. To be completely contextual runs the risk of being relevant but having no substantive meaning or purpose. Craig Van Gelder's provocative edited collection of essays, *The Missional Church in Context*, discusses the importance of text and context in understanding what the church is and what it is about.[7] Two of its essays are of particular significance to our discussion in this volume.

Mark Lau Branson's contribution directs us to the texts of the faith.[8] He writes:

> God's grace—that is God's initiatives, throughout Scripture, God's love for the world, God's missional heart, God's great redeeming presence in Jesus Christ—is to be most clearly visible and tangible in faith communities. We have profound and rich texts from those biblical years: court records and prayers, narratives and sacred legislation, long poetic prophecies and festival liturgies, Gospel accounts, Epistles, and apocalyptic images. And I believe these texts should serve us just as they served their early recipients, as words that the Holy Breath uses to shape us as messianic communities. . . .
>
> A community's imagination, its stories and practices, its history and expectations—these are created and carried by words that

interpret everything. . . . Communities are formed and shaped—or not—by their hermeneutics.[9]

These words have an obvious connection with the art of preaching. What preachers do with (or to) the text matters. But we would be wrong if we thought that Branson merely is talking about right versus wrong hermeneutics. Remember, this is an essay about leadership in the *ecclesia*, and what he is concerned about is leadership that is increasingly formed by management theory or therapeutic models. What he's pleading for is leadership formed by greater hermeneutical skills on the part of teachers and preachers of the church. Furthermore, his concern is that hermeneutics not be the sole province of the leadership, but be the work of the congregation itself. It is this work of interpreting the texts that will form and shape the community. It is this work of interpretation that informs and forms the community in the work of spiritual growth, missional awareness, and community building. Weekly preaching, like weekly Eucharist, shapes both ministry and mission.

Sometimes it seems that we get this backwards. We do mission by demographic studies, trend studies, and niche marketing strategies. We study the context to determine the ministry, and then maybe develop a hermeneutic that bolsters our decisions. When the preacher sits down with the text, or lets the text live in her for a week, she may find herself going beyond the question of what this text says to her or to Mary or to Jerry, and allow the text to lead the congregation in pondering a deeper question: To what is this text, this God-word, calling us as Christ's body to do or be here and now? Proclamation is given to the church as a gift, but it is given for the sake of the world for whom God's Son suffered, died, and rose. Preaching is nothing less than communing with the Trinity, as Professor Chan described.

In her essay, Mary Sue Dehmlow Dreier bids the ELCA and its preachers to think imaginatively in the twenty-first century.[10] She notes the four contours of "missiology for a postmodern Western culture" developed by David Bosch: missionary, public, global, and confessional. Then she adds a fifth contour: imagination—to imagine "God's future activity."[11] Dreier contends that congregational imagination currently is trapped in the here-ness and the now-ness, the immediate context, and she maintains that a sense of God's future draws on God's own hospitality. It raises the awareness of and opens the door to a ministry of hospitality that welcomes and serves those whom God is getting ready to call out into the *missio Dei* and those whom God created in the *imago Dei*.

Dreier's insight helps us to see context beyond the here and now, beyond trends and reports, beyond a discussion of whether our purpose includes those like us and those different from us. It even moves us beyond our own provincial dreams and visions, and encourages us to open our hearts and minds to what God has in mind. Some years ago, a former mayor of New York walked around the city asking ordinary citizens, "How am I doing?" It's a great political barometer, but poor homiletics practice. Context is more than what we have or what the culture demands. The context is first of all what the Lord has made, and the direction the Lord leads us. Let us rejoice and be glad in it! Second, context heightens our expectations and anticipations of a new heaven and a new earth.

Concluding Thoughts about Text and Context

Text. The texts the preacher works with are corporate texts—written, edited, proclaimed, and interpreted by the people of God. The act of preaching is also a corporate action. It is an act that unites the preacher and the congregation with the great cloud of witnesses. This is both humbling and liberating. The "truth" of a sermon is not about what the preacher says, but what God does with what the preacher says.

The texts are creative. As they have formed and shaped communities of faith from ancient times until now, so these stories and narratives shape faith communities today. But preaching is God's creative act, not the preacher's.

Preaching the texts is a public action. It's out in the open. It invites a response.

Context. Context is not optional. It is a God-given part of the act of preaching.

The context can and should help to form and shape the particularity of a sermon, even if it's the same text in different settings. Preachers should develop ways of inviting the context to participate in the preparation and delivery of sermons, and not just invite comments after it's over.

To close, let's return to the preacher, to Brandon Oaks and Trinity Ecumenical Parish. One of the great joys of internship is seeing the students "get" it, for them to experience the connection between text and context. Preaching repeatedly to the same group of people invariably deepens and strengthens their preaching, their identity, and consequently their sense of mission and purpose. What is going on in these sermons is formation—formation of a preacher to be sure, but also formation of a community, a community that is being invited into dialogue with a preacher. These dialogues shape God's message, which shapes the community into a teaching parish, a serving parish, and a place of hospitality to the stranger.

Proclaiming Good News in Times of Transition 11

TONY S. EVERETT

It is in their role as preachers that parish pastors are the most visible to their parishioners. Craig Satterlee states that "the Sunday sermon is the chief way most practicing Christians connect their faith and daily lives."[1] How the preacher addresses the contextual realities of congregational life shapes its ongoing mission and ministry.

This chapter is based on the premise that an underlying reality of contemporary living is the experience of transition for individuals and families as well as for congregations and communities. Nancy Schlossberg defines transition as "An event or non-event that results in change of place, perspective, health, security, well-being, meaning, values, status, self-esteem."[2]

Transitions, then, may include, but are not limited to, specific events or situations that are obvious to everyone. Effective and faithful coping may require immediate changes in normal patterns of thinking and behaving. Parish examples include traumatic experiences such as natural disasters, tragedies in the lives of parish leaders, or the sudden eruption of congregational conflict. Individuals and families experience crisis events such as accidents, illness, death of loved ones, and divorce.

However, most transitions do not necessarily require an urgent time frame to address. Neither are all transitions rooted in sudden and traumatic events.[3] Examples in parish life might include changes in community demography, building needs, giving patterns, membership, staff, utility costs, mission, vision, worship style, pastoral leadership, lay leadership, and so on. Examples of this type of transition faced by individuals and families include developmental changes such as marriage, birth of a child, the oldest child starting school (or becoming a teenager, starting college, obtaining a driver's license, moving away from home), empty nest, retirement, relocation, changing jobs, and so on.

According to our definition, a transition may also be a non-event that results in change. In other words, a non-event transition is experienced as unmet expectations. What was anticipated simply did not happen and changes may occur in our perceptions of reality, well-being, status, and even self-esteem. Zack Eswine writes that this type of transition "arises when what one dreams makes contact with what actually is."[4] Some congregations may experience this when they expect a newly called pastor or staff member to recruit enough new members (or persuade inactive members to return!) in order to refill the pews and eliminate a budget deficit. Newly organized parishes notice that this transition often follows the completion of the first permanent building. Other congregations often experience this non-event transition after dedicating a new family life center only to discover that it requires added staff and program burdens. Still others face the dose of reality that often occurs when the addition of a new "contemporary" worship service does not increase attendance, but simply divides the normal attendance into two separate hours on Sunday mornings. Examples of non-event transitions for individuals and families include issues such as the anticipation of lovers who marry and discover the reality of what it takes to live together; that the joy of welcoming a new baby is also accompanied by night colic, dirty diapers, and parental exhaustion; a job offer that doesn't materialize; a loan that is rejected; or a potential for excellence that is never quite fulfilled.

In short, the experience of a non-event transition leaves one with an "almost but not quite" perception of the way things really are. Dreams are "not quite" fulfilled. Needs are "not quite" met. The best-laid plans and goals are "not quite" realized.

The significant concept inherent in all forms of transition is that of change: urgent or gradual, real or imagined, and necessary for present survival or for future well-being. From this perspective all congregations and their individual members find themselves in the midst of transitions that imply anticipation of change.

All changes have within them a dimension of loss, which is simply the perceived state of being without something or someone that was previously part of one's life. Loss includes those changes listed in our definition of transition: place, perspective, wealth, security, well-being, meaning, status, self-esteem, identity, and relationships.

Each experience of loss (each transition) results in an empty space, a hole in the soul that can never quite be filled in the same way. The process by which individuals and congregations strive to adapt to the empty space is called *grief*. Although grief has different shapes and styles that are unique to particular historical and contextual situations, grief touches all aspects of existence at varying levels of intensity.

Gary Harbaugh describes the four principal components of experience as mental, emotional, social, and physical.[5] Although each transition (or loss) results in grieving behavior, the grief responses of individuals and congregations within these components will vary in emphasis according to their specific history and context. For example, some will experience transition primarily as *mental*, a challenge to normal patterns of thinking. Here grief looks like confused and unfocused thought patterns, decreased reasoning skills, and a tendency to either minimize or maximize the significance of the transition. Frequently this also includes a deep yearning for the way things used to be prior to the transition. A preoccupation with that which was lost becomes the primary interpretive lens for both present reactions and future possibilities.

For others, the grief experience is shaped by powerful *emotions* such as anger, blame, guilt, shame, abandonment, hopelessness, helplessness, despair, and anxiety. The foundational emotional response of all grief responses is anxiety. The experience of the pain of anxiety can narrow mental ability, intensify particular emotional reactions, restrict relationship patterns, and limit our patterns of behavior, all in often self-defeating attempts to stop (or at least diminish) the painful experience of loss.

For some, grief responses may be observed primarily through changing patterns of *social relationships*. Symptoms include withdrawal and caution, scapegoating and blame, conflict and separation, or even an abnormal clinging together in order to deny the painful reality. Finally, others may experience grief through the emergence of *physical* and *behavioral symptoms*. For individuals, these may include the onset of bodily complaints, illness, accidents, or an increase of crisis occasions. For individuals and congregations, grieving often takes the form of an aimless wandering and searching for something or some person who can make the problem disappear by restoring conditions to perceived pretransition stability.

Both for congregations and for individuals, adaptation to transitions results in perceptions of instability, confusion, questioning, and searching for meaning as they attempt to cope with new life circumstances. Herein lies the spiritual or theological core inherent within transitions.

Rather than adding a separate category for the spiritual dimension of existence, Harbaugh suggests that each aspect of life (that is, mental, emotional, social, and physical) has a spiritual center. He writes: "The spiritual dimension is not a part of life but rather at the *heart* of life . . . true spirituality involves the way we care for physical needs, the way we develop our intellect, the way we strengthen our capacity to feel for and feel with others, and the way we respond to others."[6]

Harbaugh illustrates this with a circle that includes each of the four aspects of existence (physical, mental, emotional, and social) arranged so that they meet at a common "L" in the center. In Hebrew Scripture, one of the names for God is *El*. Harbaugh uses this model to indicate that not only are these life areas interrelated, but also that the very integrating center of existence is God. Thus, he states that "the spiritual is *always* involved in anything that affects our body, mind, feelings, or relationships."[7]

Continuing the analogy of hole in the soul as an experience of transition, it follows that at the very integrating center of meaning within that empty space is God's own self. Therefore, the closer a transition is to the way in which persons or congregations define themselves (identity), the more pain is experienced, the more complex it is to cope, the more time it takes to address, the more help is needed from others, and the more dependent they are upon the presence and guidance of God.

Experiencing transitional challenge also means experiencing a spiritual challenge. This challenge takes the forms of identity, discernment, and mission. Previously accepted and comfortable self-definitions and focus are questioned. Who are we? Whose are we? What kind of community are we? What difference does it make anyway? Where is God in all this? What can we do about this? How can we respond faithfully and effectively to these new and confusing circumstances in which we find ourselves?

On the one hand, each new transition can become an invitation to spiritual growth, a transformed identity, and a fresh discernment of God's presence and guidance. On the other hand, the experience of transition can result in a desperate search for a quick-fix method that promises immediate anxiety relief with little or no spiritual center or faithful mission possibilities.

Far too often, many individuals and congregations choose the latter option. Sadly, when it comes to coping effectively and faithfully with transition, it appears as if many *mainline* congregations have moved to the *sideline* (spectators) on their way to the "*humm line*"[8] (bored, confused, apathetic) and are at risk of descending to the *flatline* (no vital signs of life whatsoever).

The issues facing contemporary congregations are not based on "how-to" gimmicks to alleviate anxiety or to duplicate what used to be considered successful in past generations. Rather, the core issues facing the church today are:

1. transformational, not informational
2. spiritual, not organizational
3. theological, not numerical
4. biblical, not financial
5. missional, not methodological

Given the reality that pastors are most visible to their congregations and communities during the Sunday morning sermon, it is essential for them to be skilled in understanding and communicating both the dynamics of transition as well as God's invitation for growth that is present. Preachers need the courage to interpret what is going on, along with the biblical and theological depth to proclaim what God has done, is doing, and has promised to continue to do in the midst of God's people.

Of course, this is much easier to state than it is to accomplish. Not only do pastors themselves encounter challenging transitions in their own lives, they are simultaneously in the midst of the transitional experiences of their congregations. Parishioners expect their pastors to do something about it, right now, beginning with the Sunday sermon. During my own ministry as seminary professor and as interim pastor[9] in nine different congregations, I have discovered that most parishioners want these sermons to describe the following:

1. A specific cause of the transition, preferably placing responsibility on forces beyond their control.
2. An easy, nonthreatening method either to escape or to avoid the painful anxiety that accompanies transition.
3. A step-by-step plan that enables the congregation to move through the transition as quickly and as effectively as possible.
4. A promise from God that the congregation will return to its perceived successful and pain-free past.

At the onset of transition, parishioners often express little or no desire for their pastors to focus the sermon on the good news of what God has already done, is doing, and has promised to continue doing in and through Jesus Christ for all God's people in the midst of painful and challenging situations. This is particularly true if the sermon does not include a specific time limit for enduring and suffering in the present as well as the real possibility of change in the future.[10]

This question was addressed to parishioners in congregations where I have served as interim pastor: "What word or phrase first comes to mind when you hear the word *preaching*"? The most frequent responses included the following:

1. Teaches good, old-fashioned values
2. Gives advice on how to live
3. Tells us what Jesus wants us to do
4. Hits us where we live
5. Names a sin for what it is and lets the chips fall where they may
6. Motivates us to do better
7. Persuades us to be a better congregation

Similar words or phrases may be found in dictionary definitions[11] and thesaurus associations.[12] Here we find examples such as: advice, moralizing, indoctrinating, motivating, proselytizing, and (my personal favorite) pretentious, tedious, and obtrusive speech.[13] Only one second-level definition comes close to an understanding of preaching that is taught in seminaries: "Proclaim or make known (the gospel, good tidings, etc.) by a sermon."[14] Even in this definition the gospel, although mentioned, is at best parenthetical.

It certainly appears as if proclaiming the good news of Jesus Christ in the midst of transitions (or at all) seems to be far from the common, everyday understanding of the intended goal of Lutheran preaching. During his tenure as professor of homiletics at Lutheran Theological Southern Seminary, Tom Ridenhour's favorite sermon assessment question was, "What's the good news here, preacher?" According to common usage and expectations, a proclamation of the good news is often ignored. This seems to be particularly so during the times of anxiety, confusion, and ambiguity that accompany every transition.

It is easy for preachers to fall into the trap of attempting to meet all expectations and perceived needs of their parishioners. With tongue in cheek, Charles Merrill Smith has written that the threefold task of every preacher is to "make them laugh, make them cry, and make them feel religious."[15] Smith adds that "how-to" advice is appreciated from preachers as long as sermons have no requirement for parishioners to quit doing things they enjoy, spend money, or submit to a rigorous, time-consuming discipline that may include some measure of endurance, suffering, or change.[16]

Especially during transitions, individuals and congregations tend to confuse their needs with their wants. Elizabeth Steele describes the result: this confusion places "the church in the position of being defined not by its faith . . . but by people's wants."[17] When preachers permit their sermons to become "want focused," this not only diminishes the possibilities for faithful responses to transition, it also, writes Steele, "trivializes the Church, its mission, and its outreach."[18]

Such sermons often follow this pattern:

1. A joke, personal story, or "quasi-pious" illustration from the Internet
2. Three steps to feeling and doing better
3. A passing proof text from Scripture
4. An exhortation to have faith
5. A conclusion that revisits the introductory illustration

Steele adds that this kind of preaching "eviscerates the heart of the Church's message and cuts the Church off from its identity as the people of Christ."[19]

So then, what is a preacher to do about this? How can the preaching task help individuals and congregations move beyond making the challenge disappear and restoring previous perceptions of satisfaction, contentment, and success?

Wilderness Space and Time

Fortunately, God has already provided the church with the language to interpret what is going on and how God has promised to address it. This "language" is discerned through careful and faithful adherence to the biblical texts. One such interpretive and missional lens to address transitions is that of *wilderness*.

From the perspective of preaching in the midst of transition, wilderness is an image of space and time rather than a reference to a particular geographical place and position. The image of wilderness refers more to a general circumstance and condition rather than to a specific context and location.[20]

For God's people, wilderness is the space where transition is experienced, the probability of changes is encountered, individual and communal identity is in flux, vision is blurred, and mission is unclear. J. Bill Ratliff describes wilderness as an in-between space, a space where we are challenged to grow in our understanding of "who we are and what we value."[21] Wilderness is a space of yearning for the past, struggling with the present, and hoping for a better future.

Entering a time of transition can be compared to entering the wilderness. The preaching task itself involves a wilderness of its own. Kenneth Moe writes that this is "often like reentering a wilderness, whether it be tangled undergrowth or unforgiving deserts. Pastors (and all public ministers) are put to the test by what they encounter. They need inner strength and courage to meet what they encounter."[22]

In Scripture, the wilderness can be a very threatening, confusing, and dangerous space. At first appearance, it is quite barren and desolate, with great temperature extremes. Food and water are scarce. Wild beasts and bandits prowl about, anxious to pounce on unsuspecting and vulnerable travelers. Hunger and thirst, fear and loneliness, confusion and anxiety are common experiences of wilderness reality. God is often perceived as distant and uncaring or even as absent and forgotten.

On the other hand, at closer inspection there is hidden beauty within the biblical wilderness. Animal and plant life abound. Sources of nourishment are available. Opportunities for transformed identity and mission, both personal and communal, may be discerned in the wilderness.

Furthermore, living in transitional wilderness space is also a time for new and renewed perceptions of reality. Paul writes, "See, now is the acceptable time; see, now is the day of salvation!" (2 Cor. 6:2). A primary preaching task is to help persons and congregations see with new eyes the in-breaking of the kingdom of God within their specific circumstances.

This becomes a marvelous opportunity for the connecting of memory and hope, possibility and promise. It is a time for remembering and sharing stories that formed God's people here in their past. It is also a time for sharing stories of possibilities and promises, of hopes and dreams for the future. The wilderness is a time for discerning God's presence and guidance.

Wilderness time may be interpreted by the preacher as Paul's "acceptable time" for proclaiming the good news of what God has done, is doing, and has promised to do in the world and in this particular context. In the wilderness, God connects χρόνος (the passage of time) with καιρός (the in-breaking of the kingdom of God).

It is incumbent on the preacher to be aware that it is the Holy Spirit who is extending an invitation into the wilderness of congregational and personal life. It is the Holy Spirit who guides their travels within this new space. Here the Spirit gathers God's people into a community in which their identity as God's own children is affirmed. It is in the wilderness where the Spirit enlightens with renewed perceptions of the good, acceptable, and perfect will of God. In the wilderness the Holy Spirit presents challenges with new possibilities for God's mission and vision for a particular people.

It is important to note that God takes the initiative to meet God's children where they are. At the acceptable and kairotic time, God became flesh and lived in the wilderness space of the world. Wilderness preaching proclaims and re-presents God's missional initiative. It begins at the core of God's initiating love: the splash of refreshing grace at the font, the taste of nourishment at the altar, and the word of redemption from the pulpit. Preaching in transitional wilderness must remain centered on this good news reality.

Preaching in the Wilderness

Preachers will do well to remember that on any given Sunday, most individuals and congregations are experiencing either the reality or imminent possibility of significant changes in their lives. They are living in wilderness space and time. Gathered for worship, they find themselves yearning for what once was (or perceived to have been), hoping for a more secure and meaningful future, while simultaneously struggling with confusion and anxiety in the present. As Kathleen Smith writes, "congregations are always changing or responding to some kind of issue or dilemma."[23] Therefore, from this viewpoint, preaching in the wilderness becomes an every-Sunday occurrence. Smith concludes that "there will always be a transitional aspect to congregational life."[24]

The higher level of anxiety that occurs in the wilderness indicates both a deeper caring about the situation as well as an increase in the amount of energy expended in order to endure and survive within it. This energy, diverted from other activities, easily slides into apathy, exhaustion, frustration, and even withdrawal from participation in normal and enhancing activities of life.

Within transitions, however, the increased anxiety and focused energy can also provide a unique opportunity for new perceptions and behaviors to arise. In transitional wilderness there also exists a possibility to mobilize that energy and refocus anxiety from merely surviving and holding on to thriving and growing stronger. In Smith's words, "The potential for learning through difficulty is an opportunity that is simply not present at other times."[25] Therefore, preaching in the wilderness will acknowledge the existing and energy-draining anxiety while simultaneously proclaiming the God-given transformational and energy-enhancing possibilities that are present within every wilderness space and time.

In the wilderness, preachers are called to proclaim good news from the God who re-forms barely surviving and doubtful people into actively thriving and faithful disciples. Preaching is based on the certainty that it is God who seeks and finds us in all transitions. God's children do not need to "find" God. God was never lost. Here, in the midst of confusion and searching, God renews faith and shapes vision and mission. Faithful wilderness preaching, then, becomes a matter of entering and wandering, waiting and wondering, wading and sending.

Entering and Wandering

As previously mentioned, a wide variety of events and/or non-events may thrust individuals and congregations into unwelcoming and anxious wilderness space.

Scripture provides many examples. A guilt-ridden and fearful Jacob, facing the possibility of violent confrontation with his brother, wrestles throughout the night with an unknown stranger (Gen. 32:22-32). After killing an Egyptian, Moses abandons both his family and his position of status and flees for his life into the region of Midian. Here he finds himself with a new wife and a new occupation "beyond the wilderness" (Exod. 2:11—3:1). Following his victory over the prophets of Baal, Elijah evades the wrath of Ahab and Jezebel by escaping into the wilderness (1 Kgs. 19:4-9). Following his baptism, Jesus himself either was driven (ἐκβάλλει, Mark 1:12) or led up (ἀνήχθη, Matt. 4:1) into the wilderness to be tested by the devil.

Entering into wilderness space also becomes a wilderness time for testing and refining. It offers opportunities to encounter and to be encountered by the God who was with them in their past, who meets them in the present, and who will be with them throughout their future. Here Jacob names this place *Peniel*, saying, "for I have seen God face to face and yet my life is preserved" (Gen. 32:30). Here Elijah, in the midst of lonely pessimism, hears the voice of God arising from sheer silence (1 Kgs. 19:12-13). While Jesus is tested in the wilderness, the angels of God "waited on him" (Mark 1:13).

Here in the wilderness, identity as God's children is renewed and reshaped. Energy for God's mission is refocused and renewed. This does not simply occur for individuals. Entire communities are transformed within wilderness experiences. Perhaps the best biblical example is that of God using Moses to lead Hebrew slaves out of Egypt into the wilderness on their way to a promised new land and new ways of living. On their long journey, the Hebrew people often encountered what appeared to be insurmountable obstacles. They faced enemies of all kinds, hunger, thirst, discouragement, and despair. They yearned to return even to the certainty of Egyptian slavery rather than to face their present dangers and an uncertain future. Moses' leadership was questioned and God's presence was doubted. Even Moses himself grew angry and frustrated with God.

For the Hebrews and for congregations wandering in their own wilderness, time passes very slowly. "How long will it take to escape this mess?" is a frequent and pervasive question. The Hebrews were there for forty years (Exod. 16:35). Jesus was in the wilderness for forty days (Mark 1:13).

Perhaps the very word *forty* itself provides a clue regarding the duration of wandering time. In Hebrew, this word is used both as a particular number and often as an adjective that refers to an extended but unspecific duration of time for expanding perceptions of endurance, repentance, discernment, and guidance. The question, "How long?" may thus be answered, "As long as it takes for this growth in faithfulness to occur." Wandering time may be seen as a time when the Holy Spirit expands perception of χρόνος to include an awareness of καιρός, a time for the in-breaking of the kingdom of God.

God invites us to enter and wander with confidence, endure in faith, risk the unknown, challenge the *status quo*, and share the good news with passion! Willingly entering and wandering is not for wimpy, wishy-washy preachers who prefer to preside with comfort over humm-line parishes from the security of book-lined offices and carpeted meeting rooms. In order to wander together with their people, preachers must have a deep passion for the gospel that is both inviting and contagious for all persons they encounter on this exciting wilderness journey.

Preaching during the entering and wandering experience includes the following: (1) Articulate the real pain of transition; (2) encourage a willingness to wander in this kairotic time for a while ("forty"); and (3) proclaim that it is during this time that God finds, reveals, and renews energy and faith.

How and when does this happen? What does this look like? Here emerge the concepts of faithful waiting and wondering.

Waiting and Wondering

In Hebrew Scripture, *waiting*[26] is understood as an attitude of courageous and expectant anticipation during times of tension and uncertainty (Ps.

7:14). Such an attitude prompts endurance in the midst of difficulties (Ps. 130:6-7). It is rooted in the certainty of God's promised covenant relationship (Jer. 14:22). God promises to hear, to help, and to renew the strength of those who wait (Ps. 40:1-2, 20:22; Isa. 40:31). Waiting does not simply exist in a state of passivity and helplessness. God's people-in-waiting are expected to be faithful in keeping God's way (Ps. 37:34), turn to the Lord, and hold fast to love and justice (Hos. 12:6). God's promises can be relied on, guaranteed by God's own steadfast love (Ps. 65:11).

The posture of one who waits (or hopes) is one of certainty in the reliability of God's promised salvation (Isa. 25:9). Herein is a living bond between the God who waits for Israel to bear fruit (Isa. 5:2, 7) and the waiting of God's own people themselves.

Because waiting/hoping is not limited to a specific time or to a specific outcome, it is not eliminated by unexpected changes in the present situation. Although faithful wilderness waiting may reduce overwhelming and paralyzing anxiety, the significance of patient endurance remains. Here there is a future focus and promise without either preconceived goals and time expectations, or a diminished source of confidence in God's past, present, and promised future activity.

In the New Testament also, one who waits is one who is expecting to receive or welcome.[27] Joseph of Arimathea is one who waits expectantly for the kingdom of God (Mark 15:43). Paul describes the inward yearning of the Christian who waits for redemption. God does not abandon those who wait with patient confidence (Rom. 8:23-24).

Preaching during this waiting period must also reflect this perspective of the expectant certainty of God's transforming presence. Preachers assist their congregations in assessing their wilderness context. What are the dangers as well as the God-given invitations and opportunities within this space and time? Where is sustaining nourishment to be found? How has God's self-revelation become visible in past transitions and challenges? How is God's revelation becoming clearer within the particular situation?

Perhaps the most significant assessment question was asked by Jesus himself (Matt. 15:29-37). Thousands gathered at Jesus' feet for three days. When Jesus expressed his desire to feed the crowd, his disciples perceived only an impossible task. Then Jesus responded with this crucial question: "How many loaves have you?" (15:34). It is important to note here that Jesus did not ask his disciples what they *needed* or even what they wanted. He only asked for what they *already had*. Faithful preaching will first describe current God-given resources rather than present a list of what is yet needed.

Jesus then began to demonstrate exactly what wilderness waiting actually looks like. He *listened* to the disciples' complaints of their own confusion and helplessness (v. 33). He *received* the disciples' own resources (v. 36), *gave thanks* for them, and *broke* them. Then he did something remarkable. He *returned them back to the complaining disciples* for distribution to the hungry crowds, with much left over (vv. 36, 37). Using the meager resources of anxious and confused disciples, Jesus multiplied them into a miraculous fulfillment. This is how God acts in the midst of God's people-in-waiting. This is the wonder of good news that will preach well in any congregational wilderness.

During this waiting period, preaching must both anticipate and articulate the good news of the miraculous and fulfilling abundance in and through Jesus Christ. Waiting time is a time for sharing biblical stories of encounters with the awesome holiness of God. In addition to those mentioned previously, preachers can refer to Abram/Abraham's experiences (Genesis 12–25), Jacob's "ladder dream" (Gen. 28:10-17), covenant renewal promises (Exodus 34; Deuteronomy 29–30; Joshua 24; Jeremiah 31), the Lord's pledge of commitment to a suffering servant (Isaiah 42–43), and God's providing assistance to exhausted and frustrated leaders (Exodus 17; Numbers 11).

As preachers share these stories, they must also help parishioners make connections with their own personal and congregational stories of faith. Here is an opportunity for preachers to provide space and time in parish life to do this.[28] The intent here is to invite persons to describe how they have experienced God's presence and guidance in their own personal lives and in their congregations. Invariably, the context of these stories will be that of wilderness space and time: transitional times of chaos and confusion, ambiguity and anxiety, frustration and disappointment, loss and grief.

As these stories are shared, connections with God's good news begin to appear. Because God did not abandon God's people in their biblical wilderness then, therefore God will not leave God's people desolate in their wilderness now. Thus, preaching faithful waiting for God is accompanied by proclaiming the surprising *wonder* of God's continuing presence. Sermons can illustrate how memory becomes hope, possibility becomes promise, pessimism and apathy become awe and wonder. The experience of wonder is the experience of amazement as one is surprised by God through the Holy Spirit enlightening God's people with a glimpse of new possibilities, a true foretaste of the promised feast to come.

Indeed, such preaching is grounded in the energy arising from the center of wonder. Christ himself is present at the font, altar, and pulpit. Particularly during wilderness times, faithful preaching is rooted in the wonder of worship. Here is where stories are integrated, nourishment is given, identity is transformed, and the kingdom of God is revealed, again and again.

Wading and Sending

What does all this wandering, waiting, and wondering look like anyway? It is wading in the baptismal waters of God's love in Jesus Christ. The wilderness is a space for splashing in healing, sustaining, guiding, and reconciling water.

However, the concept of wading implies much more than floating on an ocean of good, spiritual feelings. Here, even in the wilderness, wading includes the missional dimension of "walking wet," thoroughly drenched in Christ's transforming love, *so that* others notice and want to learn more. Preaching urges parishioners to walk in a light that glistens through the shimmering baptismal droplets with a lifestyle that "shine[s] before others, so that they may see your good works and give glory to your Father in heaven" (Matt. 5:16). Sermons acknowledge and affirm communal identity so that they may join in a common mission, "giving thanks and praise to God and bearing God's creative and redeeming word to all the world."[29]

Thus, the wading component of wilderness preaching suggests a strong connection between identity *in* Christ and mission *for* Christ. This integrative connection is shaped by the Greek preposition ὅπως, translated as "so that" or "in order that." God claims us as God's own baptized children *so that* God is glorified and God's saving action continued in the world. The author of 1 Peter writes this to Christians in their wilderness of chaos and persecution: "You are a chosen race, a royal priesthood, a holy nation, God's own people, *so that* you may proclaim the mighty acts of him who called you out of the darkness into his marvelous light" (1 Peter 2:9, emphasis added).

In the wilderness, God's wading people are formed into God's "so that" people.[30] Here God's "so that" people are challenged to be God's *sent* people. Inscribed on a massive stone tablet above the pulpit in our seminary chapel are Jesus' words to all "walking wet" disciples: "As the Father has sent me, so send I you" (John 20:21). In Mark 10:16 Jesus says, "I am sending you forth as sheep in the midst of wolves." Luke writes that Jesus "sent them out to proclaim the kingdom of God and to heal" (Luke 9:2).

In the midst of their own transitional wilderness experience God still sends God's people into mission. Where? Anywhere and everywhere. God tells a young protesting Jeremiah: "You shall go to all to whom I send you" (Jer. 1:7). God sends Moses back to the very place he had escaped as a wanted man: "Come, I will send you to Pharaoh to bring my people out of Egypt" (Exod. 3:10).

How is this possible for a people who are already entering and wandering, waiting and wondering in their own wilderness? It is possible because God makes it so. It is because God is with them there. It is in steadfast love that God made a lasting covenant with God's wilderness people. "It is to this steadfast love," writes Edmond Jacob, "that every member of the covenant can appeal when [they] wish to see the covenant maintained and confirmed."[31] God's own word of steadfast love, Jesus Christ, "became flesh and lived among us . . . full of grace and truth" (John 1:14). It is through the Holy Spirit that the steadfast love of the Lord continues in the present and will extend into an unknown future. Because God keeps this covenant, therefore God's "so that and sent" people can accomplish remarkable and even impossible tasks in mission.

Preachers already have a model that describes faithful and missional wilderness wading and sending. It is clearly stated in the promises made by the assembly during the Affirmation of Baptism. Here the people promise the following:

1. To continue in the covenant God made with [them] in Holy Baptism;
2. To live among God's faithful people;
3. To hear the word of God and share in the Lord's Supper;

4. To proclaim the good news of God in Christ through word and deed;
5. To serve all people, following the example of Jesus;
6. And to strive for justice and peace in all the earth.[32]

Conclusion

Preaching good news in times of transition offers an excellent opportunity to affirm and to proclaim the good news of what God has done, is doing, and has promised to continue to do in the world. Sermons in wilderness space and time announce that God meets us right here in the center of anxious wandering and frustrating waiting. It is within this wilderness that God invites us into a new and transforming identity as God's own "so that" people. It is from within this wilderness that God sends us on exciting missions, walking wet back into the wilderness of the world.

PART FOUR

Gospel Proclamation and the Life of the Church

Preaching Ethics Ethically 12
DANIEL M. BELL JR.

Everyone knows what preaching ethics is and most of us know when we have heard a sermon about ethics. Preaching ethics is preaching about ethical dilemmas and behavior, preaching on moral issues and problems, preaching that addresses the great moral questions of the day. It is preaching that guides or informs or exhorts us on how to live and act. It is the kind of preaching that we most readily associate with prophets. It is preaching that often challenges us and nudges us out of our comfort zone.

Preaching ethics, however, entails another dimension that is both less obvious and less remarked upon. It is that dimension to which Reinhold Niebuhr gestured when he penned that famous passage during his early days in pastoral ministry:

> To speak the truth in love is a difficult, and sometimes an almost impossible, achievement. If you speak the truth unqualifiedly, that is usually because your ire has been aroused or because you have no personal attachment to the object of your strictures. Once personal contact is established you are very prone to temper your wind to the shorn sheep.[1]

The insight Niebuhr articulates here may be identified as the challenge of "ethical preaching," although Niebuhr rightly did not think this challenge was limited only to the preaching task. What is the challenge of ethical preaching? It is not the challenge that is frequently put to the hearer by the preacher when the preacher preaches about an ethical issue or dilemma. This is to say, it is not the challenge of actually doing what the preacher exhorts us to do, as challenging as that may be. Rather, what Niebuhr describes is the challenge not of preaching ethics, but of preaching ethics ethically. If the first and most readily apparent dimension of preaching ethics concerns deliberately addressing ethical issues and topics, the second dimension concerns the ethics of the preaching act itself—that which makes preaching, and in this case, preaching ethics, itself either ethical or unethical.

This essay explores both dimensions of preaching ethics in their necessary and inescapable interrelation. Preaching ethics and preaching ethically are two dimensions of a single task; one cannot happen without the other. Specifically, in this essay I will argue that ethical preaching—attention to the ethics of preaching—is a condition of possibility for preaching about ethics that is itself ethical. This is to say, without proper attention to and care for preaching ethically, the effort to preach ethics—good intentions notwithstanding—is distorted and so becomes immoral, unethical.

Preaching Ethics

The argument begins by considering what it means to preach ethics. But perhaps even to begin here is to begin too late, for before we can answer what it means to preach *ethics* we need to answer the prior question of what it means to *preach*.

What Is Preaching?

As part and parcel of the church's worship, preaching is first and foremost an act of praise, adoration, thanksgiving. Before it is anything else—*if* it is anything else—preaching is first and foremost part of the church's worship of the blessed Trinity.[2] Preaching does this—it participates in and contributes to the church's worship, specifically by proclaiming the glory of God as that glory is manifest in the word of

God. Preaching is worship to the extent that it proclaims, announces, discloses, reveals what God has done, is doing, and will do in Jesus Christ. "Christ has died; Christ is risen; Christ will come again," as the church's eucharistic prayer succinctly puts it.[3] In this regard, it is no wonder that Baptists have a reputation for good preaching, for John the Baptist provides what is the paradigm for all faithful preaching when, on the banks of the river Jordan, he lifted his bony finger, pointed to the Christ, and proclaimed, "Behold the Lamb of God who takes away the sin of the world" (John 1:29). Likewise we might recall Paul's defense of his preaching among the congregation in Corinth, "I decided to know nothing among you except Jesus Christ and him crucified" (1 Cor. 2:2), or Barbara Brown Taylor's assertion that at the conclusion of every sermon the only word on anyone's lips should be "Jesus Christ."[4]

Preaching is worship that worships by proclaiming the word. But more needs to be said, lest this be misunderstood. Sam Wells reiterates this point about the content of preaching being the word when he writes: "The sermon proclaims that the God who acted in the story of Israel, came in Jesus, and was alive in the early Church, is living and active today."[5] But he helpfully elaborates on this by reminding us that the sermon is not merely or simply a report. Rather, it is an event. As such it is not an aggregation of preacherly insights gleaned from commentaries or an amalgamation of pastoral wisdom drawn from years of experience and anecdotes. Although such insight and wisdom certainly may contribute to the preaching task, preaching is a moment more akin to an epiphany than an exposition. It is a moment of revelation. Thus, preaching is not merely reporting or remembering but announcing. It is an announcement that should make all the prophets of Baal shudder and the demons squirm. The heavens have been torn open and God has come down. *Now* is the time that God acts to redeem all of God's people. *Here* is the God who has acted before to redeem and who promised to act again. Here *is* that God! Behold the lamb! Right here! Right now! In this place! In word and water, bread and wine. In the midst of the saints and the means of grace. As Wells puts it, the act of preaching is

> an incarnational moment when God's divinity meets our humanity in the spoken word, and the congregation discovers that he became what we are, so that we might become what he is. It is a

resurrection moment, when the apparent givens of sin, death, and evil are stripped away and the possibilities of humanity in the new creation are transformed.[6]

Preaching is worship that worships by proclaiming the event of the Word incarnate here and now. Preaching is first and foremost part of the church's worship of the triune God as the announcement of the good news that the God who called Israel, was incarnate in the Messiah Jesus, and gathered the church in the Spirit, is present here and now and forever working the divine will for reconciliation in the world.

Preaching is first and foremost worship as it proclaims the event of the Word incarnate. Proclamation of the Word is what preaching is; the proclamation of the Word is the point of preaching. Period. Which means preaching is not about providing meaning, consoling, meeting felt needs, exhorting, reprimanding, teaching, motivating, or anything else other than reflecting the glory of God back to God as part of the cosmic call and response that is the proper liturgy (work, worship) of all creation. Indeed, faithful preaching is nothing more or less than pointing to Christ, telling the truth about Jesus Christ, whether the time is favorable or unfavorable, whether it is meaningful, consoling, informative, or motivating to the hearers. In this regard, the preacher is not unlike Ezekiel's sentry whose task is simply and faithfully to announce the word (Ezek. 33:7).

What Is Preaching Ethics?

I began this essay with the observation that everyone knows what preaching ethics is: it is preaching about ethical dilemmas and behavior. But now, if the argument advanced in the preceding section is correct, then exactly what preaching ethics is or should be suddenly is not quite so obvious. In fact, if my argument is correct, then it is not even clear that one *should* preach ethics. If the point of preaching is simply and solely that of proclaiming/announcing Christ, then what space is there for ethics, for focusing on what we should do or how we should act? Is there no room for ethics in the homiletical inn? Must Jesus occupy all the room in the sermon?

The immediate answer is that faithful preaching in no way detracts from but only reinforces those other practices and disciplines of the Christian life that properly make addressing ethical dilemmas and moral exhortation their primary objective. In fact, the urgent responsibility many of us feel to preach ethics is (at least in part) but a symptom and sign that in the life of too many congregations those other opportunities for engaging ethics in an appropriately theological manner have all but disappeared. To continue with the metaphor of the inn, too often the practices that rightly focus on ethical teaching and moral formation have been relegated to the stables out back, where only the determined or foolhardy dare to venture. Given such circumstances, when the moral disciplines of the Christian life have been forgotten or made voluntary/optional, is it any wonder that many a good and faithful pastor and preacher feel compelled to use the pulpit to preach ethics?

Nevertheless, recognizing that to describe preaching as I have done does not preclude teaching ethics in other forums, we may still ask, Does preaching itself rightly and properly allow any opportunity for edification and exhortation, for instruction and moral formation? The answer is a very peculiar "yes." The answer is a *peculiar* yes because it actually begins with a "no" to what frequently passes for preaching ethics, at least in mainline churches today. For a way into this puzzle, let us consider a passage from Karl Barth:

> Strange as it may seem, [the] general conception of ethics coincides exactly with the conception of sin. So we have every reason to treat it with circumspection. We do take up the question of the good and we try to answer it. But there can be no more trying to escape the grace of God. On the contrary, we have to try to prevent this escape. When we speak of ethics, the term cannot include anything more than this confirmation of the truth of the grace of God as it is addressed to man. If dogmatics, if the doctrine of God, is ethics, this means necessarily and decisively that it is the attestation of the divine ethics, the attestation of the good of the command issued to Jesus Christ and fulfilled by Him. There can be no question of any other good in addition to this.[7]

The "no" that must be uttered to preaching ethics if preaching ethics is to be faithful to its task of pointing to Christ is expressed by Barth in his claim that ethics is sin and an effort to escape the grace of God. Now, it would be both unnecessary and uncharitable for me to claim that the dominant way of preaching ethics corresponds to sin and is an effort to escape God's grace, although it is wrong and frequently fails to appreciate the centrality of grace to the Christian life (I will say more about this in the next section, "Preaching Ethics Ethically"). What is more important for the immediate task at hand is the affirmation of ethics that Barth offers. After saying "no" to ethics as it is normally conceived, Barth goes on to utter a "yes" to ethics conceived as, in his words, "the divine ethics," which is the good of the command issued to and fulfilled by Jesus Christ.

Here we discover the space for preaching ethics, and see that it does not take up any space additional to that occupied by Christ in the sermon. Here we find our answer to what preaching ethics is. Put simply, preaching ethics is preaching the divine ethics. And by this Barth does not mean preaching what God tells us to do but preaching God's ethics, what God is doing. Preaching the ethics of Christ; preaching the good that Jesus Christ fulfilled, that Jesus Christ lives. Here we see a way of preaching ethics that is faithful to the task of what faithful preaching is—pointing to Christ. Preaching ethics is not something we do in addition to (or, worse, instead of) preaching Christ. To preach ethics faithfully is to preach Christ, to proclaim what Christ has done, is doing, and will do. It is to announce what Jesus is doing ethically today, right here, right now, in this place, in our communities, in this world.

Preaching is announcing the good news; preaching ethics is announcing the good news. The good news, however, is not first and foremost an exhortation or command. It is not the posting of a work order, a notification of something we have to do, something we should, must, or ought to do. The good news is the announcement of what God in Christ is doing today. The good news is an event, something that happens for us, to us, in spite of us. For this reason, as Tom Ridenhour incessantly reminds us (see page 6 above), preaching ethics is a matter of making God the subject of the sermon's verbs.

But, I can almost hear the skeptic objecting, have you not simply found another way to evade our moral obligation? In heeding Barth's call not to escape grace, have you not simply evaded our ethical responsibility? After defining preaching in a manner that appears to exclude ethics, you turn around and concede the possibility of preaching ethics. But then you follow Barth and redefine ethics so that it excludes our agency, making it still all about Jesus and letting us off the moral hook, so to speak. Surely this cannot be right? After all, Jesus does not call us simply to stand on the sidelines, if you will, as spectators announcing what *he* is doing in the world.

To preach ethics as the divine ethics, as the good that Christ embodies, is not to exclude human agency or moral responsibility. On the contrary, it is to establish the ground for human agency and the only possible means whereby Christians could live the moral life of discipleship to which they collectively have been called. This is to say, ethics or the Christian moral life is not a matter of our following Jesus' example. Neither is it a matter of merely learning from Jesus certain values or rules or principles, like "love," that we then take out into the world and put into practice. Nor is it a matter of our being inspired or motivated by Jesus. Such ethical visions, like the question of whether we can talk about our responsibility in addition to Jesus in a sermon, too sharply distinguish between Jesus and us.[8] The notion that we can preach about what Jesus does *and* (or) we can preach about what we are to do presumes that we can do anything—at least anything that looks like discipleship—apart from Christ. But this is not the case, and this was the point Barth was making in his passage. We say *no* to preaching ethics when preaching ethics presumes we exercise moral agency independent of Christ (even if inspired or motivated by his teaching and example). This is what Barth meant when he warned against escaping from grace. Rather, the Christian moral life at its very heart is about living *in Christ*. So the church is exhorted in Colossians, "As you . . . have received Christ Jesus the Lord, continue *to live your lives in him*" (Col. 2:6, emphasis added; see also Gal. 2:20). Through the waters of baptism we are incorporated into Christ (Rom. 6:1-6). The Christian life consists of being joined to Christ, as a member of Christ's body (1 Cor. 12:27; cf. Col. 1:18; Rom. 12:3-8; Eph. 4:1-16).

All of this means that preaching ethics, preaching about *our* moral responsibilities or ethical obligations, can only be done rightly in the greater context of what Christ is doing in the world, in us and through us. After all, in a very real sense our moral agency is not ours but rather is our graciously sharing in Christ's moral agency. Justified by Christ, we are joined to Christ and so join what *Christ* is doing in the world. There can be no question of preaching any ethics in addition to preaching Christ. To preach ethics is to preach divine ethics, in which we graciously participate.

So, the skeptic is correct. We are not called to stand on the side-lines merely announcing what Christ is doing. But, then again, the sermon is not merely a report, like you might see on the six o'clock news. It is an event, an incarnational moment when in the midst of our praise and worship, even through our very words of praise and worship, the word of God comes to us with the offer, the invitation, to be joined to Christ and so to what Christ is doing in the world. And it is here, at this moment *and not before*, that the preacher may exhort and judge and forgive (or in a different setting, console or offer meaning or teach, and so forth), not because this is what we must do or because this is what the preacher wants to say, but because that is what God in Christ is doing here and now at this moment in this place. The preacher calls for conversion, exhorts or judges or forgives, like a faithful sentinel, not because that is what the people clamor for or because that is what the preacher feels like doing but because that is what the word of God in this time and place is both offering us and enabling us to do.

Preaching Ethics Ethically

Having worked through both what preaching and preaching ethics are, we may now turn to consider the issue of preaching ethics ethically. In the introduction I suggested that preaching ethics and preaching ethics ethically were necessarily interrelated, so much so that I called them a single task, which we might further denominate simply as "faithful preaching." Because of the necessary interrelation, what follows could rightly be understood as mere elaboration upon what it means to preach and to preach ethics against a particular backdrop. That backdrop is what I will call the problem of preaching in mainline Protestantism, which I further specify in terms of the twin errors of therapeutic senti-mentality and moralism. As my organizing trope I borrow from Ephesians 4:15 the exhortation to "speak the truth in love."

Speak the Truth: Against Love Alone

In his well-known and justly famous "Letter from Birmingham Jail," Martin Luther King Jr. chastised those preachers whose tepid words from the pulpit amounted to little more than "pious irrelevancies" and "sanctimonious trivialities."[9] He lamented the prevalence of the kind of preaching that floated around in the realm of abstraction, that actually kept the word at bay, that stayed safely above the fray of human existence and the concrete struggle against sin, death, and the devil. When I was in seminary one of my teachers used to remark on the popularity amongst preachers of what he called "fudge divinity." By this he meant the kind of preaching that would wax long and eloquent about God's love, perhaps moving the congregation with rhetorical flash and flourish, but that was soon forgotten because, like fudge, it might feel good while being consumed but in truth it provided no real energy, no lasting benefit, no encounter with the Lord that could possibly leave one limping, like Jacob, changed for life. It is the kind of preaching that is quickly forgotten, that other than a cute anecdote is rarely remembered three days later. In 1966, Philip Rieff prophesied the advent of a therapeutic culture in the church in which faith became a kind of shorthand for affirmed humanity and the gospel was made synonymous with an altered self-understanding.[10] In 1993, Marsha Witten's study of mainline preaching displays the fruit of that therapeutic culture as it is manifest in mainline Protestantism's preaching: sentimentality passed off as the key to self-realization, the gospel as emotional catharsis and consolation.[11]

In Ephesians the church is instructed to speak the truth in love. Insofar as the church's proclamation, its preaching, is captured by the cult and culture of therapeutic sentimentality, insofar as it is dominated by what King called "pious irrelevancies," it is nothing less (or more) than love shorn of truth. Although some might question this, I think it fair to call this preaching a form of love because there is no reason to believe that we preachers who are so fond of fudge divinity are anything other than the deeply caring pastors whom Niebuhr so insightfully described in the passage that opened this essay.[12]

What has this to do with preaching ethics and preaching ethics ethically? King certainly thought that preaching pious irrelevancies had everything to do with ethics. So did the prophets who denounced the no-doubt caring pastors and priests who tried sincerely and valiantly to console their trembling flocks with soothing words of assurance, "Peace, peace" or "Is not the Lord in this place?" when there was no peace and when the Lord was indeed present, but as a lion and not as the cuddly lamb they desired (Jer. 6:14, 8:19).

The point is that preaching ethics ethically must not stay safely above the fray. It must risk incarnation. Get concrete and specific. After all, if preaching ethics means preaching Christ and what Christ is doing, well, we know something about what Christ is doing. Emmanuel. God with us. And this God is with us not by hanging out in the greeting-card shops of his day, uttering pious platitudes and soothing self-help nostrums so we may live at our full potential now. Preach love alone and the prophets of Baal do not shudder; they hardly pay attention. No one gets crucified for uttering such sentimental trivialities. Instead, they get fat book contracts, television shows, and fawning attention from politicians (at least *before* the elections); they may get an invitation to the National Cathedral, but they do not get a cross. This God with us shows up in the concrete and specific messiness of life, among the least, first Israel and then also the church where the foolish and the weak and the low and despised, things that are not, were gathered and continue to be gathered.

Preaching ethics ethically means speaking the Truth who is Christ. Tell the truth about Jesus: he did not come to offer cheap therapy or cheap grace.[13] He did not come so that we might be self-fulfilled, self-realized, or self-actualized. He did not come so that we might learn a few coping strategies for handling the stresses of our harried, middle-class, terminally consumerist lives. He preached good news to the poor, release to the captives, recovering of sight to the blind. He set at liberty those who are oppressed. He healed the sick, fed the hungry, and ate with sinners. He blessed the poor and warned the wealthy. He proclaimed good news that got himself and those whom he loves killed.

To preach ethics ethically means preaching the Truth that turns the world upside down (Acts 17:6), that makes the prophets of lesser gods, be they named Baal or Mammon or Mars, shudder. To preach ethics ethically means to refrain from preaching love alone, to renounce preaching abstractions, like "Peace, peace" or "Justice, justice" or "Can't we all just get along," that may make us feel better but do not change anything because they do not announce the event of Jesus Christ whose gracious call, "Follow me," changes everything. In this regard, Albert Camus puts the challenge of preaching ethics ethically to us about as well as anyone when he wrote:

> What the world expects of Christians is that Christians should speak out, loud and clear, and that they should voice their condemnation in such a way that never a doubt, never the slightest doubt, could rise in the heart of the simplest man. That they should get

away from abstraction and confront the blood-stained face history has taken on today. The grouping we need is a grouping of men resolved to speak out clearly and pay up personally.[14]

Although we must forgive him for suggesting that the word we proclaim is always or even primarily one of condemnation, even in the midst of the horrors of Europe in the 1930s and 1940s, his point is well taken. Preaching ethics ethically means proclaiming the Truth, without evasion or abstraction, in all of the Truth's incarnate reality.

Speak in Love: Against Truth Alone

If preaching a therapeutic sentimentality that stays safely above the fray, refusing the risk of incarnation, constitutes a form of speaking love without adequate connection to the Truth of God with us, it is moralism that runs afoul of the inverse injunction drawn from Ephesians against speaking the truth without love. Moralism, that laundry list of shoulds, oughtas, gottas, and musts that preachers, whose ire is up or whose consciences are pricked, gently but firmly, like any good parent, urge upon their flock. Moralism is preaching a message, the core and climax of which is earnest exhortations like "Follow Jesus' example," or "We have to learn to . . . ," or "We are going to have to . . . ," or "We need to step up," "You should give a little more," "You have to believe," "Don't limit yourself," "Step beyond your expectations," or "Find what you are looking for."

Moralism is preaching ethics—but preaching ethics without the power. It is preaching the truth, but the truth that is preached is truth with a small "t." By this I mean that oftentimes the action or outcome or change that the moralizer seeks to encourage is not in itself wrong. For instance, at least most of the examples just given touch on something that is or should be true about the Christian life. It is true that we should believe, we should love, step up, follow Jesus, and give a little (or a lot) more. But when these heartfelt exhortations and paternal guidance become the focus and finale of the sermon, then they fall short of preaching ethics ethically. They speak only the small "t" truth and they speak it without love.

From what has already been said, we know that when we preach ethics, if we are to do so ethically, then we need to preach the Truth with a capital "T." We proclaim Christ incarnate and what Christ incarnate has done, is doing, and will do. This means that when moralizers preach truths about us, about what we should or ought or must do, they may be preaching ethics, but they are not doing so ethically.

This critique of moralizing, of course, does not preclude preaching small "t" truths. It only means that we have to bring the small "t" truths into right relation with the capital "T" Truth who is Christ, God with us. The way to do this was suggested in the conclusion to the first section of this essay. There it was argued that ethical exhortation—small "t" truths—find their appropriate place in the sermon only when they are *clearly* set within the proclamation of Christ, of what Christ is doing, offering, and enabling. And it *must* be clear, because we fallen humans are so adept at twisting everything so that it is first and foremost about us. Ethical exhortation is appropriate when it is clearly elicited by the word and is clearly in response to what the word does and makes possible for us to do.

To state this in more formal but perhaps memorable terms: preaching ethics is ethical when it proclaims a human imperative that clearly arises out of the divine indicative. One of the things the early modern philosopher David Hume is famous for is his declaration that no "ought" may be derived from what "is." Put simply, you cannot look at the way things are, he argued, and know what ought morally to be done. For an atheist such as Hume, that was indisputably true. But for those of us who have been baptized into Christ, the moral imperative does follow from the indicative. *Because* of what God in Christ has done, is doing, and will do, including what God in Christ is doing to us (the divine indicative), *therefore* we must, we can, we are able to, we get to . . . (the human imperative). Lest anyone think I am making this up, it is the moral structure of the argument Paul makes when he writes to the church in Corinth, saying—after naming several immoral behaviors, some of which marred the life of the Corinthian congregation—"And this is what some of you used to be. But you were washed, you were sanctified, you were justified in the name of the Lord Jesus Christ and in the Spirit of our God" (1 Cor. 6:1). Paul derives a human imperative out of the divine indicative. "See what Jesus has done! See what he has done to you! Therefore, it does not make sense to live like or do x, y, or z." Because of what Christ has done to us, we can live differently. We can believe, love, give, and so forth. And the word for preaching ethics that follows this pattern is not moralism, but sanctification.

And this returns us to love. When I suggested that moralizing was a matter of speaking the truth without love I was not implying that moralizers are cynical or are categorically unconcerned about their congregations. Far from it. What I mean is that moralizing—insofar as it puts the emphasis on us, on our agency to do those things we should, have to, or must do—fails to name rightly the power that enables us to do the good works that God has prepared beforehand to be our way of life (Eph. 2:10). Love, specifically the divine love that took cruciform shape in Christ, is the power that enables us to be better than we otherwise would be. It is the sanctifying love of God that is ours in the Spirit that makes preaching ethics anything more than wishful thinking or sadistic browbeating. It is the assurance of the presence of Christ as the love of God that makes preaching ethics ethical, and that makes the preacher as God's sentinel something other than just another taskmaster working for just another pharaoh, expecting more from the people than is humanly possible. Indeed, it is only the presence of this love that makes the ethics God's sentinels are commanded to preach more than divine drudgery, that makes the moral law something in which God's people could actually take delight (cf. Pss. 1:2, 19:10). Look what we get to do! Sin need no longer bind or frighten us. Alleluia! This is the love that frees us for joyful obedience.

For this reason, because of this joy, we must tamper with Camus's challenge to Christians in the face of the worst horrors, his call for unambiguous condemnation. For even in the face of the worst evil, preaching ethics ethically entails proclaiming a truth that is not fundamentally negative, condemning, threatening—although when peering at it from the darkness of sin we may well perceive the blinding radiance of holiness as threatening and condemning. Rather, the event that preaching ethics announces when it is done ethically is the appearance of the Truth that in love emptied himself and died on the cross in an act of pure affirmation. The Truth spoken in love is the reconciling word (2 Cor. 5:18-20).[15] This is what God's sentinels are finally about. For this reason, and this reason alone, God's sentinels are charged with the obligation of preaching ethics: that all the followers of Baal, whether they be outside the church or in the pews or even standing behind the pulpit, may indeed shudder when they hear the word announced. Mind you, they shudder, we earnestly hope and desire, not out of fear for their lives but in sheer, insuppressible, barely containable excitement for the offer and opportunity that has been graciously set before them. "And I will show you a still more excellent way . . ." (1 Cor. 12:31). Such is preaching ethics ethically.

Conclusion: Hearing the Truth in Love

There is a sense in which the argument of the essay begins too late and ends too early, for preaching ethics ethically is not simply a matter of the preacher standing up with something ethical to say and then saying it in an ethical way. Rather, preaching is a communal practice. The best preaching, according to homiletical commonplace, arises out of and gives voice to the faith of the congregation; it is intimately connected to the rhythms and currents of its life. This brings us full circle, back to the claim that preaching is part of the church's praise and worship of God in response to and in gratitude for the gift of the Word that was first received.

If preaching ethics ethically is part of the church's response to the word, then the obvious precondition of the preaching act is the preacher's having heard God's ethical word. To turn Niebuhr's insight inside out, preaching ethics ethically—speaking the truth in love—should never be easy. If every preacher of ethics does not literally limp into the pulpit, certainly every preacher who hopes to preach ethics ethically will only dare speak after they have wrestled like Jacob with the word.

Hearing the Truth in love as the precondition for preaching ethics ethically, then, means two things. First, preaching ethics ethically is integrally connected to the spiritual disciplines and practices of discipleship through which the word is encountered: study to be sure, but also prayer and fasting and Christian conference and worship and the works of mercy and so forth. Second, the preacher who would preach ethics ethically cannot stand self-righteously aloft or apart from the people but instead must stand with them under the word, for it is to the community that the word comes and in the community that it is heard.[16]

If preaching ethics ethically is inescapably linked to hearing the word, then ending with the preaching act itself is indeed to end too soon. Insofar as preaching is part of the church's worship, it entails not just the preacher preaching but the congregation hearing. Accordingly, preaching ethics ethically requires attention not only to the preacher's own formation in hearing the word, but to the congregation's as well.

In other words, preaching ethics ethically is not simply a labor of the pastor but of the whole congregation. No less than the pastor, with the pastor, a congregation that desires preaching ethics that is ethical to be part of its worship and praise of God will be immersed in the disciplines and practices of the Christian life through which God gives them ears to hear the word. To put yet one last twist on Niebuhr's wisdom, this time from the perspective of the shorn sheep, preaching ethics ethically entails a congregation formed such that it does not respond to any and every sermon with the same generic, friendly "Nice sermon, pastor," but instead is more likely to look the pastor in the eye and exclaim (with all its fallen ambiguity, but also promise of faithful possibilities), "Jesus Christ, pastor!?!"

Such is the labor, the risk, and ultimately the joy of announcing what God has done, is doing, and will do in Jesus Christ.

Preaching and Evocative Objects for Faith Formation 13

H. FREDERICK REISZ JR.

The Out-Flow of the Sermon and the Objective Correlative

The story is told at the University of Chicago Divinity School that Lutheran theologian Joseph Sittler had lunch with Paul Tillich. Tillich seemed to be preoccupied and, perhaps, upset. "Paulus," Sittler inquired, "you seem concerned. What is the matter?" "Yes," replied Tillich, "I have to preach on Sunday." "Oh, Paulus," Sittler replied, "you have published so much on theology, and a three-volume systematics." "Yes," Tillich said, "but that is the plumbing. On Sunday, the waters must flow."

When you preach, you do so from the midst of the stream of word-presencing and witness. Your words, inflections, presence, organization, clarity, style, and meaningful power are the performative action of the word. You preach from the waters of creation, the crossing of the Red Sea, the divine rain of blessing on parched land and souls, the womb-waters of Mary's ministering, the Cana waters of transformation, the Jordan waters of Jesus' baptism, the well waters as a setting for theological discussion and liberation, the healing pool waters, the lake waters of preaching and faith walking, the waters of Pilate's bowl, the waters washing a dead corpse, the lakeshore waters of resurrected breakfast, and baptism's continual stream even unto that new Jerusalem to which the waters of the world will flow. Christ uses your preaching to release the healing waters of the Spirit's renewal, the inspiring waters of possibilities as we are engrafted into Christ, the hopeful waters of refreshment, and the joyous waters of grace's ocean's depth. Do not get stuck in the fixtures of the plumbing! Let the waters flow from Christ.

As one aspect of preaching, occasionally we can place before our hearers objects and events in their lives that can evoke the presence of the Holy with them, and help them follow in the way of Christ. In his writings on literary criticism, the poet T. S. Eliot used the term "objective correlative." In an essay titled "Hamlet and His Problems," Eliot defined his use of "objective correlative" as follows:

> The only way of expressing emotion in the form of art is by finding an "objective correlative"; in other words, a set of objects, a situation, a chain of events which shall be the formula of that *particular* emotion; such that when the external facts, which must terminate in sensory experience, are given, the emotion is immediately evoked.[1]

Eliot specifies how writers work to evoke emotions in us that add content and texture to the poem or work of writing. Effective communication intends to penetrate us and shape or channel our thinking and feeling. People may speak of being "touched," "moved," "motivated," "inspired," or "challenged" by a sermon. Beyond rational thought, much of this feeling is evoked by the use of "objective correlatives" for the emotions we wish to convey or inspire. Thus, our preaching has to "impress" by way of its "expression." Taking this notion used by Eliot and others, I will suggest how we can be more intentional in writing sermons for the sake of utilizing objects/situations that correlate with emotions, thoughts, and theological states. This intentional employment of these objects and situations can: (1) evoke more often the presence of Christ with us and for us, and (2) increase our spiritual formation as we are engrafted into Christ for the sake of God's mission. In this suggestive process, I will write first of the sermon as a whole, and then of more specific examples within sermons of the use of evocative objects for faith formation.

Preaching and the Evocation of Imagination for Creative Faithfulness

We preach within the biblical and a confessional or theological tradition and to a specific congregation. Pastorally, we seek to "be" the presence of the living word through Christ, to convey the teachings and practices of a tradition, and to inspire ourselves and our hearers. We seek to form Christians who live conscious of Christ's accompaniment and faithful to the call of the Spirit in Christ for the mission of God. Increasingly, for many of our listeners, there is minimal knowledge of any tradition and little of the actual biblical accounts and teachings. The Bible, church, and even Christ are practically peripheral to their consciousness and living. We participate in the work of the Spirit drawing them into Christ. Thus, sermons have to teach. I believe that often, this teaching needs to be winsome and incisive. It must be winsome to attract hearing, authentically conveying the faith struggles of the preacher, and incisive to draw listeners into being hearers of the word and toward being in Christ. We are mentoring persons toward creative faithfulness, appropriate to the Christian tradition and relevant to contemporary life. Thus, we want to provide creative support of our hearers, prophetic critique of culture and the world, and intentionality to participate in the mission of God. With the Holy Spirit, we are breaking people out of their current presuppositions about how to live. Participating with them, we do this for the sake of fuller life in Christ for all of us and for the whole world. Preaching to inspire creative faithfulness will require sage use of our imaginations as well as our biblical-theological interpretation and formation skills.

Nurturing this movement toward creative faithfulness is a communal task, and not one for the solitary preacher. Preachers preach not just "to" their communities but "from" their communities. Preachers participate in the struggle to be creatively faithful in their lives to the call of Christ. The new life in Christ is ever new. Through the body of Christ, the church regnant in each congregation, the womb of faithfulness contains the embryonic fluid of imagination, the placental blood of word and tradition, the genetic heritage and promise of life in this place at this time, and the gestational Host, the resurrected Christ working through the Holy Spirit. Sermons preached can evoke Christ's promise and hope in this birthing of new life. That evocation requires a reorientation of our imaginations. It is to this process that this essay speaks.

The contemporary theologian David Kelsey has written about the development of Christian imagination in his book *Imagining Redemption*.[2] Kelsey writes that we have to be redeemed from our own captivities through imagining our living into God's truthful promise. This imagination is specifically "Christian." It is absolutely dependent on the gift of grace—the divine love. Kelsey exhorts us to live into God's promise in the intermediate time. I want to be clear that our imaginative creations are subsets of *God's* promises and *God's* envisioning. Out of living in God's promises and hoping in the light of God's mission to redeem, we preach in part to evoke that Christian imagination. This new imagination can draw us into giving up our preoccupations, open us to the actual accompaniment of Christ, motivate us into convictions of new possibilities, and fructify our trust in Christ's leading. Thus, by the Spirit's work in and through Christ, we are led from our accustomed style of living *into* the style of Christ's life. Then, we live *from* our being engrafted into Christ. We are new beings. In this essay, I explore how objects and situations from our "normal" living can be used to evoke aspects of this Christian imagination.

The Sermon and Poetical Evocation

In limited situations, the sermon can be a work of literary art in the form of a story. Few people have such advanced literary skills, particularly to write a story as sermon effectively. Those who can, should, at least on occasion. Certainly, I have admired the work of Walter Wangerin, and some of John Updike's shorter works approach a form of this mode. Still fewer persons have been able effectively to write sermons as poetry. In my own experience, Barrie Shepherd and Harvey Mozolak both excel. My own "poetical" sermons are lower literary forms of this type.[3] Using these higher literary art forms, the sermon can convey both biblical-theological content and a range of emotional qualities. Poetry condenses the number of words to concentrate their evocative power. By the juxtaposition of words, their contrasts and relationships, their sound, the use of space and breath, good poetry evokes deeper and wider meaning. The multiple possible meanings overreach the text itself. The literary use of objective correlatives enliven preaching and create a valance of influence that attracts the listener. As the listeners are drawn into the experience and hear analogies to their own experiences conveyed in the text, they become more involved and intense hearers of the word.

Throughout my career as a preacher, I have composed poetical sermons. I believe that this form is so foreign to a congregation that initially people have difficulty responding to it. Normally, after the worship service, I make available the text so that it can be used for contemplative purposes beyond its preaching. The auditory nature of the text is important. Thus, normally, I have not preached poetical sermons to congregations unless they have become accustomed to my preaching, and to my use of poetical images within other nonpoetical sermons. Then they have a trust in me as preacher and will open themselves to the possibilities of words.

Let me give you some short examples that will be inadequate because they come from sermons composed to be poetical as a whole. At Lutheran Theological Southern Seminary, there is an annual Advent service of Lessons and Carols. The worship features the seminary choir. The liturgy is at the close of the day: late afternoon or early evening. My poetical sermon "Birthing Advent Light"[4] has a tight structure. It begins with a "Prelude:"

> What world
> Waits birth?
> What God
> Suffers life?
> What hope
> Crosses time?
> What Christ
> Rises light?

Then the poem continues with two extended sections, "Earth" and "Birth." Within these sections, the classical elements of earth, air, fire, and water each frame a section of meditation. Each subsection begins with a variant of the verses:

> Hang a candle
> In the window
> To light
> The Savior's way.

The first subsection includes meditations on desperation and waiting, exhaustion and praying, destruction and listening, and isolation and watching. Thus, the problematic of Advent is placed before the congregation.

Then, the second subsection, "Birthing," reverses the order as couplets of the elements (now, air, earth, water, and fire) from the first section and provides responses to its problematic: inspiration and watching, meditation and listening, anticipation and praying, and expectation and waiting. In each of these sections, God is active and there is a meditation on Mary's process toward giving birth.

In the "Postlude," all these elements are brought together, as it were, around the Advent candle's flickering and fragile flame:

> Isolation to inspiration
> Destruction to meditation
> Exhaustion to anticipation
> Desperation to expectation
> Hang a candle
> In the window
> To light
> The Savior's way.
>
> For God
> Hangs a Savior
> Crèched and crossed
> At your window,
> As your way
> To bring
> The light—
> The growing,
> Cleansing,
> Warming
> Light
> Of day—
> Dawn
> Birthing
> Hope.
> Near.
> Now.

As the flame at the top of the candle, the sermon condenses to single words and silence between "Hope," "Near," and "Now." This condensation echoes the movement of birth toward the one last push, the crowning, the moment of birth, and the one baby. It also echoes God's action toward the One, Jesus Christ. Advent's atmosphere is gathered together in these words: *hope, near,* and *now.*

I preached another Advent sermon, "The Weighted Waiting,"[5] following the September 11, 2001, terrorist attacks in the U.S.A. In this sermon, the waiting of Advent had to be set within the context of the shock and fear generated by 9/11. I tied these emotions also to the wondering of Mary as she awaits birth. In this context, it seemed that an ordinary sermonic discursive text might not reach the depth of feelings in the surrounding context and the evocative possibilities of the season. One short section of this sermon follows:

> In the world's wound,
> God works wonder.
> In the woman's womb,
> God gestates grace.
> In the world's wreck,
> God hides hope.
> In the woman's wondering,
> God rests redemption.
> In the world's whimpering,
> God embraces empathy.
> In the woman's waiting,
> God gods God.

In another short section, I use the traditional symbols included in renaissance paintings of the annunciation: the angel Gabriel's wings, the lily, a snuffed-out candle representing the end of one time and (perhaps) the smoke of prayers arising, a pitcher representing Mary's womb and all the water symbolism, a ray of light from the window above or an angel to Mary's ear, and Mary meditating on an open book—the word.

> Righteous representer, rise!
> On Gabriel's wings rise!
> Upon the lily's bloom, rise!
> On the snuffed candle's smoke, rise!
> Upon the empty pitcher's need, rise!

On the open book, rise!
Upon the ear of Mary, rise!
Out of the Lord
Have we called,
To the deep,
Have we cried,
"O, depths,
It is God."

Of course, few preachers will preach entire sermons that are poems. However, the use of poetical expression within sermons and whole brief poems in sermons have a long tradition. Unfortunately, in some cases, the poems have been trite and not sufficiently evocative. Because of the power of poetry and its ability to be remembered, even to haunt one, it is important to be sensitive to the texts that a preacher uses so that they are appropriate to the occasion, the thought, and the meaning desired. As with any portion of a sermon, listener-hearers may grab that segment of the sermon and work with it in their mind as the preacher continues on. Give them substance!

Through images, metaphors, sounds in the words, juxtapositions, pauses, silences, and breath, these poetical sermons seek to reach the hearers at a deeper level and have a continuing resonance. Their compression paradoxically enables expansive meaning. Their expressive power requires artful reading or "performance" out loud. The written text can be taken by a hearer and used for contemplation over time.

The Sermon as Objective Correlative

In rare instances, I think it is possible to compose an entire sermon that functions as an "objective correlative." Such a sermon evokes in the hearers a strongly predominating emotion or a set of emotions appropriate to the intent of the sermon. Such a sermon might be most appropriate for special occasions where shorter sermons are required and the time is saturated with special and specific feelings, whether of joy, blessing, or sadness. On limited occasions, I have tried to craft such a sermon to mark the beginning of a liturgical season, or to highlight a feast day with a particular emotional resonance, or perhaps within the Commemoration and Burial of the Dead liturgy. In writing such a sermon, more than writing a didactic sermon or engaging primarily in biblical exegesis, the preacher seeks to evoke a specified emotion or narrow range of emotions in the hearers. However, both Bible and theology are used because we are proclaiming the word. In limited instances, Jesus engaged in such speaking, which resulted in his listeners coming away primarily with a predominant emotional impact. The Beatitudes in Matthew may not be an actually preached unit, but as a unit, I feel that they have as much an emotional and attitudinal impact as they have a rational didactic impact. Mistakenly, many people immediately interpret Jesus' parables as moralistic tales. Because usually they are telling of extravagant and totally surprising actions, however, I suspect that their original impact was one of an emotional shock: "How could anyone do this!" and "Why would anyone take such an extravagant action?" Thus, Jesus shakes up his hearers' preconceptions of the limited action of God. He dramatically discloses new possibilities that are actual in God's graceful love.

While preaching for fourteen years at University Lutheran Church in Cambridge, Massachusetts, I used this sermonic form as well as others that I have mentioned. During Holy Week, we developed a weeklong sequence of evening worship services. We tried to shape each day in a special manner to convey the theological moment through the use of art, liturgy, hymns, the lighting of the sanctuary and narthex, and the preaching. To be truthful, only a handful of congregation members besides the pastors and staff were at all the liturgies. Thus, each night had to have its own integrity. All of this culminated in a full Easter Vigil and feast lasting hours, and the Easter morning liturgy. As the week progressed, the lighting in the sanctuary got dimmer and dimmer until, at the final reading of the Tenebrae liturgy on Good Friday evening, all was in total darkness (or as dark as one can achieve on a side street in Harvard Square). The final reading was done in as dark a condition as possible. We were blessed some years to have an African graduate student who was blind and had the Braille text. Then, we had total darkness as we entered the reality of Jesus' death and, paradoxically, we entered into this student's daily living reality of blindness. The service ended in silence and darkness, and the congregants left in silence out into the dangerous night of the city—God's night. Then, the lights remained off in the sanctuary so that after the lighting of new fire outside the church at the Easter Vigil, we processed into the total darkness bearing the light of Christ. In this case, the entire visual aspect of the worship space along with auditory accompaniment became a limited and fragile objective correlative to the death of Christ and the emotions of his followers as they buried the dead body. We were in the cave grave. There was no preaching during the Good Friday evening liturgy as we waited on God's word to come anew at the Easter Vigil. Jesus was dead.

In this context, one year, on Maundy Thursday at the evening liturgy as the lights became very dim and the sanctuary dark, I decided to preach a sermon that would be the objective correlative of total despair, death, and darkness. Such a sermon was a great risk, and I prefaced it by reminding the congregation of the liturgical time and the sequence of our liturgies as a journey-pilgrimage to cross and Easter. This sermon was one step in that awful and awe-filled journey. It ended in darkness and despair. "My God, my God! Why have you forsaken me?" The sermon moved downward, inward, and counter to hope. The risky nature of the sermon paralleled the more substantial risk of God and the risking way upon which Jesus was leading his disciples.

Evocative Objects for Faith Formation

In our living, Dr. Tony Everett urges us to ask the question: "Where is God in all this?" (WIGIAT). It is one of the phrases that students carry forever with them from Lutheran Theological Southern Seminary. The phrase has called many of us to theological reflection in circumstances within which we might have been tempted to theological negligence. In my own preaching, often I use the admonition that God calls us to see the world with the eyes of Christ, to feel the world from the heart of Christ, to think the world with the mind and imagination of Christ, and to be the hands of Christ now in God's mission. In my ministry, I came to believe that one aspect of my preaching could be shaping the theological consciousness of people so that certain objects or recurrent events that they encountered in life became luminous with theological meaning or, more importantly, the presence of Christ with and for them. I believe that most of us go about most of our lives with no consciousness of the accompaniment of Christ. In our time, or any time, a part of the responsibility of the body of Christ, the church, is to have *that* bodily awareness. The discipline of this intentional awareness of Christ with us in the everyday should be accompanied by a trained way of "being" in the world—seeing it through the eyes of Christ. Unknown to most, the objective of such disciplined training of the imagination and intentional consciousness of the people of Christ became a major theme of my ministering. Within that calling, my sermons presented appropriate contexts for suggesting ways of shaping Christ-consciousness and living in the style of Christ—as Joseph Sittler was wont to call the essence of ethics for Christians. I would conduct workshops on "Prayer for Busy People." We had laity speak about how their "work" was ministry. We had an active ministry with homeless women and men housed in our church basement every winter. For me, this actuality in our midst meant that each of us walked in any city in a new way, seeing it as Christ would, looking into its forgotten corners and noticing its rejected persons. As a young "powerhouse" couple with a small boy said to me, "We come to this church in part so that our child will not grow up not knowing that there are homeless people." In fact, he knew them by name!

At University Lutheran Church, women and men who were homeless were treated with human dignity and invited not just into the building but into the life of the body of Christ. Our ecumenical ministries kept many homeless people in Boston alive. One or two died at our building, a sort of home, and the University Lutheran people accompanied them through their funerals. A few of these homeless people had no family who would claim the bodies or be with them. They were people often abandoned by all and little noticed as authentic humans in the city. This was being in the world with the eyes and heart of Christ. It was not easy. It was a part of God's mission.

From time to time in my sermons, I suggested how specific objects or everyday events could aid in being aware of Christ with us and lead us into expressing that Christic being into which the Holy Spirit was engrafting us. It is important not to think about this process as using "object lessons." I find that many object lessons quickly become moralistic and lack theological depth. It is the curse of many children's sermons. For a preacher, often, using object lessons of this sort is a temptation toward the easy and the lazy. They may be perceived as clever or cute, but normally they do not have enduring impress or impact. They are almost dead ends, and in being "moralistic" are "dead" ends theologically. The fact that many adults hear only the children's sermon makes these sermons even harder for the preacher to compose. Authentically telling the Bible's stories in carefully chosen language actually understood by children is probably a better strategy. The pastor or a lay member of the church also can introduce children to practices of the faith and their meanings. I am writing about "objective correlatives" and "evocative objects" to form and to deepen faith formation. In the Small Catechism, Luther urged us to rise in the morning and make the sign of the cross, and ask the Trinity to watch over us.[6] As we use water in our morning washings, we can remember our baptisms. This simple suggestion deeply contextualizes our living from the start each morning. In what follows, I will mention a few other examples of this usage in sermons.

1. Back in the time before we had a mechanical dishwasher, I was the dishwasher for the family. We had two young daughters. The family seemed to use an amazing number of glasses during the day. I washed the dishes at night. In one of my sermons, I related to the congregation a little ritual that I used to remind myself of the growing population of the world, and especially of those crowded into refugee camps, often starving. I would put three or four glasses in the sink. Then, as I washed and rinsed one glass, I would put two more into the sink. The population of glasses would quickly fill the sink to overflowing! As I washed a glass, I would think of a region or place in the world or in the city, a place of overcrowding and poverty. As I rinsed a glass, I would think of God's waters of grace in that place and God calling me/us to minister refreshing and renewing grace. There are other opportunities in our lives for such Christian mindfulness: counting coins in a container, clothes in the washing machine, bottles in the recycle bin, magazines and catalogs piling up from the mail. In each instance, besides the phenomenon of geometric progression, the object itself evokes reminders of our relative wealth and its responsibilities.

Today, how can the bottle of water that is a constant companion of many people be an icon of the sweat of our repentance, the tears of the world's suffering, and the hope of the renewing waters of grace? We can see the world with the eyes of Christ! We also could suggest that before drinking from the water bottle, people pour a few drops of water on their palm. This action will remind them of the life of God poured into the world in Jesus Christ, even to nail prints in his palms. Through that life, that presence accompanying us, and through those nail holes, we see the world. God so loved the world that God gave, and gave, and gave. In baptism, through the Holy Spirit, we are called into that mission to redeem the world and to bring new life, grace, hope, love, and justice as refreshing waters.

2. During Lent, in a sermon preached at Lutheran Theological Southern Seminary, Dr. Marty Stevens used the analogy of preparing a garden for spring to talk about God's process of renewing the world and each of us through Christ. In more artistically arranged words than these, Dr. Stevens related how the gardener has to clear away the debris of winter. Then, you have to identify the weeds and remnants of growing things that are not desired in the garden. You have to plunge your hands into the midst and dig down deep and get them dirty. This digging in the soil and turning it over is labor intensive and, in a manner, costly. These actions are followed by fertilizing and planting as the Spirit of God works gracefully. Her sermon used this process of preparation and planting as the "objective correlative" to raise in her hearers the feelings of labor, change, plunging in the midst, overturning, rooting out, digging deep, enriching, and changing. In the sermon, it was clear that we were the garden. We were being dug up and exposed. We were being overturned and renewed. We were being cleared and cleansed. These were the processes of the Lenten journey to the cross. As I garden now, I do not forget!

3. I think it is important to suggest to people things from their normal lives that can help them toward the disciplines of living in the style of Jesus Christ. For daily disciplining in the faith, we can mention in our sermons the use of specific evocative objects that members of the congregation can easily obtain and carry with them each day. These objects are then imbued with theological or spiritually enhancing meaning.

Recently, I spoke at Abundant Life Church, a Lutheran mission in Pooler, Georgia. At the morning worship, children gave each one of us a round, hole-punched reinforcer sticker. We were to stick it on something we saw each day: a watch, a bracelet, and so on. I put mine on the front of my appointment book. I am sure some went on iPods, cell phones, or PDAs. The idea was that each time you saw the sticker, you were to remember to pray, even a short prayer. In my workshops on "Prayer for Busy People," I have people think about the times during the week when they stand in lines: at the grocery store, at the ATM, at traffic lights, at the Eucharist, and so on. Then, I suggest these are occasions for short prayers . . . granted, with your eyes wide open!

Please note that while not strictly speaking of objective correlatives in Eliot's terms, the above use of objects and occasions are analogous to the string tied around your finger. They are reminders, but ones given special meaning as opportunities or invitations to prayer and Christ-consciousness. I see them as aids in our quest to pray without ceasing. Note that none of these suggestions (reinforcement stickers, lines) runs the danger of getting in the way of deeper theological meaning or Christian practices. The object gives way to the meaning or practice.

4. As a final example, I want to mention an "evocative object" that is a Christian symbol in the deepest sense, the cross. This is an example from my preaching of the use of a sacred and evocative object that only partially was helpful. We all take risks in preaching. Lord, have mercy!

On one Holy Cross Sunday, I preached a theological teaching sermon on the meaning of the cross. I wanted to remind the congregation of what many of them knew, and also deepen the theology of the cross for many. In the last part of the sermon, I explained to the congregation that the variety of types of crosses that I wore on Sunday morning were so because each had been given to me by someone. Along with the theological resonances of these crosses were the stories, places, and events of which they reminded me: relationships within the body of Christ, special occasions, places where Jesus walked, artistic forming of specific meanings of the cross, and the different weights of the crosses. Then, I said that I wanted to make a suggestion in which members of the congregation could elect to participate or not.

Every Sunday, after the liturgy, an individual could come to me in public or private and volunteer to take for a week the cross I was wearing that Sunday. Their commitments were as follows: (1) they were to carry that cross with them each day of the next week (either visibly or in a pocket or purse); (2) I asked them to be conscious of the cross with them during the week as the presence of Christ with them; (3) I asked that they keep a daily journal or write a few phrases each day about what the presence of the cross with them meant or felt like; (4) privately, they were to return the cross to me the next Sunday; and

(5) if they wished to talk with me about their experience or share their writings, this was their option; I would not expect it. I also assured them that nothing from their experiences or writings would be shared in sermons unless they gave me permission or if they had shared things within the congregation or elsewhere.

After the sermon that Sunday, one young adult who worked in a hospital asked to take for a week the cross that I had worn. She was a woman who was deeply struggling with her faith. She was a person of real integrity. After the week, she shared her detailed journal with me. For her, the cross was blessing and curse. She kept the cross mostly in a pocket, or clutched in her hand, yet the cross brought her closer to and more attentive of her patients. There were times when she felt it as a burning in her hand, a curse, either because it accused her, or convicted her, or because she could not accept the maleness of Christ as fully redeeming for herself. There was a period when she could not carry it, but then picked it up again. This experience called forth deep probing of her beliefs and her struggles in life and faith. It was not an easy week for her, but memorable.

I said that this experiment was partially a failure. I do not feel that it was a failure for this young adult who so intentionally bore this little cross. However, no other member of the congregation ever asked to carry my Sunday's cross through the week with intentionality. Was that too threatening for them? Did they feel it was just a gimmick? I do not know. I do know that it was an authentic attempt to break through the cultural curse of cross as jewelry. I think that a preacher might try this strategy with another twist. Perhaps members of the congregation could carry, through the week, the pastor's little cross worn on Sunday as a mindful symbol of bearing the burdens and joys of the congregation's ministries and as a reminder to pray for the pastor.

"The world is charged with the grandeur of God"[7]

Hopkins had it right! However, our preoccupations, lack of vision, and weak trust in God, not to mention our theological perversions, blind us to the presence of Christ who accompanies us. In fact, cultures work hard to place blinders on us and lead us, if not away from Christ, at least into unthinking byways. Every preacher must work to get the attention of her congregation, center them in Christ, and open them to the

Spirit's ministrations. Of course, it is the Word that works, Christ who indwells, and the Spirit who inspires and encourages—gives us courage to break out. In this essay, I have written how my preaching and that of others used objective correlatives, evocative objects and occasions as everyday worldly instigators for formation in the faith. I agree with Hopkins in his poem "God's Grandeur": "there lives the freshness deep down things." As preachers, in part, we can open feelings, eyes, minds, and hearts to the accompaniment and call of Christ. This essay suggests how we might be more creative and effective in doing that. May what our words, inflections, compositions, and lives evoke be fully the inescapable inevitability of God in Christ.

The Interplay of Preaching and Mission

14

PHILLIP BAKER

It seemed so simple. Yet, there I sat stymied, a professor of mission, and one who loves preaching. What was my problem?

The more I thought about it, the more I realized the block to my writing could not be removed without first addressing deeper, more foundational issues. The deeper issues concerned the nature and goal of mission, as well as the nature and goal of preaching. Is mission the crossing of geographical boundaries, going to other nations with the gospel of Jesus Christ, to bring them to a saving knowledge of him? Is mission working to overcome injustice, establish hospitals and schools, and work for the end of oppression in all of its forms? Is mission church planting? Is mission the embodiment of a new reality: the reign, or kingdom, of God? The role of preaching in relationship to mission depends on how one understands the nature and goal of mission. It is both false and misleading to assume that everyone knows what mission is. David Bosch has noted thirteen different dimensions of mission, and seventy-nine different definitions of evangelism.[1] Furthermore, the differences in the understanding of the nature and goal of mission have led to controversies within the church. There is not one definition of mission, either. Several authors of essays in this book have written about how they understand preaching. For me, there is a sacramental nature to preaching in that I understand the primary preacher to be God. The one who stands in the pulpit, the one who may walk up and down the aisle, or the one who stands in the middle of the chancel is the fallible, finite human being God uses to make known the good news of what God has done, is doing, and promises yet to do.

I begin this essay by showing how two common and popular understandings of mission lead to two very different understandings of the purpose of preaching. I will then argue that either of these visions by itself is deficient and that they need to be integrated. In what follows I will draw on Lesslie Newbigin's trinitarian understanding of mission, and show how the Christian proclamation of what he calls the "open secret" of necessity includes both visions to be faithful.

Mission as Saving Souls and Extending the Church: Preaching for Conversion

If mission is identified with conversion and bringing people to a saving knowledge of Jesus Christ, preaching will have a particular focus and goal. Preaching will emphasize a call to faith among unbelievers, or a call to a renewal and/or deepening of faith among believers. There is biblical warrant for such an understanding.

. . . if you confess with your lips that Jesus is Lord and believe in your heart that God raised him from the dead, you will be saved. For one believes with the heart and so is justified, and one confesses with the mouth and so is saved. The scripture says, "No one who believes in him will be put to shame." For there is no distinction between Jew and Greek; the same Lord is Lord of all and is generous to all who call on him. For "Everyone who calls on the name of the Lord will be saved."

But how are they to call on one in whom they have not believed? And how are they to believe in one of whom they have never heard? And how are they to hear without someone to proclaim him? And how are they to proclaim him unless they are sent? As it is written, "How beautiful are the feet of those who bring good news!" But not all have obeyed the good news; for Isaiah says, "Lord, who has believed our message?" So faith comes from what is heard, and what is heard comes through the word of Christ. (Rom. 10:9-17)

On the basis of passages such as this people who understood mission as bringing others to know and to believe in Jesus as Savior and Lord have gone to the four corners of the earth. They have endured trials and tribulations, heartache and despair. They left homelands and family to go to a new land. They contracted disease and faced death in order that people who had never heard of Jesus might come to know him, believe in him, confess him, and be saved. One of the old missionary hymns, the text of which was written by Mary Thomas, declares,

> He comes again! O Zion, ere you meet him,
> make known to ev'ry heart his saving grace;
> let none whom he has ransomed fail to greet him,
> through your neglect, unfit to see his face.
> *Refrain:*
> Publish glad tidings, tidings of peace,
> tidings of Jesus, redemption and release.[2]

If one understands the nature and goal of mission to win others to faith in Jesus Christ, then the goal of preaching would be: (1) to inspire believers to become involved in cross-cultural mission; (2) to renew and strengthen faith in believers; and (3) to motivate unbelievers to accept Jesus Christ as their personal Savior and Lord, decide to follow him, and join the church. This understanding of mission, and of preaching in relationship to mission, is most typical among those who are called evangelicals. Thus, Carl Braaten writes,

> The evangelicals have spoken in a steady stream of publications from Lausanne to Pattaya and beyond. Their chief concern is to retain what they call the classical view of mission, based on the Bible. They define the classical biblical way of regarding mission as "carrying the gospel across cultural boundaries to those who owe no allegiance to Jesus Christ, and encourage them to accept Him as Lord and Savior, and to become responsible members of His church, working, as the Holy Spirit leads, at both evangelism and justice, at making God's will done on earth as it is in heaven."[3]

Braaten supports his understanding of the evangelicals' understanding as to the nature and goal of mission by reference to Arthur Glasser and Donald McGavran's book, *Contemporary Theologies of Mission.*[4]

As has already been noted, the evangelicals' understanding of the nature and goal of mission has biblical support. This understanding of the nature and goal of mission is also probably the one most evident in Lutheran congregations. It was certainly evident in the thinking of some members of our extended family when, in 1981, we accepted a call issued from the then Division for World Mission and Interchurch Cooperation of the American Lutheran Church to serve in Nigeria. By the standards of some in our family, my wife, our children, and I were not "real" missionaries. Although we had crossed the Atlantic Ocean, and although we had crossed racial and cultural boundaries, we were not considered to be "real" missionaries because we were not out trying to convert unbelievers and bring them to faith in Jesus Christ. We were teaching in a theological seminary.

Mission as Justice and Renewing the Earth: Preaching for Action in Society

The evangelicals' understanding of the nature and goal of mission is not the only one to be found among believers, or having biblical warrant. There are those who insist that the nature and goal of mission has to do with promoting justice and working against injustice, establishing schools and contending with ignorance, building hospitals and attacking diseases. Some people will point to how in Exodus God calls Moses to fight against Pharaoh, end the oppression of the people in Egypt, and lead them out of bondage into the freedom of the promised land. Other people will point out how the Old Testament prophets make clear God's abhorrence of oppression and injustice. For example, in the book of Amos God declares,

> I hate, I despise your festivals,
>> and take no delight in your solemn assemblies.
> Even though you offer me your burnt offerings and
>> grain offerings, I will not accept them;
> and the offerings of well-being of your fatted animals
>> I will not look upon.
> Take away from me the noise of your songs;
>> I will not listen to the melody of your harps.
> But let justice roll down like waters,
>> and righteousness like an ever-flowing stream. (Amos 5:21-24)

Such sentiments, however, are not limited to writers and/or speakers in the Old Testament. Christians who want to spiritualize the New Testament, and not see its political importance, might not recognize the confrontive nature of some of the passages in the Synoptic Gospels, especially that of Luke, something recognized by some of the liberation theologians who talk about God's preferential treatment of the poor.

The late Chilean general and dictator Augusto Pinochet found one passage in Luke so inflammatory that he forbade its use in Spanish. The words he thought might incite the people to rise up and overthrow him were these:

> He has shown strength with his arm;
>> he has scattered the proud in the thoughts of their hearts.
> He has brought down the powerful from their thrones,
>> and lifted up the lowly.
> He has filled the hungry with good things,
>> and sent the rich away empty. (Luke 2:51-53)

When I taught as Visiting Professor of Missiology and Systematic Theology at Gurukul Lutheran Theological College and Research Institute in Chennai, India, I discovered there was another passage from the Lukan witness that many people understood to address issues of oppression and injustice. I learned that among the Dalit Christians of India, those who were once called "untouchables" or "outcasts," there is talk about the "Nazareth Manifesto" of Luke 4:16-21:

> When he came to Nazareth, where he had been brought up, he went to the synagogue on the sabbath day, as was his custom. He stood up to read, and the scroll of the prophet Isaiah was given to him. He unrolled the scroll and found the place where it was written:
>
>> The Spirit of the Lord is upon me,
>>> because he has anointed me
>>> to bring good news to the poor.
>> He has sent me to proclaim release to the captives
>>> and recovery of sight to the blind,
>>> to let the oppressed go free,
>> to proclaim the year of the Lord's favor.

And he rolled up the scroll, gave it back to the attendant, and sat down. The eyes of all in the synagogue were fixed on him. Then he began to say to them, "Today this scripture has been fulfilled in your hearing."

As one reads various liberation theologians, whether Gustavo Gutiérrez or Leonardo Boff, Jon Sobrino or Naim Ateek, one is confronted with an understanding of the nature and goal of mission having to do with correcting social and/or economic injustice, overcoming various kinds of oppression, and so on. If this is one's understanding of the nature and goal of mission, preaching takes the role of encouragement and empowerment to the poor and downtrodden. Preaching is then intended to comfort, console, encourage, and sometimes incite to action those who are believers. Preaching with this understanding of the nature and goal of mission is not about conversion, or an individual soul's salvation, but about the betterment of all God's creation.

Mission as Accompaniment and Embodiment of a New Reality: Preaching for Empowerment

The temptation is to set the two understandings of the nature and goal of mission—that of conversion and that of justice (and therefore the role of preaching in relation to mission)—in opposition to each other. There is a temptation to set them up in an either/or contrast: either mission is conversion and bringing others to confess Jesus as Lord, or it is working for the betterment of God's creation against all the forces of evil and injustice. As I have already noted, both understandings have biblical foundation. To set one in opposition to the other, or to focus on one to the exclusion of the other, however, is both truncated and, I would say, heretical. About this, Lesslie Newbigin, whom I consider to be the father of modern missiology, writes,

> On the one hand, there are those who place exclusive emphasis on the winning of individuals to conversion, baptism, and church membership. The numerical growth of the Church becomes the central goal of mission. Action for justice and peace in the world is a secondary matter. . . . The emphasis here is exclusively on the salvation of the individual soul and the growth of the Church. The primary task is evangelism, the direct preaching of the gospel

202 A, Proclaiming the Gospel

in words—spoken or written. . . . The preaching of the gospel of salvation from sin and the offer of eternal life is the primary business of the Church.

On the other hand, there are those who condemn this as irrelevant or wrong. The gospel, they will say, is about God's kingdom, God's reign over all nations and all things. . . . It [the central responsibility of the church] is to seek the doing of God's will of righteousness and peace in this world. . . . [T]he conflict between these two ways of understanding mission is profoundly weakening the Church's witness. The conflict continues because both parties have hold of important truth. And I am suggesting that both parties are inadequately aware of the central reality, namely that mission is not primarily our work—whether of preaching or social action—but primarily the mighty work of God.[5]

In Newbigin's understanding of mission, God is and remains central. In his little book *The Open Secret: An Introduction to the Theology of Mission*,[6] Newbigin writes of the nature and goal of mission under three categories: (1) Proclaiming the Kingdom of the Father: Mission as Faith in Action; (2) Sharing the Life of the Son: Mission as Love in Action; and (3) Bearing the Witness of the Spirit: Mission as Hope in Action.

There are a number of things I appreciate about Newbigin's understanding of mission, as well as his approach to the church being missional by its very nature. First, Newbigin's approach is decidedly trinitarian. Second, it focuses mission in the actions of God: past, present, and promised. Third, Newbigin understands the missional activities of the church as derivative from God's mission in and for the sake of God's creation. It is the *missio Dei*, not the mission of the church. Newbigin writes,

The Bible . . . is covered with God's purpose of blessing for all the nations. It is concerned with the completion of God's purpose in the creation of the world and of man [*sic*] within the world. It is not—to put it crudely—concerned with offering a way of escape for the redeemed soul out of history, but with the action of God to bring history to its true end.[7]

Thus, the *missio Dei* is rooted in the nature of God—love. This love is manifest in the life, death, resurrection, and ascension of Jesus. Further, this love is embodied in the church, the body of Christ. From the opening words of Genesis through the closing words of Revelation, God's nature is witnessed to in the mighty acts of God, acts that are seen in the past, experienced in the present, and expected in the future. These acts, furthermore, are not simply for the sake of a particular people, but for the sake of all creation.

This does not mean that specific people are unimportant. From the covenant God makes with Abraham through the covenant God makes with the New Israel, God calls out, empowers, and sends a particular people in order that all creation may be blessed. Newbigin writes,

> But this universal purpose of blessing is not to be effected by means of a universal revelation to all humanity. There is, as we have seen, a process of selection: a few are chosen to be bearers of the purpose; they are chosen, not for themselves, but for the sake of all.[8]

The people of God, both Israel and the New Israel, are called out to make known God's revelation and be bearers of what Newbigin calls God's "Open Secret." Thus, he writes,

> Bearers—not exclusive beneficiaries. There lay the constant temptation. Again and again it had to be said that election is for responsibility, not for privilege. Again and again unfaithful Israel had to be threatened with punishment *because* it was the elect of God. . . . The meaning of Israel's election and of its misunderstanding of it is depicted with supreme dramatic power in the story of Jonah, which is perhaps the most moving interpretation of the missionary calling of God's people to be found in the Bible.[9]

The temptation to turn the call to bearers into beneficiaries has been a constant temptation for the people of God, past and present. Christians today are constantly tempted to think they are the ones specially loved by God, the only ones who are the apple of God's eye. We are always in danger of turning in upon ourselves, which is the nature of sin, and to think we have God's love while others, unless they are Christian, do not.

In his little book, *Foolishness to the Greeks: The Gospel and Western Culture*, Newbigin writes,

> The church is the bearer to all the nations of a gospel that announces the kingdom, the reign, and the sovereignty of God.

It calls men and women to repent of their false loyalty to other powers, to become believers in the one true sovereignty, and so to become corporately a sign, instrument, and foretaste of the one true and living God over all nature, all nations, and all human lives. It is not meant to call men and women out of the world into a safe religious enclave but to call them out in order to send them back as agents of God's kingdom.[10]

Note first, the church is not simply a collection of individual believers. The church is a corporate body, a community that is more than the sum total of its parts. Second, the church is ". . . corporately a sign, instrument, and foretaste. . . ." Third, the church does not remove people from the world, but rather equips, empowers, and sends people back into God's world to be ". . . agents of God's kingdom."

There is something significantly and uniquely different about the church. While the church is where the gospel is purely taught and the sacraments rightly administered, the church is also the people of God sent out from the liturgy to be involved in God's work in God's world. The liturgy ends with the words, "Go in peace. Serve the Lord."

I admit that I do not like the word *instrument*. On the one hand, too many Christians believe that the church is simply a means to an end, whatever that end may be, whether heaven, eternal life, the reign of God, or whatever. On the other hand, other Christians believe the church is an end in itself. The church is neither a means (instrument) to an end, nor is it an end in itself. The church is a new creation, God's new reality, called out of the world and sent back into the world to embody a new reality. Paul speaks of this new creation in 2 Corinthians 5:17 when he writes, "if anyone is in Christ, there is a new creation: everything old has passed away; see, everything has become new!" This is consistent with the understanding in John's Gospel that the church is to be in the world, but not of it. The church, as God's new creation, is different in its very nature. Christians sing about this new creation in the words of Samuel J. Stone:

The church's one foundation is Jesus Christ, her Lord;
she is his new creation by water and the word.
From heav'n he came and sought her to be his holy bride,
with his own blood he bought her, and for her life he died.[11]

To those who understand the nature and goal of mission to be the embodiment of a new reality, preaching takes on several dimensions, verbal and nonverbal. First, preaching as the proclamation of the gospel will always focus on God's actions: past, present, and promised.

Second, and a corollary of the first dimension, the focus of preaching will only secondarily and derivatively be about human beings. Gospel preaching is not anthropocentric. Nonetheless, focusing on what God has done, is doing, and promises yet to do calls for a response on the part of the listener.

Third, the listeners will be both those who have heard the gospel, and those who have never heard—both believers and unbelievers. One remembers the hymn "I Love to Tell the Story." In verse one the words refer to those who have never heard the message of salvation from God's word. In verse three the words refer to those who know the message of salvation, hungering and thirsting to hear the message of salvation.

Fourth, the response to the gospel is always invitational. It neither tries to scare "the hell out of people," or entice them with the promise of future rewards. Neither the threat of hell, nor the hope of heaven, creates faith and response. The Spirit works through the gospel, which proclaims the God who has acted in love for all of God's creation, a love manifest in the incarnation of Jesus Christ, and sung about in countless hymns, such as "Alas! And Did My Savior Bleed." In the third verse Isaac Watts pointedly writes,

> Well might the sun in darkness hide and shut its glories in
> when God, the mighty maker died for his own creatures' sin.[12]

Fifth, the power to respond to the gospel, whether the response is for the first time, or for the thousandth time, always comes from God. Lutheran Christians are reminded of Luther's explanation to the Third Article of the Apostles' Creed. We come to faith by the work and power of the Holy Spirit who calls through the gospel.

Sixth, and last, the response to the gospel is both vertical and horizontal, in relation to both God and all creation. The vertical without the horizontal, or the horizontal without the vertical, is incomplete. The vertical and the horizontal are held in tension, and are clearly articulated in the "Affirmation of Baptism" in *Evangelical Lutheran Worship*. The pastor addresses all who have gathered and says,

You have made public profession of your faith. Do you intend to continue in the covenant God made with you in holy baptism:

to live among God's faithful people,
to hear the word of God and share in the Lord's supper,
to proclaim the good news of God in Christ through word
    and deed,
to serve all people, following the example of Jesus,
and to strive for justice and peace in all the earth?

To this the assembly responds, "I do, and I ask God to help and guide me."[13]

Conclusion

How one understands the interplay between preaching and mission depends on how one understands both the nature and goal of mission and the nature and goal of preaching. I believe the center of preaching, like the center of mission, is God's actions: past, present, and promised. Sometimes, by the power of the Holy Spirit at work in, with, and through the preaching of fallible, finite human beings, people will come to say they want to become followers of Jesus Christ, and become part of the community that bears his name. Sometimes, by the power of the Holy Spirit at work in, with, and through the preaching of fallible, finite human beings, believers, as well as unbelievers, will come to repentance. Sometimes, by the power of the Holy Spirit at work in, with, and through the preaching of fallible, finite human beings, individuals within the community of faith, and the community of faith itself, will be confronted with how far short they have been in understanding and doing God's will, and will hear the word of God's gracious forgiveness. Sometimes, by the power of the Holy Spirit at work in, with, and through the preaching of fallible, finite human beings, individuals within the community of faith, and the community of faith itself, will be strengthened, comforted, and reassured. Through it all, to God be the glory.

Contributors

Rev. Dr. Phillip Baker is Professor of Missiology and Evangelism (emeritus).

Rev. Dr. Daniel M. Bell Jr. is Associate Professor of Theological Ethics.

Dr. Ira Brent Driggers is Associate Professor of New Testament.

Rev. Dr. Daryl (Tony) S. Everett is Dewey F. Beam Professor of Pastoral Care.

Rev. Shauna K. Hannan is Assistant Professor of Homiletics.

Dr. Robert D. Hawkins is Leonora G. McClurg Distinguished Professor of Worship and Music and Dean of Christ Chapel.

Rev. Dr. Lamontte M. Luker is Professor of Hebrew Scriptures.

Rev. Dr. Nicholas K. Mays is Associate Professor of Contextual Education (emeritus).

Dr. Susan Wilds McArver is Professor of Church History and Educational Ministry.

Rev. Dr. Marcus J. Miller is President of Lutheran Theological Southern Seminary.

Rev. Dr. Brian K. Peterson is Professor of New Testament.

Rev. Dr. H. Frederick Reisz is President of Lutheran Theological Southern Seminary (emeritus).

Rev. Dr. Thomas Ridenhour is Professor of Homiletics (emeritus).

Dr. Michael Root is Professor of Systematic Theology.

Dr. Agneta Enermalm Tsiparis is Professor of New Testament (emeritus).

Notes

Chapter 1: Called and Sent to Preach the Gospel of God

1. *The Book of Concord*, trans. and ed. Robert Kolb and Timothy J. Wengert (Minneapolis: Fortress Press, 2000), 40.

2. Ibid.

3. Ibid., 42.

4. Ibid., 355–56.

5. For me, the Lutheran distinction between law and gospel, and biblical interpretation that focuses on God as the primary actor, are major contributions by Lutherans to the church catholic. My own teaching experience in an ecumenical context and in the Academy of Homiletics—the primary academic guild for homileticians—is that Lutherans are not always happily recognized in our insistence on these distinctions, but are listened to and respected because of them.

Chapter 2: Lutheran Preaching and the Third Use of the Law

1. *The Book of Concord*, trans. and ed. Robert Kolb and Timothy J. Wengert (Minneapolis: Fortress Press, 2000), 502. It is worth noting that the homiletical *tertius usus legis* is always "preaching to the choir."

2. C. F. W. Walther, "Why Should Our Pastors, Teachers and Professors Subscribe Unconditionally to the Symbolical Writings of Our Church," *Concordia Journal* (July 1989): 274–84. This article was first printed in *Concordia Theological Monthly* 18 (April 1947): 241–53.

3. Timothy J. Wengert and Robert Kolb, "The Future of Lutheran Confessional Studies: Reflections in Historical Context," *Dialog: A Journal of Theology* 45, no. 2 (Summer 2006): 120.

4. Erik T. R. Samuelson, "Roadmaps to Grace: Five Types of Lutheran Confessional Subscription," *Dialog: A Journal of Theology* 45, no. 2 (Summer 2006): 157–69.

5. Timothy Wengert calls these extremes "dogmatic theology" ("believe it, or else!") and "historical document" (the Lutheran equivalent of Alex Haley's *Roots*). See Timothy J. Wengert, *A Formula for Parish Practice: Using the Formula of Concord in Congregations* (Grand Rapids: Eerdmans, 2006), 1.

6. Samuelson, "Roadmaps to Grace," 166.

7. Ibid., 167.

8. Ibid.

9. Nine years before (1521), Melanchthon had written his *Loci Communes*, which pushed him into the spotlight as an evangelical theologian. Along with the Small Catechism (written by Luther himself), the Augsburg Confession remains one of the most widely accepted sections of the Lutheran confessions.

10. Günther Gassmann and Scott H. Hendrix, *Fortress Introduction to the Lutheran Confessions* (Minneapolis: Fortress Press, 1999), 55 (emphasis mine).

11. See Martin Luther, "Treatise Against the Antinomians," in Martin Luther, *Luther's Works*, vol. 47, *The Christian in Society IV*, ed. J. J. Pelikan, H. C. Oswald, & H. T. Lehmann (Philadelphia: Fortress Press, 1971), 99–119.

12. Gassmann and Hendrix, *Fortress Introduction to the Lutheran Confessions*, 57. A slogan attributed to Agricola and his followers was *Das Gesetz bleibt auf dem Rathaus* ("The law remains in city hall") (Wengert, *Formula*, 79).

13. The difference between the Gnesio-Lutherans and Agricola was that whereas the issue for Agricola was repentance, the issue for the Gnesio-Lutherans was good works.

14. Martin Luther, *Luther's Works*, vol. 35, *Word and Sacrament I*, ed. Jaroslav Pelikan and Helmut T. Lehmann (Philadelphia: Fortress Press, 1960), 370–71.

15. Kolb and Wengert, *Book of Concord*, 486.

16. It must be noted that, to this day, not all Lutherans adhere to all parts of *The Book of Concord*, including the Formula of Concord. See *Dialog: A Journal of Theology* 45, no. 2 (Spring 2006), for an informative collection of articles on "The Future of Lutheran Confessional Studies" written by international authors.

17. See Robert J. Bast, "*Je Geistlicher . . . Je Blinder*: Anticlericalism, the Law, and Social Ethics in Luther's Sermons on Matthew 22:34-41," in *Anticlericalism in Late Medieval and Early Modern Europe*, ed. Heiko A. Oberman and Peter A. Dykema (Leiden: Brill, 1993), 367–78.

18. Jane Strohl, "Law and Gospel in Preaching," *Dialog: A Journal of Theology* 39, no. 3 (2000): 167.

Chapter 3: Preaching Justification

1. See Günther Gassmann and Scott Hendrix, *Fortress Introduction to the Lutheran Confessions* (Minneapolis: Fortress Press, 1999), 173, for a discussion of such difficulties.

2. This structure of soteriology is explored in Michael Root, "The Narrative Structure of Soteriology," *Modern Theology* 2 (1986): 145–58.

3. The Lutheran World Federation and The Roman Catholic Church, *Joint Declaration on the Doctrine of Justification* (Grand Rapids: Eerdmans, 2000), para. 18.

4. Martin Luther, "Two Kinds of Righteousness," in *Career of the Reformer*, *Luther's Works*, vol. 31, ed. Harold J. Grimm, trans. Lowell J. Satre (Philadelphia: Fortress Press, 1957), 293–306.

5. *The Apology to the Augsburg Confession*, in Robert Kolb and Timothy J. Wengert, eds., *The Book of Concord: The Confessions of the Evangelical Lutheran Church* (Minneapolis: Fortress Press, 2000), 192.

6. On this point, Gerhard Forde is certainly correct: Gerhard O. Forde, *Justification by Faith—A Matter of Death and Life* (Philadelphia: Fortress Press, 1982), 13, 95.

7. See, for example, the exaggerated Lutheran resistance to any notion that grace produces a *habitus* in the self: Werner Elert, *Der christliche Glaube: Grundlinien der lutherischen Dogmatik*, 6th ed. (Erlangen: Martin Luther Verlag, 1988), 25; or Dietz Lange, ed., *Überholte Verurteilungen? Die Gegensätze in der Lehre von Rechtfertigung, Abendmahl und Amt zwischen dem Konzil von Trient und der Reformation—damals und heute* (Göttingen: Vandenhoeck & Ruprecht, 1991), 43. On the analytic/synthetic justification distinction, see Gerhard Sauter, "God Creating Faith: The Doctrine of Justification from the Reformation to the Present," *Lutheran Quarterly* 11 (1997): 59.

8. For example, John Wesley, "Sermon 85: On Working Out Our Own Salvation," in *The Works of John Wesley; Vol. 3, Sermons III: 71–114*, ed. Albert C. Outler (Nashville: Abingdon, 1986), 204.

9. The oddity of such a sermon as Jonathan Edwards's "Sinners in the Hands of an Angry God" is that it is a conversion sermon preached to the converted. It thus must persuade some of its hearers that they still need conversion by raising the possibility that some who appear to be faithful Christians really are not: "Thus are all of you that have never passed under a great Change of Heart . . . (however you may have reformed your Life in many Things, and may have had religious Affections, and may keep up a Form of Religion in your

Families and Closets, and in the House of God, and may be strict in it), you are thus in the Hands of an angry God" (Jonathan Edwards, "Sinners in the Hands of an Angry God," in *American Sermons: The Pilgrims to Martin Luther King, Jr*, ed. Michael Warner [New York: Library of America, 1999], 356). While there certainly are nominal Christians who still need conversion, one wonders whether regularly arguing that hearers should doubt whether they actually have faith is a truly evangelical homiletical strategy.

10. Michael Reu, *Homiletics: A Manual of the Theory and Practice of Preaching*, trans. Albert Steinhaeuser (1924; repr., Minneapolis: Augsburg, 1950), 3, italics in original.

11. The best recent summary of what I believe to be an adequate doctrine of justification is Bruce D. Marshall, "Justification as Declaration and Deification," *International Journal of Systematic Theology* 4 (2002): 3–28.

12. Martin Luther, *Lectures on Romans: Glosses and Scholia, Luther's Works*, vol. 25, ed. Hilton C. Oswald (St. Louis: Concordia, 1972), 131.

13. Luther lays out this understanding in the sermon referred to above on "The Two Kinds of Righteousness" (above, n. 4). A Lutheran understanding of justification is best understood as the theological expression of the attitude of the sinner who pleads Christ before the judgment of God, rather than as the attempt at a third-person and objective description of Christian righteousness. This observation does not mean that the Lutheran understanding does not claim truth, but that its linguistic form remains tied to first-person confession and that the explication of its truth claim must not lose sight of that tie. I have explored this connection in my essay "Continuing the Conversation: Deeper Agreement on Justification as Criterion and on the Christian as *Simul Justus et Peccator*," in *The Gospel of Justification in Christ: Where Does the Church Stand Today?* ed. Wayne C. Stumme (Grand Rapids: Eerdmans, 2006), 42–61.

14. Leonhard Hutter, *Compend of Lutheran Theology*, trans. H. E. Jacobs and G. F. Spieker (Philadelphia: Lutheran Book Store, 1868), 103f.

15. Heinrich Schmid, *The Doctrinal Theology of the Evangelical Lutheran Church*, 3d ed., trans. Charles A. Hay and Henry E. Jacobs (1875; repr., Minneapolis: Augsburg, 1961), 410f.

16. Martin Luther, "The Freedom of a Christian," in *Career of the Reformer I, Luther's Works*, vol. 31, ed. Harold J. Grimm (Philadelphia: Fortress Press, 1957), 351.

17. On mystical union, see David S. Yeago, "The Doctrine of the Mystical Union," *Lutheran Forum* 18 (Advent 1984): 18–22. Lutherans have debated whether the mystical union is logically prior or subsequent to justification. While there may be senses in which justification is prior to mystical union, mystical union is inherent within justification, not a distinct, logically subsequent,

even if simultaneous, aspect. See the citations in Schmid, *The Doctrinal Theology of the Evangelical Lutheran Church*, 481.

18. It has been the great merit of recent Finnish Luther scholarship to reassert the centrality of this indwelling to a Reformation understanding of justification. See Tuomo Mannermaa, *Christ Present in Faith: Luther's View of Justification*, ed. Kirsi Stjerna (Minneapolis: Fortress Press, 2005).

19. A point of agreement between the understanding here presented and that of Forde is the importance of union with Christ's death and resurrection for justification. See Forde, *Justification by Faith*, 1–3. My contention, however, is that the resurrection of the new self with Christ is systematically undercut in Forde's understanding, as will be noted below.

20. Paul R. Hinlicky, "Luther's New Language of the Spirit: Trinitarian Theology as Critical Dogmatics," in Hinlicky, ed., *The Substance of the Faith: Luther's Doctrinal Theology for Today* (Minneapolis: Fortress Press, 2008), 142.

21. Ibid., 143.

22. A strength of Forde's theology of preaching is his emphasis on the need to move from third-person description, speaking about Christ, to second-person address, speaking Christ to the addressee. See Gerhard Forde, *Theology Is for Proclamation* (Minneapolis: Fortress Press, 1990), 2.

23. As Reu puts it: "The minister acts . . . as the divinely appointed organ for the public administration of Word and sacrament by which God enters into communion with the congregation" (Reu, *Homiletics*, 40).

24. Luther, *Lectures on Romans*, 478.

25. Reu, *Homiletics*, 14.

26. Kolb and Wengert, eds., *Book of Concord*, 133.

27. Martin Luther, "Theses Concerning Faith and Law," in *Career of the Reformer IV*, *Luther's Works*, vol. 34, ed. and trans. Lewis W. Spitz (Philadelphia: Muhlenberg Press, 1960), 113.

28. Reu, *Homiletics*, 12.

29. "The purpose of the sermon is the edification of the congregation, both as a whole and with respect to its individual members" (ibid., 99).

30. Ibid., 102.

31. Quoted in ibid., 49.

32. Susan K. Wood, "The Liturgy: Participatory Knowledge of God in the Liturgy," in *Knowing the Triune God: The Work of the Spirit in the Practices of the Church*, ed. James J. Buckley and David S. Yeago (Grand Rapids: Eerdmans, 2001), 109.

33. Among those who follow in Forde's footsteps in this areas, see Steven D. Paulson, "Categorical Preaching," *Lutheran Quarterly* 3 (Autumn 2007): 268–93.

34. On the meaning of this phrase, see the important work of Theodor Dieter, *Der junge Luther und Aristoteles: Eine historisch-systematische Untersuchung zum Verhältnis von Theologie und Philosophie*, Theologische Bibliothek Töpelmann (Berlin: W. de Gruyter, 2001), 317–25.

35. Forde, *Justification by Faith*, 50.

36. David S. Yeago, "Theological Impasse and Ecclesial Future," *Lutheran Forum* 26, no. 4 (November 1992): 37.

37. Ibid.

38. Gerhard O. Forde, *The Law-Gospel Debate: An Interpretation of Its Historical Development* (Minneapolis: Augsburg, 1969), 223f., italics added.

39. David S. Yeago, "Gnosticism, Antinomianism, and Reformation Theology: Reflections on the Cost of a Construal," *Pro Ecclesia* 2 (1993): 37–49.

40. Yeago explores the similar logic in the work of such Lutheran theologians as Adolf von Harless and Gerhard Ebeling in his essay "The Church as Polity? The Lutheran Context of Robert W. Jenson's Ecclesiology," in *Trinity, Time, and Church: A Response to the Theology of Robert W. Jenson*, ed. Colin E. Gunton (Grand Rapids: Eerdmans, 2000), 201–37. Yeago's analysis of Forde and his predecessors strikes me as conceptually devastating. That Forde and his defenders have never responded to it is interesting.

Chapter 4: Preparing to Preach the Gospels

1. Irenaeus, *Against Heresies*, III.11.8. See *The Ante-Nicene Fathers*, ed. Alexander Roberts and James Donaldson (Grand Rapids: Eerdmans, 1950), 1:428–29.

2. *Against Heresies*, III.11.7. See *The Ante-Nicene Fathers* 1:428.

3. See Frances Watson, "The Fourfold Gospel," in *The Cambridge Companion to the Gospels*, ed. Stephen C. Barton (Cambridge: Cambridge University Press, 2006), 44–46.

4. Ibid., 35; cf. Graham Stanton, "The Fourfold Gospel," *New Testament Studies* 43 (1997): 317–46.

5. See John J. O'Keefe and R. R. Reno, *Sanctified Vision: An Introduction to Early Christian Interpretation of the Bible* (Baltimore: Johns Hopkins University Press, 2005).

6. The hermeneutic and philosophical limitations of historical criticism have become clearer, even among historical critics, in recent decades, particularly with the advent of postmodernism. Prior to this, it was characterized by the disparagement of allegory based on the assumption of its own methodological hegemony. See David C. Steinmetz, "The Superiority of Pre-Critical Exegesis," *Theology Today* 37 (April 1980): 27–38.

7. See Oscar Cullmann, "The Plurality of the Gospels as a Theological Problem in Antiquity," in *The Early Church: Studies in Early Christian History and Theology*, ed. A. J. B. Higgins (Philadelphia: Westminster, 1956), 40–50.

8. In the ancient church, for example, the so-called school of Antioch, of which Theodore of Mopsuestia is the best-known representative. See Robert M. Grant and David Tracy, *A Short History of the Interpretation of the Bible*, rev. ed. (Philadelphia: Fortress Press, 1984), 63–72.

9. The analogy of "boundary" emerged out of a conversation with my colleagues Dan Bell, Ginger Barfield, and Brian Peterson.

10. Irenaeus, *Against Heresies* III.11.8. See *The Ante-Nicene Fathers* 1:428.

11. Following the theory accepted by the vast majority of scholars, I hold that Matthew and Luke both used Mark as a source and redacted it to fit their particular concerns and circumstances.

12. This dynamic is common to the history of interpretation of Mark. See, for example, Robert Fowler, *Let the Reader Understand: Reader-Response Criticism and the Gospel of Mark* (Harrisburg: Trinity, 2001), 228–60.

13. Matthew is the only Gospel to use the term *church* (16:18, 18:17), rather anachronistically, to describe the community of followers during Jesus' earthly ministry. Both occurrences of the term come in conjunction with the granting of authority to "bind and loose."

14. As form criticism has shown, the oral traditions themselves were already doing this prior to being incorporated into the Gospel narratives.

15. The question is somewhat trickier with respect to Paul insofar as he is the single author of multiple letters. While the exegete must honor how each letter is occasioned by particular circumstances, there is more room for a cautious peaking into other Pauline letters. Interpreters often do this in analyzing Paul's view of women, for instance. The issue is further complicated, however, by debates over which letters are genuinely Pauline.

Chapter 5: From Gospels to Sermon

1. The writer is a layperson who until January 2007 served as professor of New Testament at the Lutheran Theological Southern Seminary and upon retirement returned to her country of origin, Sweden. Therefore, some issues raised in this essay derive from a European context rather than the American one I was privileged to claim as mine for many years.

2. Per Beskow, "The Bible in the Church or the Hermeneutical Circle," (in Swedish) in *Bibeltolkning och bibelbruk i västerlandets kulturella historia* [*Biblical Interpretation and Use of the Bible in the History of Western Civilization*], ed. Tryggve Kronholm and Anders Piltz (Stockholm: Almqvist & Wiksell, 1999), 46.

3. *Evangelical Lutheran Worship* (Minneapolis: Augsburg Fortress, 2006).

4. Gottlob Schrenk, ἱεράτευμα, *Theological Dictionary of the New Testament* 3:250, ed. Gerhard Kittel, trans. Geoffrey W. Bromiley (Grand Rapids: Eerdmans, 1965). See also Leonhard Goppelt, *A Commentary on 1 Peter*, ed. F. Hahn, trans. J. E. Alsup (Grand Rapids: Eerdmans, 1993), 148–49.

5. The English word *church* derives from the Greek adjective κυριακή, "of the Lord," the feminine form to go with an assumed οἰκία ("house"); *Webster's New World College Dictionary*, 4th ed. (Foster City, Calif.: IDG Books, 1999), 263.

6. Goppelt, *1 Peter*, 148–49.

7. See for example Hans-Ruedi Weber, *Experiments with Bible Study* (Philadelphia: Westminster, 1982), 225–28.

8. *Evangelical Lutheran Worship*, 6.

9. The ecclesial features are obvious in 28:19-20: making disciples, teaching, baptizing.

10. Ulrich Luz, *Matthew 1–7*, Hermeneia, ed. Helmut Koester, trans. J. E. Crouch (Minneapolis: Fortress Press, 2007), 96. See also David D. Kupp, *Matthew's Emmanuel: Divine Presence and God's People in the First Gospel*, Society for New Testament Studies Monograph Series 90 (Cambridge: Cambridge University Press, 1996).

11. Hobst Dietrich Preuss, "'. . . ich will mit dir sein,'" *Zeitschrift für die alttestamentliche Wissenschaft* 80 (1968): 139–73.

12. Lars Hartman, "ὄνομα," *Exegetical Dictionary of the New Testament* [hereafter *EDNT*], ed. Horst Balz and Gerhard Schneider (Grand Rapids: Eerdmans, 1981), 2:522: "Jesus is the fundamental condition determining the gathering."

13. Horacio E. Lona, "'In meinem Namen versammelt.' Mt 18:20 und liturgisches Handeln," *Archiv für Liturgiewissenschaft* 27 (1985): 373–404 (389).

14. John P. Meier, *The Vision of Matthew: Christ, Church, and Morality in the First Gospel* (New York: Crossroad, 1991), 135.

15. Ulrich Luz, *Matthew 8–20*, Hermeneia, trans. Wilhelm C. Linss (Minneapolis: Fortress Press, 2001), 433.

16. James P. Martin, "The Church in Matthew," *Interpretation* 29 (1975): 47.

17. Krister Stendahl, *Energy for Life* (Brewster, Mass.: Paraclete, 1999), 43.

18. Meier, *The Vision of Matthew*, 216.

19. H. Frankemölle, λαός, *EDNT* 2:341: "Luke has consciously and intentionally inserted λαός in his double work."

20. Lars Hartman, *Markusevangeliet 8:27-16:20*, Kommentar till Nya Testamentet (Stockholm: EFS-forlaget, 2005), 512–13 and 403–08.

21. Hans von Campenhausen, "Das Bekenntnis im Urchristentum," *ZNW* 63 (1972). The author states that the earliest Christian confession was an affirmation of Jesus (for example, Mark 8:38) and an acknowledgment of one's personal relationship to him, the expression of which varied.

22. Gerhard Lohfink, *Jesus and Community* (Philadelphia: Fortress Press, 1984), 49.

23. Joel Marcus, *Mark 1–8*, Anchor Bible (New York: Doubleday, 2000), 148–49.

24. Petr Pokorný, " 'Anfang des Evangeliums.' Zum Problem des Anfangs und des Schlusses des Markusevangelium," in Pokorný and Sou ek, *Bibelauslegung als Theologie* (Tübingen: Mohr [Siebeck], 1996), 164–65.

25. Quoted in E. H. van Olst, *The Bible and Liturgy* (Grand Rapids: Eerdmans, 1991), 4.

26. Günther Bornkamm, "Stilling the Storm in Matthew," in *Tradition and Interpretation*, ed. G. Bornkamm, G. Barth, and H. J. Held (Philadelphia: Westminster, 1963), 52–57.

27. For the cited examples and the discussion of them, I am indebted to two articles by Arland Hultgren. For the infancy narrative, "Matthew's Infancy Narrative and the Nativity of an Emerging Community," in *Horizons in Biblical Theology* 19 (1997): 91–108; and "Liturgy and Literature: The Liturgical Factor in Matthew's Literary and Communicative Art," in *Texts and Context: Essays in Honor of Lars Hartman*, ed. Tord Fornberg and David Hellholm (Oslo and elsewhere: Scandinavian University Press, 1995), 659–73.

Chapter 6: Gospel Happenings

1. James W. Thompson, *Preaching Like Paul* (Louisville: Westminster John Knox, 2001), 3 (citing M. L. Stirewalt).

2. This expression is unique to 1 Thessalonians among Paul's letters. Far more common for Paul is the verb εὐαγγελίζομαι, which points to the same active reality. One might also recall the frequent refrain in the Old Testament regarding the prophets, that "the word of the Lord came to ____" (2 Sam. 7:4; 1 Kgs. 13:20; Isa. 38:4; Jer. 1:4; Ezek. 1:3; Jon. 1:1; Zech. 1:1).

3. Leander E. Keck, *Romans*, Abingdon New Testament Commentaries (Nashville: Abingdon, 2005), 257.

4. Richard Lischer, "The Interrupted Sermon," *Interpretation* 50 (1996): 178.

5. Thompson, *Preaching Like Paul*, 141.

6. Abraham Smith, "The First Letter to the Thessalonians," in *The New Interpreter's Bible*, vol. 11 (Nashville: Abingdon, 2000), 728.

7. Michael J. Gorman, *Cruciformity: Paul's Narrative Spirituality of the Cross* (Grand Rapids: Eerdmans, 2001), 353.

8. See Lischer, "The Interrupted Sermon," 175.

9. Arthur Van Seters, "The Problematic of Preaching in the Third Millennium," *Interpretation* 45 (1991): 273–74.

10. John William Beaudean Jr., *Paul's Theology of Preaching* (Macon, Ga.: Mercer University Press, 1988), 193–94.

11. Abraham J. Malherbe, *The Letters to the Thessalonians*, The Anchor Bible (New York: Doubleday, 2000), 156.

12. Beaudean, *Paul's Theology of Preaching*, 193–94.

13. Beverly Gaventa, *First and Second Thessalonians*, Interpretation: A Bible Commentary for Teaching and Preaching (Louisville: John Knox, 1998), 50.

14. Unless, of course, we include the southern expressions of "y'all" and "all y'all." See also Marva J. Dawn, *Reaching Out Without Dumbing Down* (Grand Rapids: Eerdmans, 1995), 212.

15. Thompson, *Preaching Like Paul*, 97, emphasis added.

16. Johannes Munck, "I Thess. I.9-10 and the Missionary Preaching of Paul," *New Testament Studies* 9 (1962): 96.

17. Peter Stuhlmacher, *Paul's Letter to the Romans* (Louisville: Westminster John Knox, 1994), 214–15.

18. See Gaventa, *First and Second Thessalonians*, 15.

19. Richard Hays, *The Moral Vision of the New Testament: A Contemporary Introduction to New Testament Ethics* (San Francisco: HarperCollins, 1996), 36.

20. One may be reminded of the (apocryphal?) story about a Lutheran pastor on his deathbed, who was at peace in the assurance of his redemption because he could not remember ever doing a single good work. Or, for a more scholarly example, see Gerhard O. Forde, *Justification: A Matter of Death and Life* (Philadelphia: Fortress Press, 1982), 25. In contrast, one might read Article 6 (*New Obedience*) and Article 20 (*Faith and Good Works*) from the Augsburg Confession (see Robert Kolb and Timothy J. Wengert, eds., *The Book of Concord: The Confessions of the Evangelical Lutheran Church* [Minneapolis: Fortress Press, 2000], 40–41, 52–57); see also Michael Root, "Is the Reformation Over? And What If It Is?" *Pro Ecclesia* 16 (2007): 340.

21. Martin Luther, "Preface to the Epistle of St. Paul to the Romans" (1522 [1546]), in *Luther's Works*, vol. 35, ed. E. Theodore Bachmann, trans. Charles M. Jacobs (Philadelphia: Fortress Press, 1960), 370.

22. See, for example, *Union with Christ: The New Finnish Interpretation of Luther*, ed. Carl E. Braaten and Robert W. Jenson (Grand Rapids: Eerdmans, 1998). One might also note Melanchthon's remark in the *Apology to*

the Augsburg Confession (72): "And because 'to be justified' means that out of unrighteous people righteous people are made or regenerated, it also means that they are pronounced or regarded as righteous. For Scripture speaks both ways" (Kolb and Wengert, *The Book of Concord*, 132). In 1559, Melanchthon also translated the Augsburg Confession into Greek and sent it to the Patriarch of Constantinople, translating the teaching about justification into the more typically Orthodox language of deification (*theosis*) through union with Christ; see David E. Aune, "Recent Readings of Paul Relating to Justification by Faith," in *Rereading Paul Together: Protestant and Catholic Perspectives on Justification*, ed. David E. Aune (Grand Rapids: Baker Academic, 2006), 224–25.

23. E. P. Sanders, *Paul and Palestinian Judaism* (Philadelphia: Fortress Press, 1977), 506; so also Richard B. Hays, "PISTIS and Pauline Christology. What Is At Stake?" in *Pauline Theology, Volume 4: Looking Back, Pressing On*, ed. E. Elizabeth Johnson and David M. Hay (Atlanta: Scholars Press, 1997), 49–50.

24. Argued cogently by Michael J. Gorman in "Justification by Co-Crucifixion: The Logic of Paul's Soteriology," Society of Biblical Literature Annual Meeting, Washington, D.C., 2006.

25. Malherbe, *The Letters to the Thessalonians*, 273.

Chapter 7: Preaching the Gospel and the Law in the First Testament

1. I shall use the terms *First Testament, Old Testament, Hebrew Bible*, and *Hebrew Scriptures* purposefully and interchangeably as synonyms that each carry their own helpful and truthful connotations.

2. Gerhard von Rad, *Old Testament Theology*, Vol. 1 (Edinburgh: Oliver and Boyd, 1962), 163–64.

3. D. Winton Thomas, ed., *Documents from Old Testament Times* (New York: Harper & Row, 1961), 31 (see "The Law Code of Hammurabi," paragraph 132).

4. Ruth became the great-grandmother of David, who founded the messianic dynasty (see Ruth 4:17), and Esther saved the Jewish nation (see Est. 4:14).

5. Norman Perrin, *Rediscovering the Teaching of Jesus* (London: SCM, 1967), 55.

6. *Evangelical Lutheran Worship* (Minneapolis: Augsburg Fortress, 2006).

7. Song of Songs, a celebration of human love, does not mention God except in 8:6, the climactic verse where love is described as a "flame of Yah." In Hosea, "knowing the LORD" is marriage language, and in 11:1-9 God's passion for God's people is described in terms of fatherly love.

8. Hans W. Frei, *The Eclipse of Biblical Narrative: A Study in Eighteenth and Nineteenth Century Hermeneutics* (New Haven: Yale University Press, 1974).

9. Frank G. Honeycutt, *Preaching to Skeptics and Seekers* (Nashville: Abingdon, 2001); *Preaching for Adult Conversion and Commitment: Invitation to a Life Transformed* (Nashville: Abingdon, 2003); *Marry a Pregnant Virgin: Unusual Bible Stories for New and Curious Christians* (Minneapolis: Augsburg, 2008).

10. When exegeting and preaching on eschatological passages, such as Jer. 31:31-34 ("The days are surely coming, says the LORD, when I will make a new covenant with the house of Israel and the house of Judah . . ."), it is important to do so in such a way as not to rob the text from a vibrant and faithful Judaism. These eschatological hopes remain also Jewish texts, and God has never relinquished the first covenant (see, for example, Romans 9–11 and the fine essay by David S. Yeago, "Messiah's People: The Culture of the Church in the Midst of the Nations," *Taproot* 11 (1995): 4–34.

Chapter 8: Sermonic Song

1. Martin Luther, "Concerning the Order of Public Worship (1523)," in *Liturgy and Hymns, Luther Works*, vol. 53, American Edition (Philadelphia: Fortress Press, 1965), 11. The volume includes his reforming pamphlets, hymns, and prefaces to hymnals. Hereafter cited as LW 53.

2. LW 53, "The German Mass and Order of Service (1526)," 62.

3. Ibid., 62–64.

4. Nicholas Temperley's *The Music of the English Parish Church*, vols. 1 and 2 (Cambridge: Cambridge University Press, 1979), discusses musicologists' tendencies to focus on cathedral and large municipal parish church music, often omitting or giving only cursory notice of the musical life of smaller congregations.

5. LW 53, "Concerning the Order of Public Worship (1523)," 11.

6. Martin Luther, "The Large Catechism," in *The Book of Concord*, ed. Robert Kolb and Timothy J. Wengert (Minneapolis: Fortress Press, 2000), 386, #25. Hereafter cited as *Book of Concord*.

7. LW 53, "Concerning the Order of Public Worship (1523)," 12.

8. Martin Luther, "Sermon on 24 January 1529," in *D. Martin Luthers Werke: kritische Gesamtausgabe*, 29 Band (Weimar: Hermann Böhlaus Nachfolger, 1904), 44.

9. LW 53, "Preface to the Wittenberg Hymnal (1524)," 316.

10. LW 53, "Preface to the Burial Hymns (1542)," 328.

11. Götz Harbsmeier, "Theologie und Liturgie," *Theologische Rundshau*, new series, 20.3 (1952): 271ff. Walter Blankenburg, "Kann Singen Verkündigung sein?" *Kirche und Musik: Gesammelte Aufsätze zur Geschichte der gottesdienstlichen*

Musik, ed. E. Hübner and R. Steiger (Göttingen: Vandenhoeck & Ruprecht, 1979), 298–313.

12. Friedrich Blume's *Protestant Church Music: A History* (New York: Norton, 1974) remains a respected, comprehensive study of the various reforming movements' influence on the music of the church and may be consulted for detailed assessment of the various theologians' positions. Also, Markus Jenny's *Luther, Zwingli, Calvin in ihren Liedern* (Zürich: Theologisher Verlag Zürich, 1983) investigates the reformers' hymns individually, providing not only historical context but theological evaluations of the hymns.

13. Miriam Therese Winter's *Why Sing? Toward a Theology of Catholic Church Music* (Washington, D.C.: Pastoral Press, 1984) is a helpful overview of the evolution of Roman Catholic understanding of congregational song.

14. LW 53, "Preface to the Wittenberg Hymnal (1524)," 316.

15. "Eight Sermons at Wittenberg (1522)," in *Selected Writings of Martin Luther: 1520–1523*, ed. Theodore G. Tappert (Philadelphia: Fortress Press, 1967), *Invocavit Sermons* II and III, 239–47.

16. LW 53, "Preface to Georg Rhau's *Symphoniae Iucundae* (1538)," 323.

17. Martin Rössler, *Die Liedpredigt: Geschichte einer Predigtgattung* (Göttingen: Vandenhoeck & Ruprecht, 1976), particularly 48–51. Lutheran "song sermons" developed as the carefully constructed interweaving of appointed pericope, sermonic treatment of the text, and hymn stanzas that both furthered the exegetical and interpretive process. This was only possible with hymns based on extended, informed treatment of the biblical text. The Bach cantata corpus might appropriately be considered a related homiletic development, given the interplay of hymn and biblical texts coupled with interpretive recitatives.

18. Martin Luther, trans. Richard Massie, in *Lutheran Book of Worship* (Minneapolis: Augsburg/Philadelphia: Board of Publication, Lutheran Church in America, 1978), #299.

19. Gustaf Aulén, *Christus Victor*, with a new introduction by Jaroslav Pelikan (New York: Collier, 1969), 103–11.

20. *Union with Christ: The New Finnish Interpretation of Luther*, ed. Carl E. Braaten and Robert W. Jenson (Grand Rapids: Eerdmans, 1998).

21. My dissertation, *The Liturgical Expression of Sanctification: The Hymnic Complement to the Lutheran Concordia* (Notre Dame, 1988), is a thorough study of the relationship of Reformation hymnody, their liturgical context, and the Lutheran confessions.

22. Paul F. Bradshaw, *The Search for the Origins of Christian Worship* (Oxford: Oxford University Press, 2002), 43f. Lawrence A. Hoffman, *The Way into Jewish Prayer* (Woodstock, Vt.: Jewish Lights, 2000), provides helpful commentary to the style and content of Jewish prayer forms.

23. David Hiley, "Alleluias," in *Western Plainchant: A Handbook* (New York: Oxford University Press, 1993), 130–37.

24. Jehan Alain, "Litanies," *L'Œuvre d'Orgue de Jehan Alain*, Tome II (Paris: Alphonse Leduc, 1971), 31.

25. In liturgical usage, the word *ceremonial* refers specifically to the prescribed and formal actions of worship.

26. Third Commandment, from "The Large Catechism," in *Book of Concord*, 399, #94.

27. Ibid., 400, #99.

28. Article XI, "Election," from "Formula of Concord, Solid Declaration," in *Book of Concord*, 245f., #28–32.

Chapter 9: "The Sound of the Gospel"

1. Rachel Muller Bernhard, "David H. Bernhard Journal," First Sabbath in April, 1863, South Caroliniana Library, University of South Carolina, Columbia (hereafter SCL).

2. John Belton O'Neall and John A. Chapman, *The Annals of Newberry, in Two Parts* (Newberry, S.C.: Aull & Houseal, 1892), 659. For additional information on former sheriff George Haltiwanger, see Edwin J. Scott, *Random Recollections of a Long Life 1806–1876* (Columbia, S.C.: George A. Calvo Jr., 1884), 87.

3. Ibid., 660, 663.

4. H. George Anderson, "Reconstruction and After, 1866–1885," in *A History of the Lutheran Church in South Carolina*, ed. Paul G. McCullough (Columbia, S.C.: R. L. Bryan, 1971), 324.

5. Joseph Hamilton Fesperman, *The Life of a Sufferer: An Autobiography* (Utica: The Young Lutheran Company, 1892), 18. Italics added to book titles for clarity.

6. Ibid., 20–21.

7. Ibid., 20.

8. Ibid., 24. Italics added for clarity.

9. Ibid., 24–28.

10. Ibid., 32, 34.

11. Junius B. Fox, *Biography of Alfred J. Fox, M.D.* (Philadelphia: Lutheran Publication Society, 1885), 24.

12. Ibid., 18, 22.

13. "Report of the Ministerium," Evangelical Lutheran Synod of South Carolina and Adjacent States, 1832, James R. Crumley Jr. Archives, Lutheran Theological Southern Seminary, Columbia (hereafter JRCA).

14. George Haltiwanger (also spelled Haltewanger), "Annual Report," Evangelical Lutheran Synod of South Carolina and Adjacent States, 1832,

JRCA. Italics added for clarity. Horne's *Introduction* is probably T. H. Horne, *Introduction to the Critical Study and Knowledge of the Scriptures*, first published in 1818, a well-known standard text for theological students across many denominations in the nineteenth century.

15. Herman Aull, "Annual Report," Evangelical Lutheran Synod of South Carolina and Adjacent States, 1832, JRCA.

16. "Report of the Ministerium," 1832.

17. Godfrey Dreher, letter to Daniel Efird, August 23, 1851, Summer Family Papers, SCL.

18. Rachel Bernhard, "Journal," 2nd Sunday July, 1855; 2nd Sunday December, 1857; 4th Sunday June, 1857. All biblical citations are in the King James Version, the version used at the time.

19. Cyprian M. Efird, *A Short Biography of Reverend Daniel Efird* (Lexington, S.C.: G. M. Harman, Book, Newspaper, and Job Printer, 1893), 9.

20. Fox, *Biography of Rev. Alfred J. Fox*, 106–07, 51.

21. O'Neall and Chapman, *The Annals of Newberry*, 660, 662–63.

22. "Report of the Committee on the Sermons and Journals of the Students of Divinity," Evangelical Lutheran Synod of South Carolina and Adjacent States, 1833, JRCA.

23. Very few southern pastors ever studied at Hartwick. Gettysburg, and Southern provided the large majority of seminary-trained pastors in the antebellum period. Although the term is anachronistic, the seminary will be referred to as "Southern Seminary" throughout this essay.

24. A Junior, *Lutheran Observer*, October 13, 1848, as quoted in William R. Fritz, "How the Lutheran Seminary Came To Columbia Seventy Five Years Ago . . . And Why It Is Not Likely To Leave" (unpublished essay, JRCA, c. 1986), 2.

25. William Houck, tribute to Ernest Hazelius on his retirement, 1853, Shuler Family Papers, SCL.

26. Scott, *Random Recollections*, 145.

27. "Appendix B: Constitution of the Theological Seminary of the Evangelical Lutheran Church of South-Carolina and Adjacent States" (1833), in *Minutes of the South Carolina Synod* (1837), 42.

28. Ibid., 43.

29. Thaddeus Street Boinest, "Journal," May 7, 1849, JRCA. Boinest's first name is sometimes spelled "Thadeus."

30. William Alexander Houck to Mary M. Haigler, September 5, 1850, Shuler Family Papers, SCL. See also his letter to Mary Haigler dated January 15, 1851.

31. "Appendix B: Constitution," 46.

32. *Amended Constitution of the Classical and Theological Seminary* (South Carolina Synod, 1850), 65–66.

33. Thaddeus Street Boinest, "Student Notebooks," JRCA; and "Appendix B: Constitution," 43.

34. John Phillips Margart, "Journal," March 13 and 14, 1838, JRCA.

35. James L. Kugel, *How to Read the Bible: A Guide to Scripture, Then and Now* (New York: Free Press, 2007), 23.

36. Richard Lischer, *Theories of Preaching: Selected Readings in the Homiletical Tradition* (Durham: Labyrinth Press, 1987), 151.

37. Martin Luther, *Table Talk*, *Luther's Works*, vol. 54, ed. and trans. Theodore G. Tappert (Philadelphia: Fortress Press, 1967), 160.

38. Charles E. Hambrick Stowe, "The Ordinances of Public Worship," in *American Spiritualities: A Reader*, ed. Catherine L. Albanese (Bloomington: Indiana University Press, 2001), 76.

39. Ronald J. Allen, ed., *Patterns of Preaching: A Sermon Sampler* (St. Louis: Chalice, 1998), x.

40. O'Neall and Chapman, *The Annals of Newberry*, 659.

41. Josiah Smeltzer, "Journal," October 25, 1863, and December 13, 1863, Newberry College Archives, Newberry, S.C.

42. "Appendix B: Constitution," 43.

43. *Minutes of the South Carolina Synod* (1853), 8.

44. R. Bernhard, "Journal," 2nd Sunday February, 1854, and 3rd Saturday April, 1854. Many similar examples fill Bernhard's journal.

45. Margart, "Journal," December 11, 1859; July 15, 1860; July 22, 1860; July 22, 1860; January 13, 1861; February 10, 1861; March 17, 1861; March 24, 1861.

46. R. Bernhard, "Journal," 1rst (sic) Sabbath August, 1853.

47. Margart, "Journal," July 3, 1841; December 17, 1843; September 11, 1859; December 18, 1842.

48. R. Bernhard, "Journal," 3rd Sunday May, 1854.

49. Ibid., April, 1857.

50. Smeltzer, "Journal," June 22, 1854.

51. Ibid., June 19, 1854; March 2, 1854; August 14, 1854; May 10, 1857.

52. David H. Bernhard, "Journal," Baptism of Coloured Persons for 1838–39, SCL. The journals of Godfrey Dreher (December 1819, February 1820, and June 1820, for example), John Margart (see his records on church discipline in 1842), Josiah Smeltzer, and Thaddeus Boinest contain dozens of similar entries.

53. *Minutes of the South Carolina Synod* (1859), "Parochial Reports." The fullest account of black Lutheranism to date is Jeff Johnson, *Black Christians: The Untold Lutheran Story* (St. Louis: Concordia, 1991).

54. "Appendix B: Constitution," 43.

55. See R. Bernhard, "Journal," 3rd Sunday June, 1857. See also 1rst (sic) Sunday January, 1858, for example.

56. Ted Ownby, *Subduing Satan: Religion, Recreation, and Manhood in the Rural South, 1865-1920*, Fred W. Morrison Series in Southern Studies (Chapel Hill: University of North Carolina Press, 1990), 127–28. Roman Catholicism, of course, was still beyond the pale.

57. The journals of Boinest, Margart, Smeltzer, and Dreher all show these characteristics. Quotation is from Charles Shealy Jr., "Rev. Thadeus Street Boinest and His Times" (paper presented at Bethlehem [Pomaria] Lutheran Church Homecoming, July 11, 1976), 3, JRCA.

58. Smeltzer, "Diary," December 7, 1879. Smeltzer's "Diary" is part of his larger "Journal," located in the Newberry College Archive, Newberry, S.C.

59. R. Bernhard, 3rd Sabbath September, 1853.

60. Joseph Hamilton Fesperman, *Practical Lessons and Devotional Thoughts: A Continuation of the Life of a Sufferer* (York, Pa.: P. Anstadt & Sons, 1894), 17.

61. Margart, "Journal," May 28, 1841.

62. Ibid., January 30–31, 1841; September 17, 1842; August 10, 1844. Margart preached at many protracted meetings throughout the course of his exceptionally long career. See, for example, September 12, 1841, and November 20, 1859.

63. J. I. M., "The Nature and Method of Special Services," *Lutheran Church Visitor*, February 10, 1910, 7.

64. *Lutheran Church Visitor*, March 16, 1916, 4–5, and June 8, 1916, 8.

65. Smeltzer, "Diary," September 4, 1851.

66. See, in this volume, Daniel M. Bell Jr., "Preaching Ethics Ethically," p. 171, below.

67. Raymond M. Bost and Jeff L. Norris, *All One Body: The Story of the North Carolina Lutheran Synod* (Salisbury, N.C.: Historical Committee, North Carolina Synod, Evangelical Lutheran Church in America, 1994), 37.

68. Socrates Henkel, *History of the Evangelical Lutheran Tennessee Synod* (New Market, Va.: Henkel & Co., 1890), 4.

69. Ibid., 8–9.

70. Paul Henkel to Solomon Henkel, June 13, 1820, in *Letters of Paul Henkel*, ed. Richard H. Baur (St. Louis: Lutheran Historical Conference, 2003), 32.

71. See, in this volume, Brian K. Peterson, "Gospel Happenings," p. 68, above.

72. See, in this volume, Robert D. Hawkins, "Sermonic Song," p. 100, above.

73. O'Neall and Chapman, *The Annals of Newberry*, 663.

74. A full description of the shift from licensure and home study to seminary education in the years 1860–1886 may be found in Anderson, *Southeastern States*, 172–87.

75. Jackson Carroll, Barbara Wheeler, Daniel Aleshire, and Penny Long Marler, *Being There: Culture and Formation in Two Theological Schools* (New York: Oxford University Press, 1997).

Chapter 10: Look and See

1. Simon Chan, "The Mission of the Holy Trinity," *Christianity Today* (June 2007): 48–51.

2. Ibid., 48.

3. Michael Foss is an ELCA pastor, writer, consultant, and speaker. His books include *Power Surge: Six Marks of Discipleship for a Changing Church* (Minneapolis: Fortress Press, 2000), *A Servant's Manual: Christian Leadership for Tomorrow* (Minneapolis: Fortress Press, 2002), and *Real Faith for Real People: Living the Six Marks of Discipleship* (Minneapolis: Augsburg, 2004). Foss is widely recognized and highly regarded as a church leader who helps pastors and lay ministers to develop their own vision and passion for ministry.

4. Eric W. Gritsch and Robert W. Jenson, *Lutheranism: The Theological Movement and Its Confessional Writings* (Philadelphia: Fortress Press, 1976), 8.

5. Ibid., 12–13.

6. John Milton, "On His Blindness," in *The New Oxford Book of English Verse 1250–1950* (New York: Oxford University Press, 1972), 297.

7. Craig Van Gelder, ed., *The Missional Church in Context: Helping Congregations Develop Contextual Ministry* (Grand Rapids: Eerdmans, 2007).

8. Mark Lau Branson, "Ecclesiology and Leadership for the Missional Church," in ibid., 94–125. Branson is Homer L. Goddard Associate Professor of the Ministry of the Laity at Fuller Theological Seminary in Pasadena, California.

9. Ibid., 94–95.

10. Mary Sue Dehmlow Dreier, "An Old New Church in the Marketplace," in Van Gelder, ed., *The Missional Church in Context*, 189–218; see p. 211. Dreier is Associate Professor of Congregational Mission and Leadership at Luther Seminary, St. Paul, Minnesota.

11. Ibid., 216–17.

Chapter 11: Proclaiming Good News in Times of Transition

1. Craig A. Satterlee, *When God Speaks Through You: How Faith Convictions Shape Preaching and Mission* (Herndon, Va.: Alban Institute, 2008), 13.

2. Nancy Schlossberg, *Counseling Adults in Transition: Linking Practice With Theory* (New York: Springer, 1984), 44ff.

3. Kathleen S. Smith. *Stilling the Storm: Worship and Congregational Leadership in Difficult Times* (Herndon, Va.: Alban Institute, 2006), 42.

4. Zack Eswine, *Preaching to a Post-Everything World: Crafting Biblical Sermons That Connect with Our Culture* (Grand Rapids: Baker, 2008), 10.

5. Gary L. Harbaugh, *The Faith-Hardy Christian: How to Face The Challenges of Life with Confidence* (Minneapolis: Augsburg, 1986), 35–37.

6. Ibid., 37.

7. Ibid.

8. I use this phrase to describe an aimless, meaningless, and barely viable existence.

9. This term itself indicates that a congregation is in the midst of transition—one pastor has left for various reasons: conflict, retirement, illness, death, new call, and so on. Interim ministry is a ministry "in between" the times of what was and what is yet to come. Loss, grief, and change are realities within this period. As previously stated in this chapter, each individual and each congregation addresses these common issues according to their own unique history and context.

10. Of course, these are natural and normal reactions to the loss and grief experience within every transition. Both pastors and their parishioners will have similar reactions.

11. *The Random House College Dictionary: Revised Edition* (New York: Random House, 1982), 1042.

12. *Bartlett's Roget's Thesaurus* (Boston: Little, Brown, 1996), 4, 48, 84, 176, 209, 431, 508, 670, 1202.

13. *Random House College Dictionary*, 1042, 1202.

14. Ibid., 1042.

15. Charles Merrill Smith, *How to Become a Bishop Without Being Religious* (New York: Doubleday, 1965), 32.

16. Ibid., 40f.

17. Elizabeth I. Steele, "How Responding to People's Needs Hurts the Church," *Congregations: Learning, Leading, Changing* 34, no. 2 (Spring 2008): 11.

18. Ibid., 11.

19. Ibid., 12.

20. Examples of specific geographical locations of wilderness in Scripture may be found in *The Interpreter's Dictionary of the Bible* (Nashville: Abingdon, 1962), 2:98–99, 3:632–33, 4:844.

21. J. Bill Ratliff, *When You Are Facing Change* (Louisville: Westminster John Knox, 1989), 49.

22. Kenneth Alan Moe, *The Pastor's Survival Manual* (Bethesda, Md.: Alban Institute, 1995), xiv.

23. Smith, *How to Become a Bishop*, xxii.

24. Ibid., 9.

25. Ibid., 10.

26. The Hebrew word here is קָוָה, derived from the noun תִּקְוָה, which is often translated as "hope."

27. Translated from the Greek ἐκδέχομαι, ἀποδέχομαι, προσδέχομαι. cf. δέχομαι, "receive."

28. Specific times for this can occur during council and committee meetings, choir rehearsals, women's and men's gatherings, and so on. Many congregations in transition have accomplished this through a combination of cottage meetings and individual home visits.

29. "Holy Baptism," in *Evangelical Lutheran Worship* (Minneapolis: Augsburg Fortress, 2006), 231.

30. For additional references, see 1 Tim. 4:15; 2 Tim. 2:10; Titus 2:1-3; 1 Peter 2:21, 4:11.

31. Edmond Jacob, *Theology of the Old Testament* (New York: Harper & Row, 1958), 105.

32. "Affimation of Baptism," in *Evangelical Lutheran Worship*, 237.

Chapter 12: Preaching Ethics Ethically

1. Reinhold Niebuhr, *Leaves From the Notebook of a Tamed Cynic* (San Francisco: Harper & Row, 1957), 47.

2. Space precludes an adequate treatment of how preaching as participation in the church's worship is in turn participation through the Spirit in the Son's communion with the Father. On this important point, see James B. Torrance, *Worship, Community, and the Triune God of Grace* (Carlisle, UK: Pasternoster, 1996).

3. *The United Methodist Hymnal* (Nashville: United Methodist Publishing House, 1989), 10.

4. Barbara Brown Taylor, "Preaching Christ Crucified," *Circuit Rider* (January/February 2006): 21.

5. Samuel Wells, *God's Companions* (Malden, Mass.: Blackwell, 2006), 165.

6. Ibid., 165–66.

7. Karl Barth, *Church Dogmatics* (Edinburgh: T&T Clark, 1957), II.2, 518.

8. This is not to deny that there is an appropriate distinction to be made between Christ and us, which is the distinction between the head and the body. This distinction is different from that drawn between two competing agencies.

For a helpful treatment of divine and human agency, see William Placher, *The Domestication of Transcendence* (Louisville: Westminster John Knox, 1996).

9. Martin Luther King Jr., *Why We Can't Wait* (New York: Signet, 1964), 90.

10. Philip Rieff, *The Triumph of the Therapeutic: Uses of Faith after Freud* (New York: Harper & Row, 1966).

11. Marsha Witten, *All is Forgiven: The Secular Message in American Protestantism* (Princeton: Princeton University Press, 1993).

12. Note that identifying this as love does not diminish its harmfulness. After all, as Augustine noted, sin is nothing but disordered love.

13. On cheap grace, see Dietrich Bonhoeffer, *The Cost of Discipleship* (New York: Macmillan, 1963), 45–47.

14. Albert Camus, *Resistance, Rebellion, and Death* (New York: Knopf, 1961), 71.

15. Cf. Richard Lischer, *The End of Words* (Grand Rapids: Eerdmans, 2005).

16. This communal dimension of the preaching task precludes the vision here proposed from being an instance of what James McClure calls "sovereign preaching" (*The Roundtable Pulpit* [Nashville: Abingdon, 1995], 30f.). While I would argue that it is collaborative, neither is it an instance of McClure's "collaborative preaching" (48ff.). Rather, it is perhaps closest to "inductive preaching" (39ff.).

Chapter 13: Preaching and Evocative Objects for Faith Formation

1. T. S. Eliot, "Hamlet and His Problems," in *The Sacred Wood: Essays on Poetry and Criticism* (New York: Barnes & Noble, 1960), 100.

2. David Kelsey, *Imagining Redemption* (Louisville: Westminster John Knox, 2005).

3. H. Frederick Reisz Jr., *On the Wilderness Way: Meditations for an Advent People (Poetical Sermons)* (Cambridge: University Lutheran Church Press, 1997).

4. H. Frederick Reisz Jr., "Birthing Advent Light," unpublished sermon preached at LTSS, December 4, 2005.

5. H. Frederick Reisz Jr., "The Weighted Waiting," unpublished sermon preached at LTSS, December 2, 2001.

6. Martin Luther, "The Small Catechism," in *The Book of Concord*, ed. Robert Kolb and Timothy J. Wengert (Minneapolis: Fortress Press, 2000), 363.

7. Gerard Manley Hopkins, "God's Grandeur," in *The Poems of Gerard Manley Hopkins*, 4th ed., rev. and enl., ed. W. H. Gardner and Norman H. MacKenzie (London: Oxford University Press, 1970), 66.

Chapter 14: The Interplay of Preaching and Mission

1. David J. Bosch, *Transforming Mission: Paradigm Shifts in Theology of Mission* (Maryknoll, N.Y.: Orbis, 1991), xi–xii, 409.

2. *Evangelical Lutheran Worship* (Minneapolis: Augsburg Fortress, 2006), #668.

3. Carl Braaten, *The Apostolic Imperative* (Minneapolis: Augsburg, 1985), 63–64.

4. Arthur Glasser and Donald McGavran, *Contemporary Theologies of Mission* (Grand Rapids: Baker, 1983).

5. Lesslie Newbigin, *The Gospel in a Pluralist Society* (Grand Rapids: Eerdmans, 1989), 135–36.

6. Lesslie Newbigin, *The Open Secret: An Introduction to the Theology of Mission* (Grand Rapids: Eerdmans, 1995).

7. Ibid., 34.

8. Ibid.

9. Ibid., 32.

10. Lesslie Newbigin, *Foolishness to the Greeks: The Gospel and Western Culture* (Grand Rapids: Eerdmans, 1986), 124.

11. *Evangelical Lutheran Worship*, #654.

12. *Evangelical Lutheran Worship*, #337.

13. "Affirmation of Baptism," in *Evangelical Lutheran Worship*, 237.

Printed in the United States
154185LV00002B/2/P